WORKS ISSUED BY

The Hakluyt Society

THE VOYAGES OF
SIR JAMES LANCASTER

SECOND SERIES
No. LXXXV

COUNCIL
OF
THE HAKLUYT SOCIETY
1939/40

SIR WILLIAM FOSTER, C.I.E., *President.*
THE RIGHT HON. THE EARL BALDWIN OF BEWDLEY, K.G., P.C., *Vice-President.*
ADMIRAL SIR WILLIAM GOODENOUGH, G.C.B., M.V.O., *Vice-President.*
JAMES A. WILLIAMSON, ESQ., D.LIT., *Vice-President.*
J. N. L. BAKER, ESQ.
E. W. BOVILL, ESQ.
SIR RICHARD BURN, C.S.I.
PROF. SIR GEOFFREY CALLENDER, F.S.A.
PROF. FRANK DEBENHAM, M.A., O.B.E.
E. W. GILBERT, ESQ., B.LITT.
DR PHILIP GOSSE
PROF. VINCENT T. HARLOW, D.LITT.
MALCOLM LETTS, ESQ., F.S.A.
PROF. A. P. NEWTON, D.LIT.
PROF. EDGAR PRESTAGE, D.LITT.
S. T. SHEPPARD, ESQ.
SIR PERCY SYKES, K.C.I.E., C.B., C.M.G.
PROF. E. G. R. TAYLOR, D.SC.
R. A. WILSON, ESQ.
EDWARD HEAWOOD, ESQ., M.A., *Treasurer.*
EDWARD LYNAM, ESQ., M.R.I.A., F.S.A., *Hon. Secretary* (British Museum, W.C.).
THE PRESIDENT
THE TREASURER } *Trustees.*
WILLIAM LUTLEY SCLATER, ESQ.

Sir James Lancaster

THE VOYAGES OF
SIR JAMES LANCASTER
TO BRAZIL AND THE EAST INDIES
1591–1603

A new edition
with Introduction and Notes by
SIR WILLIAM FOSTER, C.I.E.

LANCASTER'S ARMS
*Argent, two bars, gules. On a coulon
of the second a mullet pierced, or*

LONDON
PRINTED FOR THE HAKLUYT SOCIETY
1940

PRINTED IN GREAT BRITAIN

CONTENTS

Preface	page ix
Introduction	xi
Fuller titles of works cited	xxxix

THE FIRST VOYAGE, 1591–94:

I. Barker's Narrative	1
II. May's Narrative	22

THE SECOND VOYAGE, 1594–95:

I. Hakluyt's Account	31
II. 'Lancaster His Allarums'	52

THE THIRD VOYAGE, 1601–03:

I. The Account in *Purchas*	75
II. 'A True and Large Discourse' . . .	121
III. 'A Letter...containing the estate of the East Indian Fleete'	144

Appendices:

The Company's Commission and Instructions for the Third Voyage	149
Lancaster's letter to Mr Skinner . . .	154
The Grant of Privileges by the King of Achin	155
Instructions left at Bantam by Lancaster . .	161
Lancaster's Hints for a Voyage to the East .	166
Index	169

ILLUSTRATIONS

Sir James Lancaster . . . . . *frontispiece*
From a painting at Skinners' Hall (see p. xxxvi).

Lancaster's Arms . . . . . . *title-page*

The Fight with the Carrack . . . *opposite page* xxx
From *Het Journael van Joris van Speilbergen*, p. 52.
This drawing, though contemporary, is lacking in accuracy. The large vessel in the centre is of course the Portuguese carrack. Above this are shown the three English ships—the *Red Dragon* on the right, the *Hector* on the left, and the *Ascension* between them; and to balance these the artist has depicted below three more vessels, all wearing the Dutch colours. Of the three, the one on the left is identified as Speilbergen's ship, the *Schaep*, and that on the left as the *Lam* (exaggerated in size). The last-named, however, was English property and formed part of Lancaster's squadron. The sixth vessel, explained as being Speilbergen's sloop, is not mentioned in any of the narratives, and seems to be a figment of the artist's imagination. The wind is obligingly blowing from all quarters at once.

MAPS

A general map of the Indies . . . *opposite page* xl

Key plan, illustrating the attack upon Recife . . *page* xix

Sumatra xxviii

PREFACE

A previous volume on this subject was published by the Society in 1877 (ser. I, vol. LVI), under the editorship of Mr (afterwards Sir) Clements Markham. This, however, has long been out of print; while in the sixty years that have since elapsed much additional information has accumulated. It has therefore been thought desirable to prepare a fresh account of these three voyages, of which the two directed to the East Indies were not only memorable in themselves but constituted important stages in the establishment of regular intercourse by sea between England and the Far East.

To the four narratives contained in the earlier edition, which were drawn from the pages of Hakluyt and Purchas, it has been found possible to add three more, given in contemporary pamphlets. The longest of these deals with Lancaster's raid on Pernambuco: the other two with his second voyage to the Indies. Of the first pamphlet only two copies are known to exist, and these are both in the United States. I am much indebted to the authorities of the libraries concerned—the John Carter Brown Library at Providence (Rhode Island) and the Henry E. Huntington Library in California—for permitting me to utilize them; and particularly to Mr Lawrence C. Wroth, the librarian of the former institution, who not only arranged the supply to me of photostats of the copy in his charge, but further sent a photostat of the additional matter which appears only in the Huntington Library copy. Thanks are also due to the authorities of the Bodleian Library, Oxford, for their courtesy in allowing photostats to be made of their two pamphlets relating to the voyage of 1601–3. I desire further to offer my warm thanks to the Master, Wardens, and Court of the Skinners' Company, for consenting to the reproduction of the portrait of Lancaster which hangs at Skinners' Hall. For facilities in taking the photograph, and for other assistance, my thanks are due to Mr J. J. Lambert, the Clerk of the Company.

Assistance from other quarters has been acknowledged in the

text; but I wish especially to record my gratitude to the Rev. Dr W. G. Shellabear, for allowing me to make use of his translation of the grant obtained by Lancaster at Achin, and to Mr Edward Lynam, the indefatigable secretary of the Society, for advice and help in many directions.

Sir Clements Markham's volume included also (*a*) abstracts of, and extracts from, journals preserved at the India Office of early voyages to the East; (*b*) a calendar of these journals; and (*c*) the journal kept by Captain John Knight of his voyage in 1606 in search of the North-West Passage. No attempt has been made in the present volume to deal with this extra matter, some of which has been rendered obsolete by later publications.

The index has been compiled by Miss L. M. Anstey, who has also given valuable assistance in the examination of the proofs.

INTRODUCTION

IT is now recognized that the foundation of the East India Company at the very close of the sixteenth century was a culmination, rather than a commencement, of efforts on the part of English merchants to secure a share in the sea-borne trade between the West and the East. All through the century, in fact, the need of finding fresh markets for the national products, especially the woollen cloth which was the principal manufacture, was ever present in the minds of statesmen, of merchants, and of patriots like Richard Hakluyt. The most promising field seemed to be the marts of Asia, with its varieties of climate, its vast population, and (as was generally believed) its great wealth; while the fact that return cargoes of spices would yield great profit added to the attraction. So, from the time of the Cabots onwards, schemes were constantly brought forward and ships despatched to find a way to the fabled Orient.

For reasons which are familiar, these efforts were long directed to the discovery of a shorter and less dangerous route than the one round Africa used by the Portuguese and claimed by them as their exclusive property; and so money and lives were wasted in searching for passages by the north-west (round America) or the north-east (round Siberia). As those hopes began to fade, other considerations presented themselves. In 1580 Philip II of Spain became also King of Portugal, and the latter country was forced to join the ranks of the enemies of England—a fact which removed all need of considering Portuguese susceptibilities in regard to the use of the Cape route. The closing of the Lisbon markets to the merchants of England and the Netherlands gave them a new incentive to seek a direct trade with the sources of the production of spices. Moreover, the return of Drake in 1580 from his daring voyage round the world—a feat emulated eight years later by Cavendish—showed that English vessels, small as they were, could go anywhere and do anything. This impression was deepened by the rout of the Spanish Armada, which at the same time roused the nation to a consciousness of its capabilities and gave a powerful impetus to enterprise in every direction.

As a result, in the autumn of 1589, a number of London merchants presented to Queen Elizabeth a petition for encouragement in a project for trying to penetrate to the East Indies by way of the Cape. In this it was pointed out that, without going near any Spanish or Portuguese stronghold, it should be feasible to open up commerce with many rich countries from Southern India to China and the Philippines, and thus assist the export of English manufactures, which were suffering from lack of markets; while the capture of Portuguese ships would deal a shrewd blow at the enemy's resources. The merchants concerned proposed to fit out the *Merchant Royal*, the *Susan*, and the *Edward Bonaventure*, with two or three pinnaces, to be ready by the following December; but before doing so, they required an assurance that the ships, when ready, would not be stayed for any reason, and that the promoters would be allowed to enjoy any booty acquired during the voyage. It is unfortunate that the names of the memorialists are not given; though, as the ships mentioned were all engaged in the Levant trade, it may be concluded with confidence that those concerned were mostly engaged in that traffic. Nor is there any record of the answer returned to the petition; but since the expedition was not despatched, it is evident that the desired assurances were not forthcoming. Possibly one reason was a fear lest the Spanish attack should be renewed, and a consequent unwillingness to release even three good ships for so distant a venture.

A year later, however, the projectors appear to have received sufficient encouragement to take up the scheme afresh. Accordingly the *Penelope*, the *Merchant Royal*, and the *Edward Bonaventure*[1] were fitted out, and placed under the command of George Raymond, of whom nothing is known save that he had distinguished himself in the fight against the Armada (Laughton's *Defeat of the Spanish Armada*, p. 16). He hoisted his flag in the *Penelope*; while the *Merchant Royal* was under the charge of Samuel Foxcroft (who seems to have died early

---

[1] The *Merchant Royal* was of 300 or 350 tons, and the *Edward Bonaventure* of 250. The tonnage of the *Penelope* is not on record.

in the voyage), and the *Edward Bonaventure* was commanded by James Lancaster. The voyage was naturally to be mainly one of reconnaissance. No trading was in fact attempted, and the mention of soldiers as being on board seems to show that prize-taking was held in view from the first. The absence of cargo had at least one advantage—it left more room for men and stores. In such long voyages it was thought necessary to crowd the vessels with men, in order to secure that sufficient would survive to bring the ships home; though this overcrowding increased the difficulty of feeding them and at the same time induced a heavy mortality.

Since from this point our narrative centres largely upon the personality of Lancaster, it may be well to pause and place on record the little that has been discovered concerning his early career. We know from his will that he was born in the parish of Basingstoke, in Hampshire; while the year of his birth (according to the inscription on his portrait) was either 1554 or 1555.[1] As he died in 1618, he was almost exactly contemporaneous with Richard Hakluyt (1552?–1616). Of Lancaster's parentage nothing is known; but according to a statement on p. 57 he was 'by birth of gentillity'. The records of the Skinners' Company, which might afford some information on the point, are unfortunately not available, owing to war conditions; while, although a certain James Lancaster, who is recorded as possessing property in Basingstoke in 1559 (Baigent and Millard's *History of Basingstoke*, p. 398), may not improbably have been his father, there is no actual evidence to that effect. Similarly, we have no particulars of his boyhood; though it may fairly be surmised that he attended the local grammar school, to which he afterwards left a substantial bequest.

That Lancaster spent much of his early life in Portugal appears from his own statement (recorded on p. 43): 'I have bene brought up among this people: I have lived among them as a gentleman, served with them as a souldier, and lived among them as a merchant.' In the absence of further particulars we can only fill in this outline by conjecture; but perhaps it is not giving too much rein to the imagination to surmise that he was

[1] The parish registers for that period are no longer extant.

sent as a lad to Portugal to learn the language and the mechanism of trading: that after some years spent as a merchant, he bought an estate and settled down to cultivate it: that on the outbreak of the civil war (1580) he, like many other Englishmen, espoused the cause of Don Antonio and took up arms on his behalf: and that the victory of the Spaniards drove him to England as a refugee, with the loss of his property and money. Such a course of events would explain his bitter dislike of the Portuguese and his abiding sense of grievance against that nation.

All this is regrettably indefinite. Firmer ground seems at first sight to be promised by a suggestion, made in the *Calendar of State Papers, Domestic*, 1581–90 (p. 77), that a document in that series, assigned (with a query) to 1586, is 'probably in the hand of James Lancaster the navigator'. But a conjecture based upon handwriting is always open to suspicion, and an examination of the text of the document[1] lends no support to the hypothesis. However, in 1587, we get at last solid evidence that he was then in London. On 16 February in that year the Privy Council referred to arbitration a dispute between 'James Lancaster, of London, merchant', and another person.[2] What the contention was about, and how it ended, cannot be determined.

Next came the Armada year, when everyone who was fit to do so was eager to aid in the defence of the realm against the invaders. It is with no surprise that we find Lancaster in command of the *Edward Bonaventure*, one of the London merchant ships that joined in the operations (Laughton's *Defeat of the Spanish Armada*, vol. I, p. 326). This post he may have owed to Thomas Smythe, who was one of the leading merchants engaged in overseas trade and was, like Lancaster, a member of the Skinners' Company.[3] From such an appointment it was an easy transition to the command of the same vessel in the venture of 1591, especially in view of Lancaster's experience and his thorough acquaintance with the Portuguese language.

[1] As printed in Prof. Taylor's *Writings...of the two Richard Hakluyts*, vol. II, p. 346, no. 50. The date is there definitely given as 1585.
[2] *Acts of the Privy Council*, 1586–87, p. 329.
[3] According to the tablet on the portrait at Skinners' Hall, Lancaster was admitted as a freeman in 1579.

Raymond's fleet made far too late a start (10 April 1591), and its subsequent misfortunes were partly due to this mistake. Calms and storms delayed its progress, and the Cape of Good Hope was not sighted until nearly the end of July. Contrary winds baffled every attempt to pass that point, and sickness in all the ships forced the commander to seek a harbour. This he had the good fortune to find in what became known afterwards as Table Bay;[1] and it is worth noting that this was the earliest visit of any English ship to that roadstead. About a month was spent there, to enable the sick men to recover. The mortality had, however, been so serious that a decision was taken to send back to England the *Merchant Royal* with fifty men, distributing the rest of her crew between the other two ships.

On resuming the voyage, the Cape was passed without much difficulty. Then, off Cape Correntes, a storm separated the vessels, and the *Penelope* was never seen again. Four days later the mainmast of the *Edward Bonaventure* was struck by lightning and four of her men were killed. After proceeding up the Mozambique Channel and narrowly escaping shipwreck on a dangerous shoal, a short stay was made near Mozambique, and a longer one at the principal island of the Comoro group. There a supply of water was obtained; but at the cost of the loss of a third of the ship's crew, who were killed as the result of a sudden attack by the natives.

Lancaster's next stopping place was the island of Zanzibar, where he remained in the harbour from the end of November 1591 to the middle of the following February. The English, after their recent experience, did not venture to land; but having chanced to capture a *sharīf*, to whom the Sultan was much attached, they had no difficulty in procuring an ample supply of victuals. They trimmed their ship, and also made a new boat, to replace one lost at the Comoros. The Portuguese, who had a small settlement on the island, did not judge it prudent to attack them.

Proceeding upon his voyage, Lancaster directed his course towards Cape Comorin, the southernmost point of the Indian

---

[1] The name was given by Joris van Speilbergen in 1601; but for a long time the English continued to call it by its Portuguese appellation of Saldanha Bay.

peninsula, his intention being to lie in wait there for shipping passing between Goa and the Portuguese settlements to the eastwards. Contrary winds carried the vessel out of her course and, as victuals were running short, attempts were made in turn to reach Sokotra, the Laccadives, and the Nicobar Islands. These all failed; but finally, at the beginning of June, the ship reached the island of Gomes, near Achin (Sumatra). Lancaster was still intent upon preying on Portuguese shipping, and he made for the island of Penang, off the west coast of the Malay Peninsula, where he stayed until the beginning of September. During this time sickness took a heavy toll of his crew, which was reduced to thirty-four, of whom only two-thirds were fit for labour. Sailing again, four vessels were held up; but those carrying merely the goods of native merchants were released, and only one, which was laden with pepper belonging to some Portuguese, was detained and emptied. On proceeding further into the Straits of Malacca, a Portuguese ship from Negapatam, carrying rice for Malacca, was captured, and plundered; while another from San Thomé narrowly escaped a like fate. As some consolation for her loss, a third vessel, this time from Goa, was taken. She contained a varied cargo, much of which seems to have been plundered by the English sailors.

Fearing lest the Portuguese at Malacca, hearing of these depredations, should send out shipping too strong for his weakly manned vessel, Lancaster now left the Straits and proceeded first to Junkseylon and then to the Nicobar Islands (November 1592), where he obtained much-needed supplies. A move was next made to Point de Galle, on the south-west coast of Ceylon, where he intended to lie in wait for more Portuguese ships. His men, however, were weary of the long voyage and dismayed by their shorthandedness, and, they insisted upon returning homewards without delay. Lancaster himself was lying in his cabin 'very sicke, more like to die than to live', and he found it expedient to give way. So on 8 December the *Edward Bonaventure* made sail for the Cape. This was passed in March 1593, and early in April the island of St Helena was reached. The provisions there obtained restored the crew to health, and after a stay of nineteen days a fresh start was made.

Lancaster proposed to make for the coast of Brazil, to obtain supplies (and possibly to reconnoitre Pernambuco); but his men, now thoroughly out of hand, constrained him to lay a direct course for England. As a result, they were delayed for weeks by calms or contrary winds, until their provisions were nearly exhausted. At last in desperation they ran for Trinidad, only to find on arrival that the Spaniards had engrossed all available supplies. They then endeavoured to pass between the island and the mainland, but found themselves embayed in the Gulf of Paria. Getting out with great difficulty, in June they managed to reach the small island of Mona, which lies between Puerto Rico and San Domingo. A French ship encountered there spared them some victuals, while other supplies were obtained from the inhabitants. It was now resolved to make for Newfoundland, where they were sure to get relief from the fishing fleets; but when near the Bermudas, a gale from the north drove the *Edward Bonaventure* back to the West India Islands. In November she once again anchored off Mona; whereupon Lancaster, Barker (his second in command), and others landed to get provisions. Before they could return, the half a dozen sailors left on board cut the cable and went off with the ship to San Domingo, where they surrendered it to the Spaniards.[1]

Left marooned on shore, Lancaster and his eighteen companions spent a miserable month, living on what vegetables they could find. Then a French ship arrived, and took off twelve of the party, including their leader. A second French vessel accepted the transfer of half of the Englishmen; and aboard one or other of these ships the survivors remained, mostly off San Domingo, until April 1594. Two other French ships were met with, and in one of these (which was bound homewards) Lancaster and Barker procured passages to Dieppe. That port was reached on 19 May; and five days later the two Englishmen landed once more upon their native soil at Rye, in Sussex, after an absence of over three years.

---

[1] In his notice of Lancaster in the *Dictionary of National Biography*, Sir John Laughton said that the *Edward Bonaventure* got back to England with a rich cargo. That this view is erroneous I have shown in *England's Quest of Eastern Trade* (p. 134).

Henry May, the purser of the *Edward Bonaventure*, had been despatched in August 1593 from the West Indies in a French ship, in the hope that his early arrival in England would relieve the anxiety of the promoters of the voyage; but unfortunately the vessel in which he sailed was wrecked on the Bermudas in the middle of the following December. May was one of those who succeeded in getting ashore. The survivors managed to construct a small bark, in which, in May 1594, they set sail for Newfoundland. There May found an English ship bound for Falmouth, and in this he got back to England in August—about three months after the arrival of Lancaster and Barker. May has the distinction of having been the first of his fellow countrymen to land in the Bermudas, and his narrative, here reprinted, contains the earliest English account of those islands.

Financially, the venture had been a total failure. Only one of the three ships employed had returned to England, and she had brought back nothing but sick men. The loss of life had been heavy, and the time consumed in the voyage was discouraging. On the other hand, an English ship had for the first time roamed freely about the Indian Ocean, and had penetrated as far as the Malay Peninsula without encountering effective hindrance from the Portuguese. Truly, the voyage had been, as Hakluyt terms it, a 'memorable' one, though the results were not sufficiently favourable to induce the promoters to make a second attempt immediately.

Lancaster himself was soon again at sea. He had lost no credit by the unsuccessful issue of his first venture; indeed, he had shown himself to be a careful and capable commander, resolute, yet tactful, inspiring confidence in all who came into contact with him. He had no difficulty, therefore, in persuading a group of London merchants to finance a scheme which probably he had had in mind for some time, viz. to raid and plunder the port of Pernambuco, in Brazil. A secondary object was doubtless the capture of Spanish or Portuguese merchantmen on the way out and home. The force provided for this audacious attempt consisted of three small ships—the *Consent* (240 tons), the *Solomon* (170) and the *Virgin* (60), with crews numbering

INTRODUCTION xix

275 in all. Lancaster took command of the *Consent*, and Edmund Barker was made captain of the *Solomon*.

The expedition left the Thames in October 1594. Bad weather enforced a stay at Dartmouth, and there the aid was enlisted of Randolph Cotton, who had commanded one of the vessels of Cavendish's fleet on his last voyage. Cotton agreed to put money into the venture and to take the post of second in command. The ships proceeded to the Canaries, and thence to Cape Blanco, capturing on the way a number of vessels, some of which Lancaster added to his squadron. The pilot of one of the prizes gave information that a carrack returning from the East Indies had been cast away at Pernambuco, and her goods were stored there, awaiting conveyance to Portugal—a piece of news which whetted all appetites for the intended raid. Proceeding to Maio (one of the Cape Verd Islands), they there put together a galley-frigate which they had brought out in sections from England, to be used in landing men (the ships' boats being hardly adequate for such a purpose). The opportune arrival of Captain John Venner, with two ships, a pinnace and a Spanish prize, afforded an opportunity of strengthening the squadron; and of this Lancaster prudently availed himself, agreeing to give Venner a fourth of the booty.

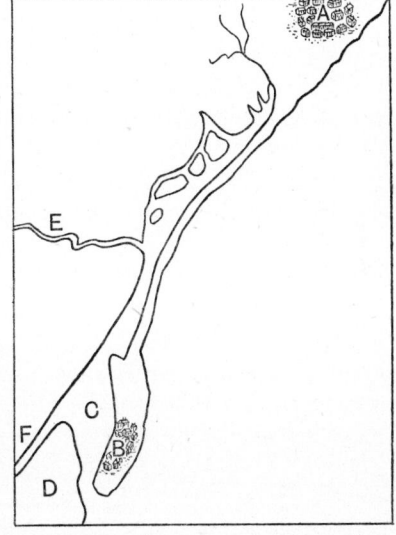

No time was now lost in making for Pernambuco, which was reached on 18 April 1595. What followed can best be explained with the aid of a rough plan,[1] on which *A* represents the head settlement of Olinda and *B* the port

---

[1] The coastline has been adapted (with the kind permission of the Hydrographer) from an Admiralty chart (no. 969). Of course, many changes have taken place since 1595.

town of Recife, the two being united by a narrow sandy isthmus. *C* is the harbour, formed by the confluence of two rivers, the Beberibe (*E*) and the Capibaribe (*F*). *D* is the island of Santo Antonio. Modern Pernambuco covers not only that island and Recife but a large tract on the neighbouring mainland.

The point of attack was Recife, the warehouses of which were filled by the Eastern produce salved from the carrack, besides the sugar and brazil-wood regularly collected for transportation to Portugal. The only defence of the place was a redoubt at the entrance of the harbour, containing seven brass cannon and manned by the local militia. Off the mouth of the harbour—which was very shallow and had a bar at the entrance—were anchored three large Dutch ships, which had been sent from Europe to carry the carrack's goods to Portugal, and their presence caused Lancaster some apprehension. However, the Dutch were evidently not disposed to be mixed up in any quarrel; for, on seeing the English preparations for an attack upon the town, they shifted their position. The first thing to be done was to capture the redoubt, and the ships' boats, carrying every available man and led by Lancaster in the galley-frigate, dashed straight for this objective. The Portuguese gunners fired one ineffective volley and then fled. Lancaster quickly occupied the position and signalled to his ships to enter the harbour. Recife was next taken possession of without opposition, the inhabitants hurrying away as the English approached. A rough wooden palisade was erected round the more vulnerable portion of the town, and a redoubt, to which the guns of the captured fort were transferred, was constructed across the isthmus on the north side of the town, to guard against attacks from Olinda. These precautions taken, all hands were set to work to lade the goods from the warehouses into the ships' boats. It was soon apparent that the vessels available would not suffice to carry all the booty; and Lancaster, with astute diplomacy, made overtures to the commanders of the Dutch squadron to take the surplus to England upon freight terms. An agreement to this effect was quickly reached and the goods were embarked.

Meanwhile the Portuguese at Olinda were not idle. Mustering

all their forces, including a number of natives, they made a sudden attack one night upon the English defences, but met with so warm a reception that they hastily retreated. During the next few days arrived five French vessels, among them being two commanded by Jean Lenoir, the kindly captain who had carried home Lancaster and Barker in the previous summer. Lancaster gave the newcomers a warm welcome and invited them to fill their ships with brazil-wood from the Recife warehouses—an invitation they were not slow to accept; and in return they joined the English in guarding both the town and the shipping. The Portuguese authorities now made overtures for negotiation, but Lancaster, who mistrusted them, declined to see the deputation. Thus rebuffed, they prepared to annoy the invaders' ships by building a fresh redoubt near the harbour. Lancaster thereupon marched out with his men, captured the unfinished trenches, and returned in triumph with four brass cannon and five country carts, which came in handy for transporting goods. Two attempts were then made to burn the English vessels by means of fireships sent down the creek at night; but these were successfully warded off, though not without difficulty.

About thirty days had now passed since the capture of the town. The ships were fully laden, and Lancaster was anxious to depart. It was discovered, however, that the Portuguese were constructing a fresh redoubt at the entrance of the harbour. Lancaster proposed to ignore this and to set sail without delay. His colleagues, however, were of a contrary opinion. They argued that, with a contrary wind (such as was then prevailing), it would in any case be a difficult process to work the ships out of the harbour, and that while so doing the new fortifications might do them much damage. They therefore deemed it imperative to make an attempt to destroy the redoubt. In the end Lancaster reluctantly gave way. He was too unwell to lead the expedition, which was accordingly committed to the charge of Randolph Cotton and Jean Lenoir, with strict injunctions not to venture beyond the range of the ships' guns. Accordingly, the joint Anglo-French forces, about three hundred in number, landed upon the island, and seized and destroyed the rudimentary fortifications. Then came disaster. Disregarding the caution given by Lancaster, they allowed themselves to be inveigled into following up the retreating enemy, with the result that they found themselves confronted with a large body of troops, who poured in a heavy fire. Cotton, Lenoir, and Barker were amongst those who were killed, and their men thereupon retreated in confusion to their boats, with a loss of thirty-five of their number.

There was now no opposition to an immediate departure, and the same evening, the wind having become favourable, the fleet, fifteen sail in all, quitted the harbour and put to sea. It was intended to take in water and other supplies at a place about forty leagues to the northward, and Lancaster, with his usual foresight, had already sent two Frenchmen thither to make arrangements with the natives. Upon arriving, however, a gale drove most of the ships to sea, and only Lancaster's vessel, with four more, succeeded in securing the desired provisions. Nevertheless, all but one of the ships reached England or France in safety with their cargoes (July 1595), and thus the audacious enterprise came to a successful conclusion. It had, we may hope, brought Lancaster not only increased reputation but also considerable pecuniary gain.

The news of the raid evidently created a sensation in Spain. A letter of 23 July 1595, included in the *Cal. S.P. Dom.* 1595–97 (p. 77), says that the Spaniards are advised that certain English ships have taken wonderful great riches at Pernambuco; which is no small grief to them. Another from the Venetian ambassadors at Madrid, 15 June 1595, is more explicit. To quote the abstract given in *Cal. S.P. Venice*, 1592–1603 (p. 162): 'News has lately been received that twelve [sic] galleons belonging to the Queen of England landed four hundred harquebusseers at Pernambuco in Brazil. They harried the country and sacked a ship belonging to the West [sic] India fleet, and made themselves masters of a small fort near Pernambuco. The booty amounts to seven thousand cases of sugar, six thousand hundredweight of pepper, and other goods to the value of about two millions in gold.' Evidently the story had not lost in proportion as it travelled eastwards.

INTRODUCTION

Of the Pernambuco expedition we have two narratives. One is contained in a pamphlet written by Henry Roberts (for whom see a note on p. 52) and published soon after the return of the fleet in 1595. Of this pamphlet only two copies are known to be now extant, and these are both in the United States—one in the John Carter Brown Library at Providence (Rhode Island) and the other in the Henry E. Huntington Library in California. The former is here reprinted, by the kind help of the Librarian, Mr Lawrence C. Wroth, who, as already recorded, supplied photostats for the purpose and gave other valuable assistance. The second account is found in Hakluyt's *Principall Navigations*. A comparison of the two makes it clear that both are drawn from the same source—a narrative written by someone who took part in the enterprise. We glean from the pamphlet some useful information which we should not otherwise have had; but it is less clear than Hakluyt's version, and there is at least one glaring discrepancy between the two accounts. Roberts represents Lancaster as leading the unsuccessful attack upon the Portuguese just before the departure of the fleet; whereas Hakluyt's account (which has the ring of truth) declares that Lancaster was not present and that the defeat was due to disregard of his express instructions. Roberts's object seems to have been to exonerate the memory of Captain Randolph Cotton, who was in command of the English contingent and lost his life in the affray; but this does not excuse the misrepresentation. We may surmise that Hakluyt, hearing the truth (possibly from Lancaster himself), thereupon took the trouble to get hold of the original manuscript, instead of trusting to the account of the voyage given in the pamphlet. This is yet another example of the pains Hakluyt always took to obtain accurate information.

For nearly four years after his return in July 1595 we hear little or nothing of Lancaster. Robert Southey, who, in his *History of Brazil* (vol. I, p. 364), gives a full account (derived from Hakluyt) of the Pernambuco raid, assumes that after its conclusion Lancaster settled down to a life of respectability, and declares that 'no further mention is made of him'. That he was not idle during the four years we may safely conclude; but practically the only fact that emerges is that in 1598 he was named in the articles of agreement for the Earl of Cumberland's Twelfth Voyage as one of the commissioners for its management (Williamson, p. 201), though there is no evidence of his actual participation in the voyage. The letter printed on p. 154 shows that Lancaster, in 1601, was drawing from the royal exchequer a pension of fifty pounds per annum, but for what services it was conferred we are quite ignorant. An entry in the *Cal. S.P. Dom.* 1603–10 (p. 607), refers to his surrender of this annuity and the grant of it to another on 6 May 1610.

In the meantime Captain Benjamin Wood had been despatched in 1596 by Sir Robert Dudley and others to follow in Lancaster's footsteps. He managed to reach the Malay Peninsula, only to lose both his vessels, with all on board. More success attended the Dutchman, Cornelisz. Houtman, who, sailing in the spring of 1595, returned two years later with three out of his four ships. He had reached Bantam, the pepper port on the north-western coast of Java, and had concluded with its ruler an agreement for trading facilities. This success roused great enthusiasm in Holland, with the result that in 1598 over twenty ships left for the East. In July 1599 four ships under Jakob Cornelisz. van Neck got back with rich cargoes, and plans were rapidly matured for further and greater efforts. The French were likewise bestirring themselves, and the merchants of St Malo were collecting funds for the despatch of two ships to the East Indies.

The threat to England's Levant trade was obvious, and once again the merchants of London took steps to counter the plans of their rivals. In the autumn of 1599 a subscription was raised for a new voyage to the East, and promises were obtained of over 30,000*l.*—equivalent to at least 300,000*l.* in modern currency. A petition was then presented to the Queen for the grant of a charter and a guarantee that the ships, when ready, should not be stayed 'uppon anie pretence'. This assurance, however, Elizabeth would not give. She was negotiating with Spain for the conclusion of a peace, and the question of English trade in Eastern waters was likely to be a stumbling-block. So the merchants were told that their demand could not be entertained for the present. Lancaster appears to have taken no part in the proceedings.

The negotiations with Spain broke down in July 1600, and in the following September the Privy Council urged the leaders of the movement to renew their endeavours, assuring them that the desired privileges would be granted and that the fleet would be allowed to sail. An instant response was made. The former subscribers met and agreed to 'goe forward'. They elected for the purpose seventeen 'committies and directors', and among these were Alderman Thomas Smythe and James Lancaster. The former, already Governor of the Levant Company, was nominated for the like post in the new body; his name was accordingly inserted in that capacity in the charter, which was sealed on the last day of the year. Lancaster was appointed in the same document one of the twenty-four 'committees' who were to assist the Governor in the management of the Company's affairs.

In the meantime Lancaster was active in assisting to fit out the fleet, which consisted of four vessels specially purchased for the voyage.[1] The largest was the *Malice Scourge* (renamed the *Red Dragon*), which the Earl of Cumberland had built in 1595. She was more of a privateer than a merchantman; her burden was at least 600 tons (on p. 117 it is estimated at a higher figure), and she carried about forty guns and two hundred men. The other three—all of which had been engaged in the Levant trade —were the *Hector* (300 tons, 108 men), the *Ascension* (260 tons, 82 men), and the *Susan* (240 tons, 88 men); the armament of each was twenty-four guns. In addition, a small vessel, called the *Gift*, was sent to carry spare stores and provisions during the first part of the voyage. The cost of buying and fitting out the fleet amounted to nearly 40,000*l*. An expenditure of 6860*l*. was incurred for goods sent out for trading, and further, since ready money would be needed for the purchase of return cargoes, a sum of 21,742*l*. was put on board for that purpose. The bulk of this was in the form of Spanish rials of eight (the European currency most familiar in the East); but the Company

---

[1] In 1611 the Company described them as 'four of the best merchant shippes of the kingdome' (*First Letter Book*, p. 430).

was unable to collect enough of these, and accordingly applied to the Queen for permission to have about 6000*l.* worth coined at the royal mint. Apparently Her Majesty hesitated to allow her mint to imitate the coins of a foreign prince, and she insisted on substituting coins of similar weight and fineness, bearing her own name and arms on the one side and on the other the Tudor emblem of a portcullis. As might have been anticipated, these unfamiliar coins failed to pass current in the East, except possibly at their bullion value. Specimens of this 'portcullis money' are nowadays eagerly bought by collectors.

The command of the fleet, as 'general', was given, almost as a matter of course, to Lancaster, whose remuneration seems to have been fixed at an immediate payment of 200*l.* and the profit on 1500*l.* adventure, with a minimum of 300*l.* In addition, he appears to have put 200*l.* of his own into the Company's stock. He himself took charge of the *Red Dragon*. John Middleton was selected for the command of the *Hector*, William Brund for that of the *Ascension*, and John Hayward (or Havard) for that of the *Susan*. The important post of pilot-major of the fleet was given to the well-known navigator, John Davis of Sandridge,[1] who had just returned from filling a like position in Houtman's second voyage in 1598, when Achin and the Malay Peninsula were visited. Considering the importance of his task and his long experience, it is somewhat strange to find that he is mentioned only once in the accounts of the voyage, and then in a rather censorious tone; but it is necessary to bear in mind that these accounts were written by merchants, and there was a longstanding jealousy between the two branches of the service.

We may be sure that Lancaster, remembering the ill effects of the late start made in his first voyage, did his best to get away in good time; yet despite his efforts the fleet did not leave Woolwich until the middle of February 1601, and then contrary winds and the necessity of calling at Dartmouth for some stores delayed the actual departure until 20 April. All went well until they drew near the Line, when calms and a south wind

---

[1] It may be noted that another John Davis (of Limehouse) also served in the fleet as a pilot. This appears from his 'Ruter' (in *Purchas*, vol. I, bk. iv, chap. vi), which contains several references to the events of the voyage.

caused the loss of a whole month. Getting away at last from this zone, and after taking a Portuguese vessel laden with wine, oil, and meal, the fleet stretched over to near the coast of Brazil, and then turned eastwards. The trade wind was picked up, and at last on 9 September the Table Mountain was sighted. The crews of most of the vessels were suffering so badly from scurvy that Lancaster (who had kept his own men fairly healthy by regular doses of lime-juice) was obliged to send assistance to his consorts to bring them into the road. The death-roll was terrible, for only three-quarters of those who had started from England still survived. However, fresh food and rest restored most of the sick men to health, and it was with confidence that the fleet set sail again at the close of October.

After passing the Cape of Good Hope, contrary winds delayed progress and sickness reappeared; so Lancaster found himself obliged once more to seek a port. A short stay was made at the island of St Mary, on the eastern side of Madagascar, and then on Christmas Day the ships anchored in the neighbouring Antongil Bay. Here they traded with the natives for supplies and built a small pinnace, the materials for which had been brought from England. However, the climate proved very unhealthy, and nearly twenty deaths occurred, while Captain Brund was slain by an unfortunate accident. His place as commander of the *Ascension* was taken by Robert Pope.

Quitting Antongil Bay on 6 March 1602, the ships passed an island, which appears to have been that now known as Agalega (or Galega), and towards the end of the month found themselves entangled in the islands and reefs of the Chagos Archipelago. Their next landfall (9 May) was in the Nicobar Islands. There about three weeks were spent, and then the fleet proceeded to Achin (Kotaraja), which was reached early in June. The outward voyage had taken nearly sixteen months.

The English were well received by the ruling monarch, to whom Lancaster presented with due ceremony a letter from Queen Elizabeth and some handsome gifts provided by the Company for that purpose. The king, who was reported to be 'desirous to intertaine strangers', was certainly in a position to plume himself on the number of Europeans now seeking his favour. There were already two Dutchmen resident in his capital, left there by Houtman on his recent visit; also a Portuguese envoy from Malacca, presumably sent to watch the moves of other European powers. The arrival of Lancaster's fleet was followed by that of a Dutch pinnace,[1] which had strayed

from the squadron of Joris van Speilbergen: of a French vessel, the *Croissant*, whose consort, the *Corbin*, had been wrecked on the Maldives: and finally of Speilbergen himself, with his remaining two ships. To his English visitors the king was especially kind, and he and Lancaster were soon on the best of terms.

---

[1] The *Lam*. This Lancaster promptly bought, as it was of a handy size for port-to-port traffic in the East.

In one respect the latter was disappointed. He had hoped for the conclusion of a formal commercial treaty between the two nations, as a basis for future trade. Such an arrangement, however, was not consonant with Oriental notions. No sovereign could bind his successor; and indeed any concession he himself might make was to be regarded as revocable at his pleasure. So Lancaster had to be content with a document in which the king authorized the English to trade freely with his people, without the payment of customs dues, and accorded them some minor concessions. The point, however, was really of small importance. It soon became apparent that Achin, though a convenient port of call for Asiatic vessels (there were eighteen such in the roads when the English arrived), was never likely to be of importance for European trade. There was no demand for the products of the West; while the pepper-producing districts, though under the rule of Achin, lay far to the south, with Priaman and Tiku as their natural outlets. At Achin itself pepper was both scarce and dear; and though the English merchants managed to procure enough to lade in part the *Ascension*, this was only effected at a considerable cost. Lancaster was anxious to send home as soon as possible at least two of his ships; and so, towards the end of July, the *Susan* was sent down the coast to Priaman, with orders to secure for herself a full lading of pepper and await the coming of the rest of the fleet.

For his remaining two ships Lancaster was hoping to obtain cargoes at Bantam in Java; but that was as yet an untried market, and he began to be seriously alarmed for the financial success of his voyage. His thoughts turned therefore to the possibility of capturing (as on his first voyage) some of the Portuguese shipping passing through the Straits of Malacca.[1] The king, whose enmity to the Portuguese was of long standing, entered heartily into his schemes, and readily undertook to prevent the Portuguese envoy from sending a warning to Malacca. The arrival of Speilbergen offered an opportunity for securing a useful ally, and he was induced to join the expedition with his

---

[1] The Company had provided him with letters of reprisal from the Lord High Admiral, authorizing him to capture the goods of the King of Spain or his subjects (*First Letter Book*, pp. 191–6).

flagship, on promise of a share in the booty. Towards the end of September, therefore, Lancaster, with the *Dragon*, *Hector*, *Ascension*, and the pinnace purchased from the Dutch, and Speilbergen in the *Schaep*, left Achin and proceeded to the Straits. Fortune favoured them, for in a few days they met and captured the *Santo Antonio*, a vessel of 1200 tons, bound from India to Malacca, with many passengers and a rich cargo, which included a stock of calicoes specially suited for the Eastern markets. Such goods as were thought to be of value were quickly transferred, and then, a storm arising, the Portuguese vessel was left riding at anchor.

By 24 October Lancaster was back at Achin, 'much bound to God, that had eased him of a very heavy care'. The lading of the *Ascension* was now completed, and there was no reason for staying longer. Lancaster took his leave of the king, who handed him a letter for Queen Elizabeth, and wished him good luck for the rest of his voyage. A picturesque incident marked the closing scene. The king and his nobles stood up and sang one of the Psalms of David—'for your prosperitie', he told Lancaster; and then, at his suggestion, Lancaster and his companions sang another in English. This done, the final leavetakings were exchanged, with cordial assurances that Englishmen and English ships would always be welcomed at Achin.

The fleet set sail on 9 November 1602. A couple of days later the *Ascension* took her departure for England. The *Dragon* and the *Hector* continued their voyage to Priaman, where they found the *Susan* almost laden. Leaving her to complete her cargo and then follow the *Ascension*, Lancaster proceeded on his way to Bantam, to fill his two remaining ships. The desired port was reached in the middle of December.

Bantam was at this period, and for long afterwards, a place of considerable commercial importance, not only as a market for the pepper-producing districts of the neighbourhood, but also as a centre of transit trade. It had a large Chinese community and carried on a regular commerce with that country and with the Moluccas. Its nominal ruler was a boy of ten, but all real power was exercised by his uncle, the *Pangeran* or Protector. Lancaster had an interview with both, and delivered a letter

THE FIGHT WITH THE CARRACK

from Queen Elizabeth and a present of plate. Terms of trade were quickly agreed upon; and not only were many of the goods brought by the English ships sold at a good price, but full cargoes of pepper were secured on terms which compared very favourably with those demanded at Achin and Priaman. Seeing the prospects of future trade so attractive, and as he had still remaining most of the goods captured from the Portuguese, Lancaster decided to leave at Bantam a group of merchants, under William Starkie, to sell the stock on hand and purchase pepper in readiness for the next fleet from England. For the same purpose the pinnace acquired from the Dutch was appointed to go to the Moluccas and there procure a supply of cloves and nutmegs. Thus was established the first English 'factory' at Bantam—destined to be for a long period the centre of English trade in the East.

The general satisfaction was saddened by the death of John Middleton, the captain of the *Hector*, who fell a victim to the pestilential climate which was the great drawback of Bantam. Warned by this and the sickly state of others, Lancaster made haste to depart; and after a farewell interview with the boy king, who gave him a letter and a present for his sovereign, the two ships set sail for home on 20 February 1603, 'with thankes to God and glad hearts'.

The homeward voyage proved long and trying. Both vessels were much in need of repairs, which it was impossible to effect in an Eastern port; and they were also poorly provisioned and undermanned. At first all went smoothly; but towards the end of April, when nearing the Cape, a furious storm smote the ships, starting leaks which gave trouble all the rest of the voyage. Five days later another tempest caused the *Dragon* to lose her rudder, and she lay driving 'up and downe in the sea like a wracke'. Attempts to provide a substitute failed, and the crew, giving up hope, clamoured to abandon the ship and take refuge in the *Hector*. Lancaster, however, declared that 'wee will yet abide Gods leasure, to see what mercie He will shew us'; and, in order to check any such attempt, he sent orders secretly to the master of the *Hector* to leave the *Dragon* to her fate and make the best of his way home, carrying with him a farewell letter to the

Company from Lancaster.[1] But the master was 'an honest and a good man, and loved the generall well and was loth to leave him in so great distresse'. So next morning, when Lancaster looked over the heaving waste of waters, he saw in the distance the *Hector*, still hovering round him like a faithful dog. 'These men regard no commission', he growled; yet he made no attempt to enforce his order, and soon the weather mended and a new rudder was fixed. A course was now laid for St Helena, and on 16 June that island was reached and a welcome respite was obtained.

After resting his men and taking in such provisions as were available, Lancaster sailed again on 5 July. The rest of the voyage was comparatively uneventful, and the two ships dropped anchor in the Downs on 11 September 1603. The *Ascension* had got home in the previous May, and the *Susan* had also arrived in safety. The return of all four ships, with good cargoes, and the news that a factory had been established in the Far East to carry on the trade, gave legitimate cause for satisfaction, and we may feel assured that the returned wanderers received a warm welcome, not only from the East India Company but also from Londoners in general.

They found at least one great change in the England they had left in 1601. The great Tudor queen was dead, and Scottish James sat upon her throne. Lancaster was accorded an interview with the new monarch at Winchester on 2 October 1603, when the honour of knighthood was conferred upon him, in recognition of his services to the nation (Shaw's *Knights of England*, vol. II, p. 129). Presumably on that occasion he presented to James the letters and presents he had brought from Achin and Bantam.

In his conferences with the Company, Lancaster doubtless urged the early despatch of a fresh fleet to follow up what had been achieved. But the position was difficult. The money

---

[1] It is interesting to note that Lancaster concluded his letter with the statement that 'the passage to the East-India lieth in 62½ degrees by the north-west on the America side'. This piece of information, passed on to his employers as a parting gift, may have been derived from the same source as the statement as to the Portuguese explorations on the coast of China (p. 21). The striking thing about it is that the latitude indicated approximates to that of the Bering Strait, and so the statement was fairly accurate.

collected for the First Voyage had all been spent; it had been found necessary to borrow 2000*l*. before the mariners of the *Ascension* could be paid off, and further and larger loans were necessitated by the arrival of the other three ships. The fact that the cargoes brought home consisted mainly of pepper was a source of embarrassment, for the commencement of the new reign had been signalized by a virulent outbreak of plague and trade was at a standstill. The home market for pepper was in any case a limited one; while exportation to the Continent offered small prospect of gain, seeing that the Dutch were bringing large quantities from the East. To add to the Company's troubles, the Crown had on hand a considerable stock of the commodity,[1] and was disposed to insist that this should take precedence of the Company's pepper in the market. In the end the Company decided to distribute most of its pepper among the members by way of dividend, at the rate of 2*s*. a pound, leaving each one to make his own arrangements for disposing of his share. The ensuing competition drove down the price to 1*s*. 2*d*., and some of the members could not get rid of their stock for six or seven years (*Court Minutes*, 29 August and 8 October 1623). When the accounts were finally made up (in 1609), it was found that the profit was 95 per cent. upon the amount invested. Considering that this was spread over nine years, and that eight per cent. interest was easily obtained upon well-secured loans, the return was not specially attractive, allowing for the risky nature of the venture.

Before leaving the subject, we may note that, despite its difficulties, the Company managed to scrape together about 60,000*l*. and to fit out the same four ships for a second voyage. This fleet departed for the East in March 1604. Doubtless, all concerned would have been glad if Lancaster had been willing to take the command; but his health was poor and he had had enough of adventure and hardship. So the new expedition was entrusted to the leadership of Henry Middleton, who had brought home the *Susan* in the previous voyage.

Lancaster continued to take an interest in the affairs of the

---

[1] Resulting probably from the capture of a carrack in the preceding year: see Monson's *Naval Tracts* (Navy Records Society), vol. II, appendix C.

East India Company and to afford it the benefit of his advice. The *Court Minutes* of that body for 1603–6, 1610–13, and 1615–17 are missing; but he was certainly serving as a 'committee' (i.e. director) in 1606–7 and 1617–18, and probably in other years as well. From time to time references occur to his being consulted on special points, and the 'Hints' printed on p. 166 show how readily he responded to an appeal for guidance. The lively interest he took in schemes for the discovery of the North-West Passage is attested by the name of Lancaster Sound, given by Baffin to an inlet found by him in 1616.

Lancaster resided in a large house situated on the eastern side of Bevis Marks, opposite the northern end of St Mary Axe Street and backing on to London Wall. This was an old house, originally built as a home for aged priests, and known as The Papey. In the reign of Edward VI the charity was suppressed and the house became a private dwelling, numbering among its subsequent tenants Sir Francis Walsingham. In February 1612 Lancaster was persuaded to stand for alderman for Cordwainer Ward; but the electors preferred another candidate, and he made no further attempt to obtain civic office.

Apparently he never married. In his will no mention is made of wife or child, and in the Latin verses on his portrait he is described as a bachelor. Such was often the case at that time with Englishmen who sought a livelihood abroad. There were many difficulties in the way of taking a wife to foreign countries; while trading bodies, such as the Levant or the East India Company, arranged for lodging and boarding their employees in 'factories', but only on a celibate basis. Marriage had therefore in most cases to be deferred until the exile returned to his own country, and by that time he had often become a confirmed bachelor.

Lancaster died, apparently after an illness lasting some months, on 6 June 1618; and three days later he was buried in the parish church of All Hallows, London Wall (*Registers*, Harleian Society, p. 194). There is no record of any monument being erected to his memory, and the church itself was taken down and rebuilt in 1765–67. The only extant memorial that has survived is his coat of arms, still displayed in Basingstoke parish church.

His will[1] (*P.C.C.*: 65 *Meade*), dated 18 April 1618, with a codicil of 4 June, shows that he died a comparatively wealthy man. Mention is made therein of an uncle, William Lancaster, and of an aunt, Mrs Izard; also of two brothers, John (dead) and Peter (surviving), a brother-in-law named Hopgood, and several cousins. To these and other relatives or friends bequests were made, totalling over 2000*l.*; while his household servants— three men and two maids—were not forgotten. A sum of 120*l.* was to be distributed among the poor of six London parishes, and grants were also made for the poor of Basingstoke and the neighbouring parish of Kingsclere, three London hospitals, and various prisons (for the benefit of the poorer inmates). Further, a sum was to be placed at the disposal of Mrs Thomasine Owfield, widow, for distribution at her discretion to poor people. To her personally Lancaster left the lease of his London dwelling and the tenement at its back gate, together with tapestry, china, and glass. His landed property (chiefly in Lincolnshire) was bequeathed in trust to the Skinners' Company. From the rents thereof the Company was to pay yearly to the churchwardens, etc. of Basingstoke 45*l.* for the poor of that town, 40*l.* for a lecturer at the parish church, 20*l.* to the free school, and 13*l.* 6*s.* 8*d.* for an additional schoolmaster at that institution. Out of the residue, four scholarships of 15*l.* apiece were to be given to lads intending to study divinity at Oxford or Cambridge; 20*l.* was to be distributed yearly to widows of poor freemen of the Company, and a similar sum to four poor preachers; 20*l.* a year was provided to maintain a schoolmaster at Kingsclere; 35*l.* was to be retained by the Company for its trouble in administering these charities; and ten marks were to be spent on an annual dinner, to be held after the transaction of such business. The executors were directed to arrange that his funeral should take place at night, to avoid trouble; and they were further to keep his household going for three months (in order to give his servants time to find other employment) and meanwhile they were to make use of the premises for the transaction of business connected with the estate.

[1] A full account of its provisions is given in Mr Wadmore's book on the Skinners' Company (p. 211).

In the main these charities are still in operation at the present day. By an arrangement, sanctioned in 1713 by a decree of the Lord Chancellor, the estates bequeathed by Lancaster were made over to the corporation of Basingstoke, subject to the payment annually to Kingsclere and to the Skinners' Company of the sums necessary for carrying out the other charitable provisions of the will. After the passing of the Municipal Corporations Act in 1835 the estates were vested in trustees, and they are now administered under a scheme sanctioned by the Charity Commissioners. The Skinners' Company still distributes yearly the 20*l.* bequeathed to the widows of freemen and the bequests for preachers and scholarships; in the two latter cases the amounts given are augmented by the bounty of the Company from its own funds.

Lancaster's connexion with the Skinners' Company is commemorated in Skinners' Hall by a large painting depicting his departure on his third voyage in 1601. This was executed by Mr Frank Brangwyn, R.A., and is a magnificent piece of colour.[1] The Company also possesses a portrait of Lancaster, copied from an original painting[2] belonging to Mrs Christie-Miller. By the kind permission of the Master, Wardens, and Court of Assistants, and with the concurrence of Mrs Christie-Miller, the Company's copy has been reproduced as the frontispiece of the present volume. As shown by the inscription at the top of the picture, this portrait was painted in 1596, when Lancaster was in his forty-second year.[3] The name of the painter is not known.

Lancaster's outstanding characteristic is his quiet efficiency. In everything he undertook, his plans were laid with the utmost care; provision was made for every contingency, and, once made, these plans were carried out with boldness and resolution. When occasion required, he did not flinch from taking risks, as

---

[1] A coloured reproduction forms the frontispiece to *The Story of Exploration*, edited by Sir Percy Sykes.

[2] A photograph of this has been reproduced in Mr Wadmore's volume (p. 211).

[3] The addition 'Obiit Jun. 6, 1618' must of course have been made after Lancaster's death. Possibly the panegyric in Latin verse in the top right-hand corner was added at the same time.

is shown by his persistence in remaining aboard the battered *Dragon* when her survival was thought to be impossible, or by his dash through the surf at Recife to head the attack upon the Portuguese redoubt; but in general he was tender of the lives of his men, and he has been credited with being the first commander to use lime-juice as an anti-scorbutic. In his relations with his subordinates he was frank and open, ever ready to explain his motives and, if necessary, to argue with recalcitrants instead of silencing them by resort to authority. In most cases, however, his decisions were accepted without demur, his officers and men alike trusting implicitly in his judgment and regarding him with both respect and affection. The reader will not fail to notice that in all the narratives in the present volume there is not a word of criticism of Lancaster personally or any questioning of his capacity as a leader.

Hardly less striking is his modesty. Looking back in his years of leisure, he may well have felt a pride in his achievements; yet not only did he refrain from writing any account of them himself, but there is no hint that he instigated or helped those who undertook that task. Fortunately, it has been adequately performed by other pens, and Lancaster's services as a pioneer of English trade in Eastern waters have been imperishably inscribed upon the scroll of fame.

FULLER TITLES OF WORKS CITED

Acts of the Privy Council of England, 1586–87. London, 1897.
Archivo Portuguez-Oriental. 7 vols. Nova Goa, 1857–77.
BAIGENT, F. J. and MILLARD, J. E. *A History of...Basingstoke.* Basingstoke, 1889.
BEST, THOMAS. *The Voyage of, to the East Indies*, 1612–14. Edited by Sir William Foster, C.I.E. Hakluyt Society, 1934.
BOWREY, THOMAS. *The Countries round the Bay of Bengal*, 1669–79. Edited by Sir Richard Temple, C.B., C.I.E. Hakluyt Society, 1905.
BRUCE, JOHN. *Annals of the Honourable East India Company.* 3 vols. London, 1810.
Calendar of State Papers, Domestic, 1581–90, 1595–97, and 1603–10. London, 1857, 1865, and 1869.
Calendar of State Papers, Venice, 1592–1603. London, 1897.
Dawn of British Trade to the East Indies. Edited by Henry Stevens. London, 1886.
DUDLEY, ROBERT. *The Voyage of, to the West Indies and Guiana.* Edited by Sir George F. Warner. Hakluyt Society, 1899.
First Letter Book of the East India Company. Edited by Sir George Birdwood, K.C.I.E. and William Foster. London, 1893.
FOSTER, WILLIAM. *England's Quest of Eastern Trade.* London, 1933.
HAKLUYT, RICHARD. *The Principall Navigations...of the English Nation.* 3 vols. London, 1598–1600.
HAKLUYTS, RICHARD. *Writings...of the two.* Edited by Prof. E. G. R. Taylor. 2 vols. Hakluyt Society, 1935.
LAUGHTON, Sir JOHN. *The Defeat of the Spanish Armada.* 2 vols. Navy Records Society, 1894.
Letters Received by the East India Company from its Servants in the East, 1602–17. Edited by William Foster. 6 vols. London, 1896–1902.
LINSCHOTEN, J. H. VAN. *The Voyage of, to the East Indies.* Edited by A. C. Burnell and P. A. Tiele. 2 vols. Hakluyt Society, 1885.
MARSDEN, WILLIAM. *History of Sumatra.* Third edition. London, 1811.
MARTIN, FRANÇOIS. *Description du premier Voyage faict aux Indes Orientales par les François.* Paris, 1604.
MYDDLETON, W. M. *Pedigree of the Family of Myddleton.* Horncastle, 1910.

PURCHAS, SAMUEL. *Purchas His Pilgrimes.* 4 vols. London, 1625.
PYRARD, FRANÇOIS. *The Voyage of.* Edited by Sir Albert Gray, K.C.B. 2 vols. Hakluyt Society, 1887–89.
ROE, Sir THOMAS. *The Embassy of, to the Great Mogul.* Edited by Sir William Foster, C.I.E. Second edition. London, 1926.
SHAW, W. A. *Knights of England.* 2 vols. London, 1906.
SMYTH, W. H. *Sailor's Word-Book.* London, 1867.
SOUTHEY, ROBERT. *History of Brazil.* 3 vols. London, 1810.
SPEILBERGEN, JORIS VAN. *Het Journael van.* Delft, 1605.
WADMORE, J. F. *Some Account of the Worshipful Company of Skinners.* London, 1902.
WILLIAMSON, G. C. *George, Third Earl of Cumberland.* Cambridge, 1920.

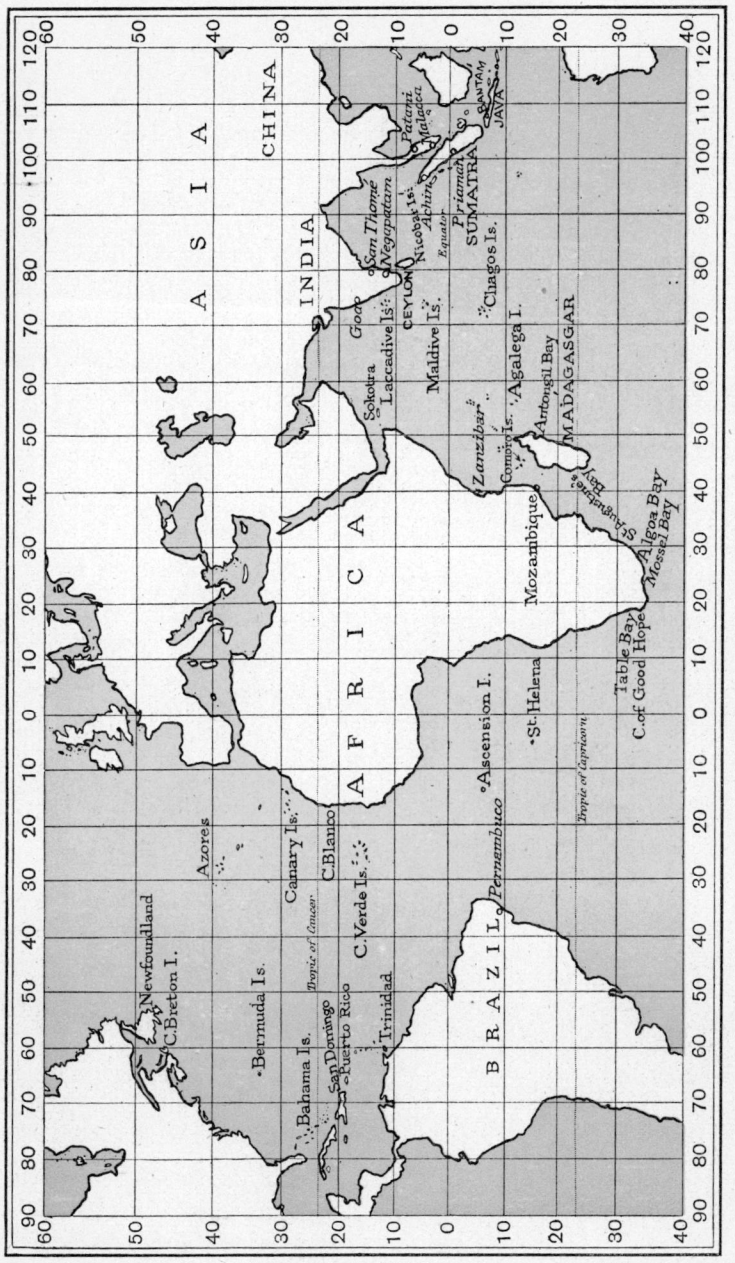

A GENERAL MAP OF THE INDIES

THE FIRST VOYAGE
1591-94

I

BARKER'S NARRATIVE[1]

A voyage with three tall ships, the Penelope, *admirall, the* Marchant Royall, *vice-admirall, and the* Edward Bonaventure, *rere-admirall, to the East Indies, by the Cape of Buona Speransa, to Quitangone, neere Mosambique, to the iles of Comoro and Zanzibar on the backeside of Africa, and beyond Cape Comori in India to the iles of Nicubar and of Gomes Pulo (within two leagues of Sumatra), to the ilands of Pulo Pinaom, and thence to the maine land of Malacca*[2]. *Begunne by M[aster] George Raymond, in the yeere* 1591, *and performed by M[aster] James Lancaster; and written from the mouth of Edmund Barker of Ipswich (his lieutenant in the sayd voyage) by M[aster] Richard Hakluyt.*

OUR FLEET of the three tall ships above-named departed from Plimmouth the 10 of April 1591, and arrived at the Canarie Ilands the 25 of the same; from whence we departed the 29 of April. The second of May we were in the height of Cape Blanco[3]. The fift we passed the Tropique of Cancer. The eight we were in the height of Cape Verde. All this time we went with a faire winde at north-east, always before the winde, untill the 13 of the same moneth, when we came within 8 degrees of the

---

[1] From Hakluyt's *Principall Navigations*, vol. II, pt. ii, p. 102.
[2] For the places here mentioned see notes on later pages.
[3] In Spanish West Africa, in lat. 20° 47′ N.

Equinoctiall Line; where we met with a contrary winde. Here we lay off and on in the sea untill the sixt of June, on which day we passed the sayd Line. While we lay thus off and on, we tooke a Portugal caravel[1], laden by marchants of Lisbon for Brasile; in which caravel we had some 60 tunnes of wine, 1200 jarres of oyle, about 100 jarres of olives, certaine barrels of capers, three fats [i.e. vats] of peason, with divers other necessaries fit for our voyage: which wine, oyle, olives, and capers were better to us then gold.

We had two men died before wee passed the Line and divers sicke, which tooke their sicknesse in those hote climates; for they be wonderful unholesome from 8 degrees of northerly latitude unto the Line at that time of the yeere; for we had nothing but ternados[2], with such thunder, lightning, and raine, that we could not keep our men drie 3 houres together; which was an occasion of the infection among them, and their eating of salt victuals, with lacke of clothes to shift them.

After we passed the Line we had the wind still at east-southeast, which caried us along the coast of Brasil, 100 leagues from the maine, til we came in 26 degrees to the southward of the Line, where the wind came up to the north; at which time we did account that the Cape of Buona Esperansa [i.e. Good Hope] did beare off us east and by south betwixt 900 and 1000 leagues. Passing this gulfe from the coast of Brasil unto the Cape we had the wind often variable, as it is upon our coast, but for the most part so that we might lie our course. The 28 of July we had sight of the foresayd Cape of Buona Esperansa. Untill the 31 wee lay off and on, with the wind contrary to double the Cape; hoping to double it and so to have gone seventie leagues further, to a place called Agoada de S. Bras[3], before we would have sought to have put into any harbour. But our men being weake and sicke in all our shippes, we thought good to seeke some place to refresh them. With which consent we bare up with the land to the northward of the Cape; and going along the shore we espied a goodly

---

[1] For a description (with illustration) of a caravel, see Sir Albert Gray's *Voyage of Pyrard de Laval*, vol. II, pt. i, p. 215.

[2] Tornadoes are common in those latitudes.

[3] Now known as Mossel Bay. It is sixty leagues from the Cape. *Aguada* means 'watering-place.'

baie with an iland lying to seawards of it; into which we did beare, and found it very commodious for our ships to ride in. This baie is called Agoada de Saldanha, lying 15 leagues northward on the hither side of the Cape[1]. The first of August, being Sunday, we came to an anker in the baie, sending our men on land; and there came unto them certaine blacke salvages, very brutish, which would not stay, but retired from them.

For the space of 15 or 20 dayes we could find no reliefe, but onely foules which wee killed with our pieces [i.e. muskets], which were cranes and geese. There was no fish but muskles and other shel-fish, which we gathered on the rockes. After 15 or 20 dayes being here, our admirall went with his pinnasse unto the iland which lieth off this baie, where hee found great store of penguines and seales; whereof he brought good plenty with him. And twise after that we sent certain of our men, which at both times brought their bots lading unto our ships. After we had bene here some time we got here a negro, whom we compelled to march into the country with us, making signs to bring us some cattell; but at this time we could come to the sight of none; so we let the negro goe, with some trifles. Within 8 dayes after, he, with 30 or 40 other negros, brought us downe some 40 bullocks and oxen, with as many sheepe; at which time we bought but few of them. But within 8 dayes after, they came downe with as many more, and then we bought some 24 oxen, with as many sheepe. We bought an oxe for two knives, a stirke[2] for a knife, and a sheepe for a knife; and some we bought for lesse value then a knife. The oxen be very large and well fleshed, but not fat. The sheepe are very big and very good meat; they have no woll on their backs, but haire, and have great tailes, like the sheepe in Syria[3]. There be divers sorts of wild beasts, as the antilope

---

[1] Doubtless they had a Portuguese chart and under its direction were seeking the watering-place which Antonio de Saldanha discovered on his way to India in 1503, and at which six years later the ex-Viceroy, Francisco de Almeira, was killed in a skirmish with the natives. This was Table Bay, long known to succeeding English fleets as Saldania Bay.

The island mentioned in the text was called by the English Penguin Island, but now bears the Dutch appellation of Robben (Seals) Island. It has recently been fortified.   [2] Young bullock or heifer.

[3] 'Their sheepe have exceeding great tailes, only of fat, weighing twelve or fourteene pounds; they have no wooll, but a long shag haire' (Davis in *Purchas*, vol. I, bk. iii, p. 118).

(whereof M[aster] Lancaster killed one of the bignes of a yong colt), the red and fallow deere, with other great beasts unknowen unto us. Here are also great store of over-growen monkeis.

As touching our proceeding upon our voyage, it was thought good rather to proceed with two ships wel manned then with three evill manned; for here wee had of sound and whole men but 198, of which there went in the *Penelope* with the admiral 101, and in the *Edward* with the Worshipfull M[aster] Captaine Lancaster 97. We left behind 50 men with the *Roiall Marchant*, whereof there were many pretily well recovered; of which ship was master and governour Abraham Kendal[1], which for many reasons we thought good to send home. The disease that hath consumed our men hath bene the skurvie. Our souldiers, which have not bene used to the sea, have best held out, but our mariners dropt away; which (in my judgement) proceedeth of their evill diet[2] at home.

Sixe dayes after our sending backe for England of the *Marchant Roiall* from Agoada de Saldanha, our admirall, M[aster] Captaine Raimond, in the *Penelope*, and M[aster] James Lancaster, in the *Edward Bonadventure*, set forward to double the Cape of Buona Esperansa; which they did very speedily. But being passed as far as Cape Dos Corrientes, the 14 of September we were encountred with a mighty storme and extreeme gusts of wind, wherein we lost our Generals companie, and could never heare of him nor his ship any more, though we did our best endevour to seeke him up and downe a long while, and staied for him certaine dayes at the iland of Comoro, where we appointed to stay one for another. Foure dayes after this uncomfortable seperation, in the morning, toward ten of the clocke, we had a terrible clap of thunder, which slew foure of our men outright, their necks being wrung in sonder without speaking any word, and of 94 men there was not one untouched; whereof

---

[1] Kendal was afterwards master of the *Bear* in Robert Dudley's voyage to the West Indies in 1594–95, and wrote an account of it which is printed in Sir George Warner's edition. Later he accompanied Drake and Hawkins in their last voyage, and died off Porto Bello on 28 January 1596 (the same day as Drake).

[2] Used here in its old sense of 'way of living.'

Sept. 1591]   A STORM   5

some were striken blind, others were bruised in their legs and armes, and others in their brests, so that they voided blood two dayes after; others were drawen out at length, as though they had bene racked. But (God be thanked) they all recovered, saving onely the foure which were slaine outright. Also with the same thunder our mainemaste was torne very grievously from the heade to the decke, and some of the spikes, that were ten inches into the timber, were melted with the extreme heate theereof[1].

From thence wee shaped our course to the north-east, and not long after we fell upon the north-west end of the mighty iland of S. Laurence[2]; which one of our men espied (by Gods good blessing) late in the evening by moonelight; who, seeing afarre off the breaking of the sea and calling to certaine of his fellowes, asked them what it was; which eftsoones told him that it was the breaking of the sea upon the shoulds; whereupon in very good time we cast about to avoyd the danger which we were like to have incurred. Thus passing on forward, it was our lucke to overshoote Mozambique and to fall with a place called Quitangone[3], two leagues to the northward of it. And we tooke three or foure barkes of Moores[4] (which barkes in their language they call pangaias[5]), laden with millio[6], hennes, and ducks, with one Portugall boy, going for the provision of Mozambique.

Within few dayes following we came to an iland, an hundred leagues to the north-east of Mozambique, called Comoro[7]; which we found exceeding full of people, which are Moores, of tawnie colour and good stature, but they be very trecherous, and

[1] The disaster was of course due to lightning; but it was customary at that period to attribute the damage to some solid body associated with the thunder ('th'all-dreaded thunder-stone').

[2] Madagascar. May (p. 23) says they were off 'the westermost part' of the island; but it would appear from a later page that they were nearly wrecked upon the *Bassas da India*, in the middle of the Mozambique Channel.

[3] Quitangonha Island, on the northern side of Conducia Bay, about ten miles north of Mozambique.

[4] In Spain and Portugal, the followers of Islam were chiefly known as invaders from Morocco, and hence the terms Moor and Muhammadan became synonymous. This usage spread to Holland and England, as witnessed by the description of Shakespeare's Othello as a Moor.

[5] Pangaia was a Portuguese name for a sailing barge, much used on the coast of East Africa. Descriptions are given on pp. 6, 23.

[6] Port. *milho da India*, maize.

[7] Great Comoro (Angasija), the principal island of the Comoro group.

diligently to be taken heed of. Here wee desired to store ourselves with water, whereof we stood in great need, and sent sixteene of our men well armed on shore in our boate; whom the people suffred quietly to land and water. And divers of them with their king came aboord our ship in a gowne of crimosine [i.e. crimson] sattin, pinked after the Moorish fashion downe to the knee; whom we entertained in the best maner, and had some conference with him of the state of the place and marchandises, using our Portugall boy which we had taken before for our interpreter; and in the end licensed the king and his company to depart, and sent our men againe for more water, who then also dispatched their businesse and returned quietly. The third time likewise we sent them for more, which also returned without any harme. And though we thought ourselves furnished, yet our master, William Mace of Radcliffe[1], pretending that it might be long before we should finde any good watering place, would needes goe himselfe on shore with thirtie men, much against the will of our captaine; and hee and 16 of his company, together with one boat (which was all that we had[2]) and 16 others that were a-washing over-against our ship, were betrayed of the perfidious Moores, and in our sight for the most part slaine, we being not able for want of a boat to yeeld them any succour.

From hence with heavie hearts we shaped our course for Zanzibar the 7[3] of November; where shortly after wee arrived, and made us a new boat of such boards as we had within boord; and rid in the road untill the 15 of February. Where during our aboad we sawe divers pangaias or boates, which are pinned with woodden pinnes and sowed together with palmito cordes, and calked with the huskes of cocos shels beaten, whereof they make occam [oakum]. At length a Portugall pangaia comming out of the harborow of Zanzibar, where they have a small factorie, sent a canoa with a Moore which had bene christened, who brought

---

[1] He is mentioned by Hakluyt as having made a voyage to the Gulf of Mexico in 1589, as master of a small vessel named the *Dog*. On that occasion he narrowly escaped losing his life at the hands of some Spaniards.

[2] This was a common practice at that period.

[3] This date is doubtful. Later it is stated that Zanzibar was reached at the end of November; while May says that they remained at the Comoros all that month.

us a letter wherein they desired to know what wee were and what we sought. We sent them word we were Englishmen come from Don Antonio[1] upon businesse to his friends in the Indies; with which answere they returned, and would not any more come at us. Whereupon not long after wee manned out our boat and tooke a pangaia of the Moores, which had a priest of theirs in it, which in their language they call a Sherife[2], whom we used very curteously; which the king tooke in very good part (having his priests in great estimation) and for his deliverance furnished us with two moneths victuals, during all which time we detained him with us. These Moores informed us of the false and spitefull dealing of the Portugals towards us, which made them beleeve that we were cruell people and men-eaters, and willed them, if they loved their safetie, in no case to come neere us; which they did onely to cut us off from all knowledge of the state and traffique of the countrey.

While we road, from the end of November until the middle of February, in this harborough (which is sufficient for a ship of 500 tuns to ride in), we set upon a Portugall pangaia with our boat; but because it was very litle and our men not able to stirre in it, we were not able to take the sayd pangaia, which was armed with 10 good shot like our long fouling pieces. This place, for the goodnesse of the harborough and watering and plentifull refreshing with fish, whereof we tooke great store with our nets, and for sundry sorts of fruits of the countrey, as cocos and others, which were brought us by the Moores, as also for oxen and hennes, is carefully to be sought for by such of our ships as shall hereafter passe that way. But our men had need to take good heed of the Portugals; for while we lay here the Portugall admiral of the coast from Melinde to Mozambique came to view and to betray our boat, if he could have taken at any time advantage, in a gallie frigate of ten tunnes, with 8 or 9 oares on a side. Of the strength of which frigate and their trecherous meaning we were advertised by an Arabian Moore which came

---

[1] The candidate for the throne of Portugal, whom Elizabeth as a matter of policy supported against Philip II. It was generally believed in England that the Portuguese overseas were in favour of Don Antonio.

[2] *Sharīf*, a descendant of the Prophet's family. The term means 'noble' and it generally connotes a man of rank or importance, apart from his descent.

from the king of Zanzibar divers times unto us about the deliverie of the priest aforesayd, and afterward by another which we caried thence along with us; for wheresoever we came, our care was to get into our hands some one or two of the countreys to learne the languages and states of those partes where we touched. Moreover, here againe we had another clap of thunder which did shake our foremast very much; which wee fisht[1] and repaired with timber from the shore, whereof there is good store thereabout of a kind of trees some fortie foote high, which is a red and tough wood and (as I suppose) a kind of cedar. Here our surgeon, Arnold, negligently catching a great heate in his head (being on land with the master to seeke oxen) fell sicke and shortly died; which might have bene cured by letting of blood before it had bin setled. Before our departure we had in this place some thousandweight [i.e. ten cwt.] of pitch, or rather a kind of gray and white gumme like unto frankincense, as clammie as turpentine; which in melting groweth as blacke as pitch, and is very brittle of itselfe, but we mingled it with oile, whereof wee had 300 jarres in the prize which we tooke to the northward of the Equinoctiall, not farre from Guinie, bound for Brasil.

Sixe dayes before wee departed hence, the cape marchant of the [Portugal] factorie wrote a letter unto our capitaine in the way of friendship, as he pretended, requesting a jarre of wine and a jarre of oyle and two or three pounds of gunpouder; which letter hee sent by a negro (his man) and [a] Moore in a canoa. We sent him his demaunds by the Moore, but tooke the negro along with us, because we understood he had bene in the East Indies and knew somewhat of the countrey. By this negro we were advertised of a small barke of some thirtie tunnes (which the Moores call a junco[2]), which was come from Goa thither, laden with pepper for the factorie and service of that kingdome.

Thus, having trimmed our shippe as we lay in this road, in the end we set forward for the coast of the East India the 15 of February aforesayd, intending, if we could, to have reached to Cape Comori [Comorin], which is the headland or promontorie

---

[1] Strengthened with a wooden support.
[2] The term junk (Malay *jong*) is now restricted to Chinese ships, but in the seventeenth century it was used of any Asiatic seagoing vessel.

of the maine of Malavar, and there to have lien off and on for such ships as should have passed from Zeilan [Ceylon], Sant Tome[1], Bengala, Pegu, Malacca, the Moluccos, the coast of China, and the ile of Japan; which ships are of exceeding wealth and riches. But in our course we were very much deceived by the currents that set into the gulfe of the Red Sea along the coast of Melinde; and the windes shortening upon us to the northeast and easterly kept us that we could not get off, and so, with the putting in of the currents from the westward, set us in further unto the northward, within fourescore leagues of the ile of Zocotora [Sokotra], farre from our determined course and expectation. But here we never wanted abundance of dolphins, bonitos[2], and flying fishes. Now while we found ourselves thus farre to the northward, and the time being so farre spent, we determined to goe for the Red Sea or for the iland of Zocotora, both to refresh ourselves and also for some purchase [i.e. booty]. But while wee were in this consultation, the winde very luckily came about to the north-west and caried us directly toward Cape Comori. Before we should have doubled this cape we were determined to touch at the ilands of Mamale[3] (of which we had advertisement that one had victuals), standing in the northerly latitude of twelve degrees. Howbeit, it was not our good lucke to finde it; which fell out partly by the obstinacie of our master[4], for the day before we fell with part of the ilands the wind came about to the south-west, and then shifting our course we missed it. So, the wind increasing southerly, we feared we should not have bene able to have doubled the cape; which would have greatly hazarded our casting away upon the coast of India, the winter season and westerne monsons already being come in, which monsons continue on that coast until August. Nevertheles, it pleased God to bring the wind more westerly, and so in the moneth of May 1592 we happily doubled Cape Comori without sight of the coast of India[5].

[1] The Portuguese settlement of San Thomé, on the Coromandel Coast. It is now a suburb of Madras.   [2] A fish of the tunny class.
[3] The Laccadives were generally called by the Portuguese the Mammale Islands, after the great Cananor merchant who controlled their trade (Gray's *Pyrard de Laval*, vol. I, p. 323).
[4] John Hall, who had succeeded Mace in that post.
[5] As a matter of fact the ship must have gone round Ceylon.

From hence, thus having doubled this cape, we directed our course for the ilands of Nicubar, which lie north and south with the westerne part of Sumatra and in the latitude of 7 degrees to the northward of the Equinoctiall. From which Cape of Comori unto the aforesayd ilands we ranne in six dayes with a very large wind, though the weather were foule, with extreme raine and gustes of windes. These ilands were missed through our masters default, for want of due observation of the south starre; and we fell to the southward of them, within the sight of the ilands of Gomes Polo[1] (which lie hard upon the great iland of Sumatra) the first of June; and at the north-east side of them we lay two or three dayes becalmed, hoping to have had a pilote from Sumatra, within two leagues whereof wee lay off and on.

Now the winter comming upon us with much contagious[2] weather, we directed our course from hence with the ilands of Pulo Pinaou[3] (where, by the way, is to be noted that Pulo in the Malaian tongue signifieth an iland); at which ilands wee arrived about the beginning of June, where we came to an anker in a very good harborough betweene three ilands; at which time our men were very sicke and many fallen. Here we determined to stay untill the winter were overpast. This place is in 6 degrees and a halfe[4] to the northward, and some five leagues from the maine betweene Malacca and Pegu. Here we continued untill the end of August. Our refreshing in this place was very smal; onely of oisters growing on rocks, great wilks, and some few fish which we tooke with our hookes. Here we landed our sicke on these uninhabited ilands for their health. Neverthelesse, 26 of them died in this place; whereof John Hall, our master, was one, and M[aster] Rainold Golding another, a marchant of great honestie and much discretion. In these ilands are abundance of trees of white wood, so right and tall that a man may make mastes of them, being an hundred foote long.

The winter passed; and having watered our ship and fitted her to goe to sea, wee had left us but 33 men and one boy, of

---

[1] Gomes, which Linschoten calls 'Gomespola'; but the writer seems to give this name to the whole group. See the map at p. xxxv of *The Voyage of Thomas Best*.   [2] In its old sense of 'foul.'
[3] A misprint for 'Pinaon.' The island of Penang is intended.
[4] Really 5° 25′.

which not past 22 were sound for labour and helpe, and of them not past a third part sailers. Thence we made saile to seeke some place of refreshing, and went over to the maine of Malacca. The next day we came to an anker in a baie in six fadomes water, some two leagues from the shore. Then Master James Lancaster, our captaine, and M[aster] Edmund Barker, his lieutenant, and other of the companie, manning the boat, went on shore to see what inhabitants might be found. And comming on land, we found the tracking of some barefooted people, which were departed thence not long before, for we sawe their fire still burning; but people we sawe none, nor any other living creature, save a certaine kind of foule, called oxe-birds, which are a gray kind of sea-foule, like a snite [i.e. snipe] in colour, but not in beake. Of these we killed some eight dozen with haile-shot, being very tame; and spending the day in search, returned toward night aboord. The next day, about two of the clocke in the afternoone, we espied a canoa which came neere unto us, but would not come aboord us; having in it some sixteen naked Indians, with whom, nevertheles, going afterward on land, we had friendly conference and promise of victuals.

The next day in the morning we espied three ships, being all of burthen 60 or 70 tunnes, one of which wee made to strike with our very boate. And understanding that they were of the towne of Martabamm[1], which is the chiefe haven towne for the great citie of Pegu, and the goods belonging to certaine Portugal Jesuites and a biscuit-baker, a Portugal, we tooke that ship, and did not force the other two, because they were laden for marchants of Pegu; but having this one at our command, we came together to an anker. The night folowing, all the men, except twelve which we tooke into our ship, being most of them borne in Pegu, fled away in their boate, leaving their ship and goods with us. The next day we weighed our anker and went to the leeward of an iland hard by, and tooke in her lading, being pepper, which shee and the other two had laden at Pera[2], which is a place on the maine 30 leagues to the south. Besides the

---

[1] Martaban, near Maulmain, on the east side of the Gulf of Martaban.
[2] Perak (pronounced Pera), a state on the Malay Peninsula about halfway between Penang and Malacca.

aforesaid three ships, we tooke another ship of Pegu, laden with pepper; and perceiving her to bee laden with marchants goods of Pegu onely, wee dismissed her without touching anything.

Thus having staied here 10 daies and discharged her goods into the *Edward* (which was about the beginning of September), our sicke men being somewhat refreshed and lustie with such reliefe as we had found in this ship, we weighed anker, determining to runne into the streights of Malacca to the ilands called Pulo Sambilam[1], which are some five and fortie leagues northward of the citie of Malacca; to which ilands the Portugals must needs come from Goa or S. Thome for the Malucos, China, and Japan. And when wee were there arrived, we lay too and agayne for such shipping as should come that way.

Thus having spent some five dayes, upon a Sunday we espied a saile, which was a Portugall ship that came from Negapatan[2], a towne on the maine of India, over-against the north-east part of the ile of Zeilan; and that night we tooke her, being of 250 tunnes. She was laden with rice for Malacca. Captaine Lancaster commanded their captaine and master aboord our shippe, and sent Edmund Barker, his lieutenant, and seven more to keepe this prize; who, being aboord the same, came to an anker in thirtie fadomes water, for in that chanell three or foure leagues from the shore you shall finde good ankorage. Being thus at an anker, and keeping out a light for the *Edward*, another Portugall ship of Sant Thome, of foure hundred tunnes, came and ankered hard by us. The *Edward* being put to leeward, for lacke of helpe of men to handle her sailes, was not able the next morning to fetch her up, until we which were in the prize with our boate went to helpe to man our shippe. Then comming aboord we went toward the shippe of Sant Thome; but our ship was so foule that shee escaped us. After we had taken out of our Portugall prize what we thought good, we turned her and all her men away, except a pilot and foure Moores.

We continued here untill the sixt of October; at which time we met with the ship of the Captaine of Malacca, of seven hundred tunnes, which came from Goa; we shot at her many shot, and at

---

[1] The Sembilan Islands, in lat. 4° N.
[2] Negapatam, 180 miles south of Madras.

last shooting her maineyard through, she came to an anker and yeelded. We commaunded her captaine, master, pilot, and purser to come aboord us. But the captaine, accompanied with one souldier, onely came, and after certaine conference with him he made excuse to fetch the master and purser, which he sayd would not come unlesse he went for them; but being gotten from us in the edge of the evening, he with all the people, which were to the number of about three hundred men, women, and children, gote ashore with two great boates and quite abandoned the ship. At our comming aboord we found in her sixteene pieces [i.e. cannon] of brasse and three hundred buts of Canarie wine and nipar wine[1], which is made of the palme trees, and raisin wine, which is also very strong; as also all kind of haberdasher wares, as hats, red caps knit of Spanish wooll, worsted stockings knit, shooes, velvets, taffataes, chamlets[2], and silkes, abundance of suckets[3], rice, Venice glasses, certaine papers full of false and counterfeit stones (which an Italian brought from Venice to deceive the rude Indians withall), abundance of playing cardes, two or three packs of French paper. Whatsoever became of the treasure, which usually is brought in roials of plate[4] in this gallion, we could not find it. After that the mariners had disordredly pilled [i.e. pillaged] this rich shippe, the captaine, because they would not follow his commandement to unlade those excellent wines into the *Edward*, abandoned her and let her drive at sea, taking out of her the choisest things that she had.

And doubting [i.e. fearing] the forces of Malaca, we departed thence to a baie in the kingdom of Junsalaomm[5], which is betweene Malacca and Pegu eight degrees to the northward, to seeke for pitch to trimme our ship. Here we sent our souldier which the captaine of the aforesaid galion had left behind him with us, because he had the Malaian language, to deale with the people for pitch; which hee did faithfully, and procured us some two or three quintals[6], with promise of more; and certaine of the

---

[1] Arrack distilled from the sap of a palm tree (Malay *nīpah*).
[2] Cloths made of silk and camel's hair.   [3] Sweetmeats.
[4] Spanish silver rials of eight, which were widely current in the East. They were worth about 5s. each. (On a later page their value is estimated at 4s. 6d.)
[5] The island of Junkceylon (or Salang) is in 8° 15′ N.
[6] The *kintār* was equal to about 100 lb. avoirdupois.

people came unto us. We sent commodities to their king to barter for ambergriese and for the hornes of abath[1], whereof the king onely hath the traffique in his hands. Now this abath is a beast which hath one horne onely in her forehead, and is thought to be the female unicorne, and is highly esteemed of all the Moores in those parts as a most soveraigne remedie against poyson. We had onely two or three of these hornes (which are of the colour of a browne gray) and some reasonable quantitie of ambergriese. At last the king went about to betray our Portugall, with our marchandise; but he, to get aboord us, told him that we had gilt armour, shirtes of maile, and halberds, which things they greatly desire; for hope whereof he let him returne aboord, and so he escaped the danger.

Thus we left this coast, and went backe againe in sight of Sumatra, and thence to the ilands of Nicubar; where we arrived, and found them inhabited with Moores[2]. And after wee came to an anker, the people daily came aboord us in their canoas with hennes, cocos, plantans, and other fruits; and within two dayes they brought unto us roials of plate, giving us them for Calicut cloth [i.e. calico]; which roials they finde by diving for them in the sea, which were lost not long before in two Portugall ships which were bound for China and were cast away there. They call in their language the coco *calambe*, the plantane *pison*, a hen *jam*, a fish *iccan*, a hog *babee*[3].

From thence we returned the 21 of November to goe for the iland of Zeilan, and arrived there about the third of December 1592, and ankered upon the south side in sixe fadomes water; where we lost our anker, the place being rockie and foule ground. Then we ranne along the south-west part of the sayd iland to a place called Punta del Galle [Point de Galle]; where we ankered, determining there to have remained untill the comming of the Bengala fleet of seven or eight ships, and the fleete of Pegu of two or three sailes, and the Portugall shippes of Tanaseri

---

[1] Rhinoceros (Port. *abada*).

[2] This is an error. The Nicobarese are mainly animistic. But possibly the English found there a Portuguese-speaking Malay to act as interpreter, and thought that he was a native.

[3] These words are not Nicobarese but (as Dr Blagden confirms) Malay (*kĕlamboi, pisang, ayam, ikan, babi*).

[Tenasserim], being a great baie to the southward of Martabam, in the kingdom of Siam; which ships, by divers intelligences which we had, were to come that way within fourteene dayes to bring commodities to serve the caraks, which commonly depart from Cochin for Portugall by the middest of Januarie. The commodities of the shippes which come from Bengala bee fine pavillions[1] for beds, wrought quilts, fine Calicut cloth, pintados[2] and other fine workes, and rice; and they make this voiage twise in the yeere. Those of Pegu bring the chiefest stones, as rubies and diamants, but their chiefe fraight is rice and certaine cloth. Those of Tanaseri are chiefly fraighted with rice and nipar wine, which is very strong, and in colour like unto rocke water, somewhat whitish, and very hote in taste, like unto aqua vitae[3]. Being shot up to the place aforesayd, called Punta del Galle, wee came to an anker in foule ground and lost the same, and lay all that night adrift, because we had nowe but two ankers left us, which were unstocked [without stocks] and in hold. Whereupon our men tooke occasion to come home, our captaine at that time lying very sicke, more like to die then to live. In the morning we set our foresaile, determining to lie up to the northward and there to keepe ourselves to and againe out of the current, which otherwise would have set us off to the southward from all knowen land. Thus having set our foresayle, and in hand to set all our other sayles to accomplish our aforesayd determination, our men made answere that they would take their direct course for England and would stay there no longer. Nowe, seeing they could not bee perswaded by any meanes possible, the captaine was constrained to give his consent to returne, leaving all hope of so great possibilities.

Thus the eight of December 1592 wee set sayle for the Cape of Buona Speransa, passing by the ilands of Maldiva and leaving the mightie iland of S. Laurence on the starreboord or northward, in the latitude of 26 degrees to the south. In our passage over from S. Laurence to the maine, we had exceeding great store of bonitos and albocores[4], which are a greater kind of fish;

---

[1] Canopies. [2] Printed cotton cloths.
[3] A general term for ardent spirits, such as brandy.
[4] Albacore, a large species of tunny.

of which our captaine, being now recovered of his sicknesse, tooke with an hooke as many in two or three howers as would serve fortie persons a whole day. And this skole [school] of fish continued with our ship for the space of five or sixe weekes, all which while we tooke to the quantitie aforesayd; which was no small refreshing to us.

In February 1593 we fell with the eastermost land of Africa, at a place called Baia de Agoa[1], some 100 leagues to the northeast of the Cape of Good Hope; and finding the winds contrary, we spent a moneth or five weekes before we could double the Cape. After wee had doubled it in March folowing, wee directed our course for the iland of Santa Helena, and arrived there the third day of Aprill; where wee staied, to our great comfort, nineteene dayes; in which meane space some one man of us tooke thirtie goodly congers in one day, and other rockie fishe and some bonitos.

After our arrivall at Santa Helena, I, Edmund Barker, went on shore with foure or five Peguins (or men of Pegu) which we had taken, and our surgion; where in an house by the chappell I found an Englishman, one John Segar of Burie[2] in Suffolke, who was left there eighteene moneths before by Abraham Kendall, who put in there with the *Roiall Marchant*, and left him there to refresh him on the iland, being otherwise like to have perished on shipboord; and at our comming wee found him as fresh in colour and in as good plight of body to our seeming as might be, but crazed in minde and halfe out of his wits, as afterward wee perceived; for whether he were put in fright of us, not knowing at first what we were, whether friends or foes, or of sudden joy when he understood we were his olde consorts and countreymen, hee became idle-headed, and for eight dayes space neither night nor day tooke any naturall rest, and so at length died for lacke of sleepe.

Here two of our men, whereof the one was diseased with the skurvie and the other had bene nine moneths sicke of the fluxe[3], in short time while they were on the iland recovered their perfect health. We found in this place great store of very holesome and excellent good greene figs, orenges, and lemons very

[1] Algoa Bay.   [2] Bury St Edmunds.   [3] Dysentery.

faire, abundance of goates and hogs, and great plentie of partriges, guiniecocks, and other wild foules.

Our mariners, somewhat discontented, being now watered and having some provision of fish, contrary to the will of the capitaine, would straight home. The capitaine, because he was desirous to goe for Phernambuc [Pernambuco], in Brasil, granted their request; and about the 12 [? 22] of Aprill 1593 we departed from S. Helena and directed our course for the place aforesayd. The next day, our capitaine calling upon the sailers to finish a foresaile which they had in hand, some of them answered that, unlesse they might goe directly home, they would lay their hands to nothing; whereupon he was constrained to folow their humour. And from thenceefoorth we directed our course for our countrey; which we kept untill we came 8 degrees to the northward of the Equinoctiall, betweene which 8 degrees and the Line we spent some sixe weekes, with many calme and contrary winds at north and somtimes to the eastward and somtimes to the westward; which losse of time and expense of our victuals (whereof we had very smal store) made us doubt to keepe our course. And some of our men, growing into a mutinie, threatned to breake up other mens chests, to the overthrow of our victuals and all ourselves; for every man had his share of his victuals before in his owne custody, that they might be sure what to trust to and husband it more thriftily. Our capitaine, seeking to prevent this mischiefe, being advertised by one of our companie, which had bene at the ile of Trinidada in M[aster] Chidleis voyage[1], that there we should be sure to have refreshing, hereupon directed his course to that iland. And not knowing the currents, we were put past it in the night into the Gulfe of Paria, in the beginning of June; wherein we were 8 dayes, finding the current continually setting in, and oftentimes we were in 3 fadomes water, and could find no going out, until the current had put us over to the western side under the maine land, where we found no current at all and more deep water; and so keeping by the shore, the wind off the shore every night did helpe us out to the northward. Being cleare, within foure or

---

[1] For a lengthy note on John Chudleigh and his disastrous voyage in 1589 to the Straits of Magellan, see the previous edition.

five dayes after we fell with the ile of Mona[1], where we ankred and rode some eighteene dayes, in which time the Indians of Mona gave us some refreshing. And in the meane space there arrived a French ship of Cane [Caen], in which was capitaine one Monsieur de Barbaterre[2], of whom wee bought some two buts of wine and bread and other victuals. Then wee watered and fitted our shippe, and stopped a great leake which broke on us as we were beating out of the Gulfe of Paria.

And having thus made ready our ship to goe to sea, we determined to goe directly for Newfoundland. But before wee departed, there arose a storme, the wind being northerly, which put us from an anker and forced us to the southward of Santo Domingo. This night we were in danger of shipwracke upon an iland called Savona[3], which is environed with flats lying 4 or 5 miles off; yet it pleased God to cleare us of them, and so we directed our course westward along the iland of Santo Domingo, and doubled Cape Tiberon[4], and passed through the old chanell betweene S. Domingo and Cuba for the Cape of Florida. And here we met againe with the French ship of Caen; whose captaine could spare us no more victuals (as he said) but only hides which he had taken by traffike upon those ilands; wherewith we were content, and gave him for them to his good satisfaction.

After this, passing the Cape of Florida and cleere of the chanell of Bahama, we directed our course for the Banke of Newfoundland. Thus running to the height of 36 degrees and as farre to the east as the isle of Bermuda the 17 of September, finding the winds there very variable, contrarie to our expectation and all mens writings, we lay there a day or two. The winde being northerly and increasing continually more and more, it grewe to be a storme and a great frete [i.e. squall] of wind, which continued with us some 24 houres, with such extremitie as it caried not onely our sayles away (being furled) but also made much water in our shippe, so that we had sixe foote water in

---

[1] A small island between Puerto Rico and San Domingo.
[2] Barbotiere, according to May (who is likely to be correct, as he knew French).
[3] Saona, an island off the south-east point of San Domingo.
[4] Tiburon, the western point of San Domingo.

holde. And having freed our ship thereof with baling, the winde shifted to the north-west and became dullerd; but presently upon it the extremitie of the storme was such that with the labouring of the ship we lost our foremaste and our ship grewe as full of water as before. The storme once ceased, and the winde contrary to goe our course, we fell to consultation what might be our best way to save our lives. Our victuals now being utterly spent, and having eaten hides 6 or 7 daies, we thought it best to beare back againe for Dominica[1] and the islands adjoyning, knowing that there we might have some reliefe; whereupon we turned backe for the said islands. But before we could get thither the winde scanted upon us, which did greatly endanger us, for lacke of fresh water and victuals; so that we were constrained to beare up to the westward to certaine other ilandes, called the Nueblas or Cloudie Ilands[2], towards the ile of S. Juan de Porto Rico; where at our arrivall we found land-crabs and fresh water and tortoyses, which come most on lande about the full of the moone. Here having refreshed ourselves some 17 or 18 dayes, and having gotten some small store of victuals into our ship, we resolved to returne againe for Mona; upon which our determination five of our men left us, remaining still on the Iles of Nueblas, for all perswasions that we could use to the contrary; which afterward came home in an English shippe.

From these iles we departed, and arrived at Mona about the twentieth of November 1593. And there comming to an anker toward two or three of the clocke in the morning, the captaine and Edmund Barker, his lieuetenant, with some few others, went on land to the houses of the olde Indian and his three sonnes, thinking to have gotten some foode, our victuals being all spent and we not able to proceede any further untill we had obteyned some new supply. We spent two or three daies in seeking provision to cary aboord to relieve the whole companie. And comming downe to go aboord, the winde then being northerly and the sea somewhat growne, they could not come on shore with the boate, which was a thing of small succour and not able to rowe in any rough sea; whereupon we stayed untill the next morning, thinking to have had lesse winde and safer

---

[1] San Domingo is meant.   [2] Not to be found in modern maps.

passage. But in the night, about twelve of the clocke, our ship did drive away, with five men and a boy onely in it. Our carpenter secretly cut their owne cable, leaving nineteene of us on land without boate or any thing, to our great discomfort. In the middest of these miseries, reposing our trust in the goodnesse of God, which many times before had succoured us in our greatest extremities, we contented ourselves with our poore estate, and sought meanes to preserve our lives. And because one place was not able to sustaine us, we tooke our leaves one of another, dividing ourselves into severall companies. The greatest reliefe that we sixe which were with the captaine could finde for the space of nine and twentie dayes was the stalkes of purselaine boyled in water, and nowe and then a pompion [i.e. pumpkin] which we found in the garden of the ould Indian, who, upon this our second arrivall, with his three sonnes stole from us and kept himselfe continually aloft in the mountaines.

After the ende of nine and twentie dayes we espied a French shippe, which afterwarde we understood to be of Diepe, called the *Luisa*, whose captaine was one Monsieur Felix; unto whom wee made a fire, at sight whereof he tooke in his topsayles, bare in with the land, and shewed us his flagge, whereby we judged him French. So comming along to the westerne ende of the island, there he ankered, we making downe with all speede unto him. At this time the Indian and his three sonnes came done to our captaine, Master James Lancaster, and went along with him to the shippe. This night he went aboord the Frenchman, who gave him good entertainement, and the next day fetched eleven more of us aboord, entreating us all very courteously. This day came another French shippe of the same towne of Diepe, which remayned there untill night, expecting our other seven mens comming downe; who, albeit we caused certaine pieces of ordinance to be shot off to call them, yet came not downe. Whereupon we departed thence, being devided, sixe into one ship and sixe into another; and leaving this island, departed for the north side of Saint Domingo, where we remained untill Aprill following (1594), and spent some two monethes in traffike with the inhabitants, by permission, for hides and other marchandises of the countrey.

In this meanewhile there came a shippe of Newhaven[1] to the place where we were; whereby we had intelligence of our seven men which wee left behinde us at the isle of Mona; which was that two of them brake their neckes with ventring to take foules upon the cliffes; other three were slaine by the Spaniards, which came from Saint Domingo, upon knowledge given by our men which went away in the *Edward*; the other two this man of Newhaven had with him in his shippe, which escaped the Spaniards bloodie hands.

From this place Captaine Lancaster and his lieutenant, Master Edmund Barker, shipped themselves in another shippe of Diepe, the captaine whereof was one John La Noe[2], which was readie first to come away. And leaving the rest of their companie in other ships (where they were well intreated) to come after him, on Sunday, the seventh of Aprill 1594, they set homewarde. And disbocking[3] through the Caiicos[4], from thence arrived safely in Diepe within two and fortie dayes after, on the 19 of May; where after we had stayed two dayes to refresh ourselves, and given humble thankes unto God, and unto our friendly neighbours, we tooke passage for Rie [Rye], and landed there on Friday, the 24 of May 1594; having spent in this voyage three yeeres, sixe weekes, and two dayes (which the Portugales performe in halfe the time), chiefely because wee lost our fit time and season to set foorth in the beginning of our voyage.

We understood in the East Indies, by certaine Portugales which we tooke, that they have lately discovered the coast of China to the latitude of nine and fiftie degrees, finding the sea still open to the northward; giving great hope of the north-east or north-west passage. Witnesse, Master James Lancaster.

---

[1] Le Havre was known to the English by this name.
[2] The form 'Noyer,' used later, suggests that the name was really Lenoir.
[3] An old form of 'disemboguing.'
[4] Passing through the Windward Passage, between Cuba and San Domingo, and south of the Caicos Islands, which are outliers of the Bahamas.

II

MAY'S NARRATIVE[1]

A briefe note of a voyage to the East Indies, begun the 10 of April 1591, *wherein were three tall ships, the* Penelope *of Captaine Raimond, admirall, the* Merchant Royall, *whereof was captaine Samuel Foxcroft, vice-admirall, the* Edward Bonaventure, *whereof was captaine M[aster] James Lancaster, rere-admirall, with a small pinnesse. Written by Henry May*[2], *who, in his returne homeward by the West Indies, suffred shipwracke upon the isle of Bermuda, wherof here is annexed a large description.*

The tenth of April 1591 we departed from Plymmouth with the ships aforesayd. In May[3] following wee arrived at Grand Canaria, one of the Fortunate Islands. Also toward the end of this moneth we tooke a Portugall shippe, being bound for Brasil, within three degrees to the northward of the Equinoctiall; which served greatly to our refreshing. The 29 of July following we came to Aguada Saldania, a good harbour neere the Cape of Buona Sperança; where we stayed about a moneth with the *Merchant Royall*, which, by reason of sicknesse in our fleet, was sent home for England with divers weake men. Here we bought an oxe for a knife of threepence, a sheepe for a broken knife or any other odde trifle, of the people, which were negros, clad in cloakes or mantles of raw hides, both men and women.

The 8 of September the *Penelope* and the *Edward Bonaventure* weyed anker, and that day we doubled the cape of Buona Sperança. The 12 following we were taken with an extreame tempest or huricano. This evening we saw a great sea breake over

---

[1] From Hakluyt's *Principall Navigations*, vol. III, p. 571. Purchas mentions that the MS. was in his possession, but what became of it is not known.

[2] According to Purchas, he was the purser of the *Edward Bonaventure*.

[3] The reader will notice that May's dates often differ from those given by Barker; as also some of his other statements.

our admirall, the *Penelope*, and their light strooke out; and after that we never saw them any more.

In October following we in the *Edward* fell with the westermost part of the isle of S. Laurence about midnight, knowing not where we were. Also the next day we came to an anker at Quitangone, a place on the mainland of Africa which is two or three leagues to the northward of Mozambique, where the Portugals of the isle of Mozambique fetch all their fresh water. Here we tooke a pangaia, with a Portugall boy in it; which is a vessell like a barge, with one mat saile of coconut leaves. The barge is sowed together with the rindes of trees, and pinned with woodden pinnes. In this pangaia we had certeine corne called millio, hennes, and some fardels [i.e. bales] of blew Calicut cloth. The Portugall boy we tooke with us and dismissed the rest.

From this place we went for an island called Comoro, upon the coast of Melinde, which standeth about 11 degrees to the south of the Equinoctial. In which island we stayed all November, finding the people blacke and very comly, but very treacherous and cruell; for the day before we departed from thence they killed thirty of our men on shore, among whom was William Mace, our master, and two of his mates; the one of them being in the boat with him to fetch water, the other being on shore against our ship; they having first betrayed our boat.

From hence we went for the isle of Zanzibar, on the coast of Melinde, whereas[1] wee stayed and wintered untill the beginning of February following.

The second of February 1592 wee weyed anker, and set saile directly for the East Indies; but having calmes and contrary windes, wee were untill the moneth of June before wee could recover the coast of India, neere Calicut; whereby many of our men died for want of refreshing. In this moneth of June we came to an anker at the isles of Pulo Pinaom; whereas we stayed untill the first day of September, our men being very sicke and dying apace. This day we set saile, and directed our course for Malaca. And wee had not bene farre at sea but wee tooke a shippe of the kingdome of Pegu of some fourescore tunnes, with wooden ankers, and about fiftie men in her, with a pinnesse of

[1] An obsolete form of 'whereat.'

some eighteene tunnes at her stearne, both laden with pepper. But their pinnesse stole from us in a gust in the morning. Here we might have taken two shippes more of Pegu, laden likewise with pepper and rice. In this moneth also we tooke a great Portugall ship of six or seven hundred tun, laden chiefly with victuals, chests of hats, pintados, and Calicut clothes. Besides this we tooke another Portugall ship of som hundred tun, laden with victuals, rice, calicos, pintados, and other commodities. These ships were bound for Malaca with victuals; for those of Goa, of S. Thomas, and of other places in the Indies doe victuall it, because that victuals there are very scarce.

In the moneth of November 1592 we shaped our course for the island of Nicubar, lying certeine leagues to the north-west of the famous island of Sumatra; whereas within short time wee came to anker. And here wee had very good refreshing; for after wee arrived there, the people (whom we found in religion Mahumetans) came aboord us in their canoas with hennes, cocos, plantans, and other fruits; and within two dayes they brought unto us reals of plate, giving us them for Calicut cloth; which reals they found by diving in the sea, which were lost not long before in two Portugall ships which were bound for China and were cast away there. This was the furthest place that we were at to the south-east.

And heere, because our company by this time was much wasted and diminished, we resolved to turne backe to the isle of Zeilan. Wherfore we weyed anker in the moneth of November, and arrived at Zeilan about the end of the same moneth. In this island groweth great store of excellent cinamom, and the best diamonds in the world[1]. Here our captaine meant to stay to make up our voyage[2]; whereof hee conceived great hope, by certeine intelligence which wee had received. But the company, which were in all but 33 men and boyes, being in a mutiny and every day ready to go together by the eares (the captaine being sicke and like for to die) would not stay, but would needs go home.

The 8 of December 1592 we set saile homeward. But some

---

[1] There are no diamonds in Ceylon.
[2] I.e. take prizes to pay the cost of the voyage.

15 dayes before we had sight of the Cape of Good Hope we were forced to share our bread, by reason we had certeine flies[1] in our ship, which devoured most part of our bread before we were aware. So that, when we came to sharing, we had but 31 pound of bread a man to cary us into England, with a small quantity of rice a day. The last of March 1593 we doubled the Cape of Bona Sperança.

In April next insuing we came to anker at the island of S. Helena; whereas we found an Englishman, a tailer, which had bene there 14 moneths before we came thither. So, we sending our boat on shore with some ten men, they found this Englishman in the chapell; who by reason of the heate of the climat was inforced to keepe himselfe out of the sun. Our company, hearing one sing in the chapell, supposing it had bene some Portugall, thrust open the doore and went in unto him; but the poore man, seeing so many come in upon him on the sudden, and thinking them to be Portugals, was first in such a feare (not having seene any man in 14 moneths before) and afterwards, knowing them to be Englishmen and some of them of his acquaintance, in such joy that, what betweene excessive sudden feare and joy, he became distracted of his wits, to our great sorowes. Here we found of his drying some 40 goats. The party had made him, for want of apparell, two sutes of goats skinnes with the hairy side outwards, like unto the savages of Canada. Here we stayed all this moneth. This man lived untill we came to the West Indies, and then he died.

In the moneth of June 1593 we arrived at the island of Trinidad, in the West Indies, hoping there to finde refreshing; but we could not get any, by reason that the Spanyards had taken it. Here we were imbayed betweene the island and the maine. And for want of victuals the company would have forsaken the ship; whereupon the captaine was inforced to sweare every man not to forsake the ship untill we should see further occasion. Out of this bay, called Boca de Dragone[2], it pleased God to deliver us; from whence we directed our course for the isle of S. Juan de

---

[1] Cockroaches?
[2] The strait between Trinidad and the mainland is still called the Serpent's Mouth.

Puerto Rico, but fell with the small isle of Mona, where we abode some fifteene dayes, finding in that place some small refreshing. And heere arrived a ship of Caen in Normandy, whereof was captaine one Monsieur Charles de la Barbotiere; who greatly refreshed us with bread and other provision, which we greatly wanted. And so we tooke our leaves the one of the other.

In July, having foule weather at Mona, we were forced to wey anker and to set saile, directing our course for Cape Tiburon. And in doubling of the cape we had a gust from the shore, which caried away all our sailes from the yardes, so that we had left but one new forecourse to helpe ourselves withall; which canvas the aforesayd Frenchman did helpe us withall. Also, having doubled the foresayd cape in the distresse aforenamed, the foresayd Capitan de la Barbotiere, with his pinnesse, gave chase unto us againe; who being come nere unto us, I went aboord him, certifying him what distresse we were in. The gentleman replied to me againe that there was not anything in his shippe, but what he could spare he would helpe us withall. So, to conclude, we agreed with him for canvas. Moreover, he sayd that, if we would go with him to an harbour called Gonnavy[1], which is to the northward of Cape Tiburon, that then he would helpe us with fresh victuals enough. Whereupon I returned aboord our ship and certified our captaine of all, who made it knowen unto the company; which no sooner heard of it but they would all go in. So here we staied with the aforesaid Frenchman 15 dayes; but small refreshing we could get, because the Spaniards stood in some feare of the French man of war, supposing our ship to be a Portugal and that we were his prize; neverthelesse, hee certified them to the contrary.

And in staying so long with him and having little refreshing, our company began to be in a mutiny, and made report that the captaine and I went aboord the Frenchman but to make good cheere, and had not any care of them; but I protest before God that our care was to get victuals, wherby we might have bene gone from him. But in the meanetime a great part of our company had conspired to take away the Frenchmans pinnesse, and with her to boord the man of warre. While these things were

[1] The island of Gonave lies in a bay on the west of San Domingo.

in complotting, one of their consorts went aboord the Frenchman and certified him of all the conspiracy; whereupon the captaine of the French ship sent for our captaine and me to come aboord to dinner; and we stayed with him all the afternoone, being invited unto supper. And being at supper, he himselfe would not a great while come to us; but at length hee came. At his comming wee asked of him what newes; who answered us that either we must depart from him or els he must goe seeke some other harborow. Whereupon I tolde Captaine Lancaster, who prayed me to tell him that, rather then we would be any hindrance unto him, we would be gone[1]. But in the meanetime, while we were thus talking together, the Frenchman weyed and set saile; which we perceived, and asked him what he meant by it. He replied to the captaine and me that he kept us for his security, and that our men had purposed as is aforesayd. When he came thwart our shippe, it blew a prety gaile of winde. The boat being asterne of them, having in her two Moores and two men of Pegu, which we had given them, brake away; then was the Frenchman worse then before, and did threaten us very sore that we should pay his voyage. In the meanetime the *Edward*, seeing us past, weyed and set saile to go for England. And they did share among them all the captaines victuals and mine, when they saw the Frenchman keepe us as prisoners.

So the next morning we went to seeke out the Frenchmans pinnesse; which being at Laguna[2], we shot off a piece, and so she came to us, having in her three more of our company, Edmund Barker, our lieutenant, and one John West, and Richard Lucland, one of the mutinous crew, the which I told the Frenchman of; and he could not deny but that there was such a thing pretended [i.e. intended]. Then I was put into the French pinnesse to seeke their boat; and in the meanetime they would go to see if they could overtake our shippe, and the next day we should meet againe at Cape S. Nicolas[3]. So the next morning we met together, all three of us; but heard no newes of his boat. So he, having Spanyards and negros aboord of us, requested to

---

[1] Evidently May knew French and acted as interpreter.
[2] Possibly Leogane, near Port-au-Prince.
[3] The north-western point of San Domingo.

have them. Our captain desired him to send his boat aboord our shippe and he should have them with all his heart; so with much adoe he sent his boat and had them. Then he demanded of them if his boat were not aboord the ship; they answered no. So that then Monsieur de la Barbotiere was satisfied; and then we were great friends againe, to all our joyes.

The 12 of August 1593 our captain was sent aboord our ship; but before his departure he requested the captaine of the French ship that he would give mee passage home with him, to certifie the owners what had passed in all the voyage, as also of the unrulinesse of the company. And this day we tooke our leaves the one of the other; the *Edward* for England, and we bare in for Gonnavy, where afterwards we found the Frenchmans boat.

The last of November 1593 Monsieur de la Barbotiere departed from a port called Laguna, in Hispaniola. The 17 of December next insuing it was his fortune to have his ship cast away, upon the north-west part of the isle of Bermuda, about midnight. The pilots, making themselves at noone to be to the southward of the island twelve leagues, certified the captaine that they were out of all danger; so they demanded of him their wine of heigth, the which they had. And being, as it should seeme, after they had their wine, carelesse of their charge which they tooke in hand, being as it were drunken, through their negligence a number of good men were cast away. And I being but a stranger among 50 and odde Frenchmen and others, it pleased God to appoint me to be one of them that were saved, I hope to His service and glory. We made account at the first that we were cast away hard by the shore, being hie clifs, but we found ourselves seven leagues off; but with our boat, and a raft which we had made and towed at our boats sterne, we were saved, some 26 of us; among whom were no more English but myselfe. Now being among so many strangers and seeing not roome for the one halfe, I durst neither presse into the boat nor upon the raft, for feare lest they should have cast me overboord, or els have killed me; so I stayed in the ship, which was almost full of water, untill the captaine, being entred the boat, called me unto him, being at hand, for that it stood upon life or death; and so I presently entred, leaving the better halfe of our company to the mercy of the sea. After this we rowed all the day until an houre or two before night yer [i.e. ere] we could come on land, towing the raft with the boat. When we came on shore, being all the day without drinke, every man tooke his way, to see if he could finde any; but it was long before any was found. At length one of the pilots, digging among a company of weeds, found fresh water, to all our great comforts; being only raine water, and this was all the fresh water that we found on shore. But there are in this island many fine bayes, wherin, if a man did dig, I thinke there might be found store of fresh water. This island is divided all into broken islands; and the greatest part I was upon, which might be some 4 or 5 miles long and two miles and a halfe over; being all woods, as cedar and other timber, but cedar is the chiefest.

Now it pleased God, before our ship did split, that we saved our carpenters tooles; or els I thinke we had bene there to this day. And having recovered the aforesaid tooles, we went roundly about the cutting downe of trees, and in the end built a small barke of some 18 tun, for the most part with tronnels[1] and very few nailes. As for tackling, we made a voyage aboord the ship before she split, and cut downe her shrowds; and so we tackled our barke and rigged her. Instead of pitch, we made lime and mixed it with the oile of tortoises; and as soone as the carpenters had calked, I and another, with ech of us a small sticke in our hands, did plaister the morter into the seames; and being in April, when it was warm and faire weather, we could no sooner lay it on but it was dry and as hard as a stone. In this moneth of Aprill 1594, the weather being very hot, we were afrayd our water should faile us, and therfore made the more haste away. And at our departure we were constrained to make two great chests, and calked them, and stowed them on ech side of our mainemast, and so put in our provision of raine water, and 13 live tortoises for our food for our voyage, which we intended to Newfoundland. In the south part of this island of Bermuda there are hogs, but they are so leane that you cannot eat them, by reason the island is so barren; but it yeeldeth great store of fowle, fish and tortoises. And to the eastward of the island are very good harbours; so that a shippe of 200 tun may ride there

[1] Treenails, i.e. wooden pins used in shipbuilding.

landlocked, without any danger, with water enough. Also in this island is as good fishing for pearles as is any in the West Indies, but that the place is subject to foule weather, as thundering, lightning, and raine; but in April and part of May we had very faire and hot weather.

The 11 of May it pleased God to set us cleere of the island, to the no little joy of us all, after we had lived in the same almost the space of 5 moneths. And the 20 of May we fell with the land nere to Cape Briton[1]; where we ran into a freshwater river (whereof there be many) and tooke in wood, water, and ballast. And heere the people of the countrey came unto us, being clothed all in furs, with the furred side unto their skins, and brought with them furres of sundry sorts to sell, besides great store of wild ducks. So some of our company, having saved some small beads, bought some of their ducks. Here we stayed not above four houres, and so departed. This should seeme to be a very good countrey; and we saw very fine champion[2] ground and woods.

From this place we ranne for the Banke of Newfoundland; whereas we met with divers [ships], but none would take in a man of us, untill it pleased God that wee met with a barke of Falmouth, which received us all for a little time. And with her we tooke a French ship, wherein I left Capitan de la Barbotier, my deere friend, and all his company, and stayed myselfe aboord the English barke; and having passage in the same, in the moneth of August I arrived at Falmouth (1594).

[1] Cape Breton Island, south-west of Newfoundland.
[2] A variant of 'champaign' (open, level).

THE SECOND VOYAGE
1594-95

I

HAKLUYT'S ACCOUNT[1]

The well governed and prosperous voyage of M[aster] James Lancaster, begun with three ships and a galley-frigat[2] from London in October 1594, and intended for Fernambuck, the port towne of Olinda[3] in Brasil; in which voyage (besides the taking of nine and twenty ships and frigats) he surprized the sayd port towne, being strongly fortified and manned, and held possession thereof thirty dayes together (notwithstanding many bolde assaults of the enemy, both by land and water) and also providently defeated their dangerous and almost inevitable fireworks. Heere he found the cargazon or freight of a rich East Indian carack, which, together with great abundance of sugars, brasil-wood[4], and cotton, he brought from thence; lading therewith fifteene sailes of tall ships and barks.

IN September 1594 the Worshipfull M[aster] John Wats[5], alderman, M[aster] Paul Banning[6], alderman, and others of worship in the city of London, victualled three good ships, to wit, the *Consent*, of the burthen of 240 tunnes or thereabout, the *Salomon*, of 170 tunnes, and the *Virgin*, of 60 tunnes; and appointed for commanders in this voyage M[aster] James Lancaster of London, gentleman, admirall of the fleet, M[aster] Edmund Barker[7] of London, vice-admirall, and M[aster] John

For notes 1–7 see next page.

Audely[8], of Poplar neere London, rere-admirall; having in their sayd ships to the number of 275 men and boyes.

Being fully furnished with all needfull provision, wee departed from Blackwall in October following, keeping our owne coast untill we came into the West Countrey, where we met with such gusts and stormes that the *Salomon*, spending her mast at the Range[9] of Dartmouth, put into harbour; but by the earnest care and industry of the generall [i.e. Lancaster] and others having charge, she was shortly againe provided; which done, having a pleasant gale for our purpose, we put foorth from Dartmouth the last of November following. But, contrary to our expectation, not fifty leagues from our owne coast, we lost the *Salomon* and the *Virgin*, by a storme of contrary winde that

---

[1] From Hakluyt's *Principall Navigations*, vol. III, p. 708. The unknown chronicler of the voyage was evidently on board the *Consent*.

[2] As we learn later, the galley was taken out in sections, and was put together at one of the Cape Verd Islands.

[3] The upper town of Pernambuco, as distinguished from the port (Recife). The previous edition has here the following note: 'A factory was originally settled at Pernambuco by a ship from Marseilles; but in 1530 the line of coast from the Rio de San Francisco to the Rio de Juraza was granted to Duarte Coelho Pereira, and he came there with his family to found a colony, landing at the port of Pernambuco. He exclaimed: *O que linda situaçam!*'; hence the town was called Olinda and the port Recife.'

Hakluyt, in his notes on South America obtained from Lopez Vaz, says (*Principall Navigations*, vol. III, p. 778): 'The first place inhabited on this coast beyonde the river of Marannon is called Fernambuck; so named by the Indians, but in Portugall it is called Villa de Olinda.' He adds later: 'To returne to Fernambuck, inhabited by a Portugall captaine called Duarte Coelio, it is the greatest towne in all that coast, and hath above three thousand houses in it, with seventie ingenios [Port. *engenho de assucar*, sugar mill] for sugar, and great store of brasill-wood and abundance of cotton. Yet are they in great want of victuals, for all their victuals come either from Portugall or from some places upon the coast of Brasill. The harbour of this towne is a barred harbour [i.e. has a bar at its mouth], and fit onely for small barkes. This place belongeth as yet unto the sonne of Duarte Coelio.'

[4] A term originally applied to a species of dye-wood imported from India, but later transferred to a similar kind of tree growing near Pernambuco. From this came the name of Brazil, bestowed upon the whole country.

[5] Afterwards Sir John Watts, Lord Mayor, 1606–7. He was Governor of the East India Company in 1601–2, and was knighted in 1603.

[6] He was a 'committee' of the East India Company in 1600–2 and 1606–7, and Treasurer in 1600–2.

[7] Lancaster's second in command in the previous voyage.

[8] Called 'Addy' and 'Awdley' later.

[9] Mr J. C. Gardner, Town Clerk of Dartmouth, has kindly informed me that the Range 'is a stretch of water outside the mouth of the river, between the two headlands.'

fell upon us. Yet, being alone, in hope to meet them about the Canaries or Cape Blank,[1] we kept on our course to the Canaries, but could heare no tidings of our consorts; which greatly grieved us.

Thence we went, bearing for the isle of Tenerif; where in the morning early we had sight of a saile, which, being becalmed under the shore, was towing with their boat ahead, having one other at her sterne. For this saile we manned our boat, appointing our men wel for fight, if need should require. The Spaniards, seeing our boat come, entred theirs and, leaving the ship, sought to save themselves by flight; but our men pursued them so fast that they boorded them and brought them with their shippe to our generall. This ship was laden with 80 tunnes of Canary wine, which came not unto us before it was welcome. We kept and manned it, plying that day and the next night thereabout. The very next morning we had sight of one other, to whome in like maner wee sent our boat. But their gunner made a shot at her, which strooke off a propper yoong mans arme; yet we inforced her to yeeld, and found 40 tunnes of wine in her. The Spaniards, having their free passage and an acquitance for the delivery of their wines, were all set on shore upon Tenerif; making a quicke returne of their long voyage intended into the West Indies.

Hence we departed toward Cape Blank. And before wee came thither, wee met againe with the *Virgin*, our rere-admirall, whose men tolde us for very trueth that the *Salomon* was returned for England; inforced so to doe, by spending her mast the second time. Which when our men understood, they were all in a maze, not knowing what to doe, and saying among themselves that their force was but small when all our strength were together, and now we had lost the one halfe of our strength, we were not able to performe the voyage. And therefore some of them came to the captain, asking him what he would now do, seeing the *Salomon* was lost (the one halfe of our strength); giving him counsell to beare up for the West Indies and prove there to make his voyage[2], because his first plat [i.e. plan], for want of strength, was cleane overthrown. The captaine, hearing this new novelty, as not unacquainted with the variable pre-

[1] Cape Blanco (see p. 1). [2] See note on p. 24.

tenses of mariners, made them this answere: Sirs, I made knowen to you all at my comming out of England what I pretended [i.e. intended], and that I meant to go for Fernambuck; and although at the present we want one of our ships, yet (God willing) I meane to go forward, not doubting but to meet her at the appointed places, which are either at Cape Blank or the islands of Cape Verde; for I am assured that M[aster] Barker, the captaine, is so resolute to performe this voyage that, his mast being repaired, he will not faile to meet us; and it were no wisdome for us to divert our course till we have sought him at those places where our appointed meeting is; for the diverting of courses is the overthrow of most of our actions; and I hope you will be all contented herewith, for to go any other course then I have determined (by Gods helpe) I will not be drawn unto. With these reasons, and many others shewed, they rested all satisfied. And at our comming to Cape Blank (God be praised) we met with the *Salomon*, with no small joy to us all. And there she had taken of Spaniards and Portugals 24 saile of ships and caravels, fishermen, and had taken out of them such necessaries as she had need of. Of these ships our captain tooke foure along with him, with another that he had taken himselfe; meaning to imploy them as occasion should serve. At this place he understood, of one of the pilots of those ships, that one of the caracks that came out of the East Indies was cast away in the rode of Fernambuc, and that all her goods were layd upon the Arraçife[1], which is the lower towne. Of these[2] newes we were all glad and rejoyced much; for our hopes were very good, seeing such a booty before us.

Of this good company and happy successe we were all joyful, and had great hope of the blessing of God in performance of our intended voyage. And so, after some parle and making frolike for joy of our meeting one with the other (praising God for all), we plied for Maio[3]. Where comming to anker, our generall and the rest of the captaines went ashore to view the place where we might in best safety set our gally-frigat together; which frame

[1] Apparently O-Recife (the Recife). 'Recife' in Portuguese means a ridge.
[2] A reminder that 'news' used to be a plural.
[3] One of the Cape Verd Islands.

wee brought from England, of purpose to land men in the country of Brasil. Here we discharged our great prize of wine, and set her on fire. But before our comming thither, you shall understand we had sight of foure sailes; which was Captaine Venner in his ship the *Peregrine*, and a proper Biskaine[1] which he tooke at Cape Blank, the *Welcome* of Plymmouth, and her pinnesse; all which stood with us. But they, seeing our flags, not expecting such good fellowes as we, did beare from us all they might; which our people tooke very unkindly that, being all friends, they would neither enquire nor tell us any newes of our friends, but without making any shew of kindnes would so depart.

As before I have said, the choice being made for the place to build the gally-frigat, ashore it was brought; where the carpenters applied their worke, still [i.e. continually] cheered unto it by the generals good gifts bestowed among them and kind usage of the rest of the commanders, not without great care of the captain for the safety of them all, by keeping good watch. Yet one negligent fellow, which had no knowledge of the country, straying from his company, was by the Portugals taken, and very kindly used and brought againe unto us; for which good the generall rewarded them well with gifts very acceptable, which they tooke as kindly. While wee were thus busily imployed about the foresayd galley, we descried at sea foure sailes, which we had good hope would have prooved Indies men[2], or some to have brought us what wee looked for. But they proved Captaine Venner with his fleet as aforesayd; who, seeing us at anker, ankered also. Where spending some time, and being acquainted with our generals determination for landing, [they] consorted with us, and their bils, according to the maner of the sea, were made and signed on either part; we to have three parts, and he the fourth, of all that should be taken; wherby our strength was increased, to all our comforts.

Three weeks or thereabouts we stayd in this place before the gally was finished; which done, putting men into her and fitting

---

[1] A vessel from Biscay, a province of Northern Spain, with Bilbao for its principal port.
[2] Portuguese carracks from India.

her with oares (having foureteene banks[1] on a side), a mast and saile, the commandement of her was committed unto M[aster] Wats, an honest, skilfull mariner.

From thence we put againe to sea and went for the ile Brava[2], where we watered; which done, we made no long stay after, but bent our course as directly as we could for the place, making our first fall with the land to the southward of Cape S. Augustine[3]. From whence wee plied still to our desired port of Fernambuck, and did so much that about midnight we came before the harbour; where some plied up and downe, holding that the best policy to forbeare the entring till day might give them light, the harborow being bard [see note 3 on p. 32], and therefore the more perillous. Our ships being in safety well arrived, God was praised; and the generall in his boat went from ship to ship, willing them to make ready such men as they could spare, with muskets, pikes, billes, bowes, arrowes, and what weapons they had, to follow him. Himselfe, with 80 men from his owne ship, imbarked himselfe in the gally, which caried in her prow a good sacar[4] and two murdering pieces.

Our admiral spent all the night in giving directions to every ship to have their men ready shipped in their boats, for he intended to enter the harborow at the breake of day, and to leave his ships without till he had gotten the fort and the towne; for he would not adventure the ships in till the harborow was gotten. Also he provided the ships which he brought from Cape Blank, and put men in them, as many as could conveniently saile them, and no more, giving them charge to enter the harborow with his boats; for at the entrance of the harborow rode three great Holland ships, which our admirall doubted would impeach his going in. And therefore he gave order to the men of these five small ships (which were not above 60 tunnes apiece), if the Hollanders did offer any resistance, to run aboord of them and to set their owne ships on fire and scape in their boats, which they had for the same purpose, that by this meanes they might not impeach our entrance. But when the morning was come, we

---

[1] Benches.   [2] The south-easternmost island of the Cape Verd group.
[3] A little to the southward of Pernambuco.
[4] The saker (so named from a species of hawk) was a small piece of artillery. The murdering piece was another kind of cannon.

were fallen above halfe a mile downe to the northward below the harborow; which was a great inconvenience unto us. So that before wee could get up againe, the ebbe was come upon us, and thereby we were forced to hover before the harborow till two of the clocke in the afternoone, in the sight of all the towne. In this meanetime our ships rode before the fort without the harborow, about a demy-colvering[1] shot off; in the which time passed many shot betweene the fort and the ships, and especially betweene the admirals ship and them; but no great harme was done on either part. All this while our admirall kept the men ready hovering in the gally and the boats. The Hollanders that rode in the mouth of the harborow, seeing our resolution, layd out haulsers [i.e. hawsers] and wound themselves out of the way of us. Our admiral was very joyfull, and gave great incouragement to all his men; for to passe these three great Hollanders, he held it the greatest danger of all.

About 12 of the clocke the governer of the towne sent a Portugall aboord the admirals ship, to know what he would have and wherefore he came. He returned him this answere: that he wanted the caracks goods, and for them he came, and them he would have, and that he should shortly see. In this processe of time the townesmen and inhabitants, which saw so much shipping and perceived us to be enemies, gathered themselves together, three or foure ensignes[2] of men, esteemed to the number of some six hundred at the least. These came to the fort or platforme lying over against the entry of the harborow, and there attended [i.e. awaited] our landing. But before our admirall set forward with his boats, he gave expresse order to all that had charge of governing the boats or galley, to run them with such violence against the shore that they should be all cast away without recovery, and not one man to stay in them; whereby our men might have no maner of retreat to trust unto, but onely to God and their weapons.

Now was the time come of the flood, being about two of the clocke in the afternoone; when our admirall set forward and

---

[1] Demi-culverin, a cannon with a bore of about four inches.
[2] An old term for a body of men serving under one banner, i.e. a company or troop.

entered the harborow with the small galley, and all the rest of the boats following him. The Hollanders that rode in the mouth of the harborow nothing impeached him; but now the fort began to play with their ordinance upon the galley and the boats, and one of their shot tooke away a great piece of our ensigne out of the galley. But our saile being set, it was no time for us to make any stay; but with all the force we could we ranne the galley upon the shore right under the fort, within a coits cast of it, with such violence that we brake her backe and she suncke presently [i.e. immediately]; for there where we landed went a breach of the sea, which presently cast her away. The boats, comming after, did the like. At our arrivall those in the fort had laden all their ordinance, being seven pieces of brasse, to discharge them upon us at our landing; which indeed they did, for, our admirall leaping into the water, all the rest following him, off came these pieces of ordinance. But (Almighty God be praised) they in the fort, with feare to see us land in their faces, had piked their ordinance so steepe downewards with their mouthes that they shot all their shot in the sand, although (as I sayd before) it was not above a coits cast at the most betweene the place wee landed and the face of the fort. So that they only shot off one of our mens armes, without doing any more hurt; which was to us a great blessing of God, for if those ordinances had bene well levelled, a great number of us had lost our lives at that instant. Our admirall, seeing this, cried out, incouraging his men: Upon them, upon them; all (by Gods helpe) is ours; and they therewith ran to the fort with all violence. Those foure ensignes of men that were set to defend [i.e. prevent] our landing, seeing this resolution, began to go backe and retire into certeine bushes that were by the same fort; and being followed, fledde thorowe a certeine oaze which was drie, being then but the beginning of the tide; and so abandoned the fort and left it with their ordinance to us. This day of our arrivall was their Good Friday[1], when by custome they usually whippe themselves; but God sent us now for a generall scourge to them all, whereby that labour among them might be well spared.

The fort being taken, with all their ordinance, the admirall

[1] 18 April 1595.

waved to the ships, willing them to wey and come in, which they did with all speed; himselfe taking order in leaving certeine men in keeping the sayd fort, and placed the ordinance toward the high towne [i.e. Olinda], from whence hee suspected the greatest danger; and putting his men in order, marched toward the low towne [i.e. Recife], which was about some foureteene score[1] from the fort; in which towne lay all their merchandize and other goods. Approching to the towne, he entered the same; the people imbarking themselves in caravels and boats, with all the expedition they could. The base towne, of above an hundred houses, being thus taken, we found in it great store of merchandizes of all sorts, as brasil-wood, sugars, calico-cloth, pepper, cynamon, cloves, mase, nutmegs, with divers other good things, to the great comfort of us all. The admirall went up and downe the towne, and placed at the south end of the same Captaine Venner and his company, himselfe and his company in the midst of the towne, and Captaine Barker and Captaine Addy at the other end of the towne; giving great charge that no man, upon paine of great punishment and losse of his shares, should breake up or enter into any warehouse, without order and direction from the admirall. And this commandement was as well kept as ever any was kept, where so great spoile and booty was found; for it was not knowen, in all the time of our being there, that any disorder was committed, or any lodge or warehouse broken open, or any spoile was made or pillaging of anything; which is a note[2] much to be observed in such an action, for common mariners and souldiers are much given to pillaging and spoiling, making greater account of the same then of their shares.

Order being put in all things, we kept a very sure watch this first night. And the morning being come, our admirall and Captaine Venner, with the rest of the captaines, went about the towne, and gave order for the fortifying of it with all expedition; so that within two dayes it was surrounded with posts and planks, all that part of the towne next the maineland, at least nine foot high; for (God be thanked) we found provision in the towne sufficient store for it. Now it is to be understood that this

---

[1] An old term for 'twenty paces.' [2] Noteworthy thing.

towne is environed on the one part by the sea and on the backside by a river[1] that runneth behinde it; so that, to come at it by land, you must enter it by a small narrow passage, not above forty paces over at an high water. At this passage we built a fort, and planted in it five pieces of ordinance, which we tooke out of the first fort we wan at our comming into the harborow.

Now, we having the towne in possession, our admirall sent for the Hollanders by his chyrurgian, which had bene brought up in that countrey, a man knowing their conditions [i.e. dispositions], and sober and discreet of his owne cariage. At his first comming aboord of them, they seemed to stand upon their owne guard and defence, for they were three great and strong ships; but he used himselfe so, that they at the last willed him to come into the greatest of their ships, which was above 450 tunnes. Then he declared to them our intent of comming thither, and that they should be there as sure from any shew of violence or injury offered them as if they were in their owne houses; and if they should thinke so good, his admirall would fraight them for England, if they would be content with fraight reasonable and as they should agree; and it should be at their owne choise whether to go or not; he would not force them, unlesse it were to their benefit and good liking. Although this people were somewhat stubburne at the first (as that nation is in these causes), yet, being satisfied with good words and good dealing, they came aland and, after conference had with the admirall, they were so satisfied that they went thorow with a fraight; and then we joyned with them and they with us, and they served us as truely and as faithfully as our owne people did, both at watch and ward by sea and all other services.

Within two dayes after our comming in, about midnight a great number of Portugals, and Indians with them, came downe upon us with a very great cry and noise. But (God be thanked) we were ready for them; for our admirall, supposing some such assault, had provided all our muskets with haile shot, which did so gaule both the Indians and the Portugals that they made them presently retreat. And this is to be noted, that there was both the horse and his rider slaine, both with one of these shot. Our men followed them some five or sixe score [paces], but no further.

[1] The Rio Beberibe.

We lost in this conflict but onely one man, but had divers hurt. What was lost of their part we could not tell, for they had before day, after our retreat, caried away all their dead.

Within three or foure dayes after our comming in, appeared before the harborow 3 ships and 2 pinnesses. The pinnesses, being somewhat nere, descried our flags; and one of them came in, which was a French pinnesse, declaring all the rest to be French bottoms; which our admirall willed should come in, and so they did. These were French men of war[1], and came thither for purchase [i.e. prize-taking]. The captaines came aland and were welcomed; amongst whom was one Captaine John Noyer, of Diepe, that the yere before had taken in our admirall at the iland of Mona in the West Indies, where his ship was cast away, comming out of the East Indies. To this man our admirall offered great kindnes, and performed it, and was not ungratefull for his former benefit shewed unto him. This captaine desired of our admirall to bestow upon him his ships lading of Fernambuc-wood[2]; which he granted him and also his pinnesse, and more gave him a caravel of about 50 tuns, and bid him lade her with wood also; which with other benefits he gratefully received. To the other two captaines he granted their ladings of wood, the one captaine being of Diepe, the other of Rochel. The captain of Diepe confessed that he met Abraham Cocke[3] certein moneths before, and being distressed for want of water, gave him some, and went with him to a watering place, where he had water enough; and so departed from him, saying that his men were very weake[4].

The comming in of these ships did much strengthen us; for our admiral appointed both these French and the Flemings to

---

[1] Privateers. [2] Brazil-wood.
[3] 'Going for the River of Plate' (marginal note).
[4] From references in Hakluyt and Purchas we learn that Abraham Cock, born at Leigh (Essex) and afterwards a resident of Limehouse (London), was left at the River Plate by the *Minion* in 1581, settled down there, and married. In Jan. 1587, while acting as master of a small Portuguese vessel, he was captured near the River Plate by a squadron sent out by the Earl of Cumberland, and was carried to England. In the spring of 1589 he was despatched to South America in command of two pinnaces, but his voyage was unsuccessful. When last we hear of him, he was captain of one of Lord Cumberland's vessels and assisted in the capture of the *Madre de Dios* (August 1592); but the reference in the text suggests that he made yet another voyage to South American waters.

keepe watch upon the river by night with their boats, every boat having in her 12 men at the least, and the boats well provided. This was for feare of fired ships or barks to come downe; which our admirall had great care unto, and caused our ships to ride by cables and haulsers, at all advantages to shun them, if by that meanes they should attempt to put us out of the harborow; giving commandement to us that watched in the towne, that what fires soever we should espy or see, not one man to start from his watch or quarter, unlesse we were by himselfe commanded to the contrary.

Now this order put in all things, and having viewed all the goods in the towne, and thinkinge ourselves sufficiently fortified, we began to unlade our ships, which came as full laden in as they went foorth, but not with so good merchandize. And this order was taken about the unlading of them, and also the lading of goods out of the towne: our men were divided into halves, and the one halfe wrought one day and the other halfe the other day. Alwayes those that wrought not kept the watch, with their furniture[1] in their hands and about them, and none stept far off or wandred from his colours. And those that wrought had all their weapons in good order set and placed by them, so that at an instant every one knew where to go to his furniture; and this was very carefully looked unto.

The third day after our comming in, came down from the higher towne (which might be about foure miles off upon a hill) three or foure of the principall gentlemen of the countrey, and sayd that from the bishop, themselves and the rest they would have some conference with our admirall. This newes being brought to the admirall, he hung downe his head for a small season; and when he had muzed awhile, he answered: I must go aboord of the Flemings upon busines that importeth me, and therefore let them stay if they will. And so he went, and sate there with the Flemings from nine of the clocke till two at the afternoone. In this space divers messengers went to the admirall to come away, for these gentlemen stayd; to whom he gave this answere: Are they not gone yet? And about two of the clocke he came aland, and then they tolde him they were departed. Many

---

[1] Military equipment.

of the better sort of our men marvelled and thought much, because he would not vouchsafe to come and have conference with such men of account as they seemed to be. But the admiral made them this answere: Sirs, I have bene brought up among this people: I have lived among them as a gentleman, served with them as a souldier, and lived among them as a merchant; so that I should have some understanding of their demeanors and nature, and I know, when they cannot prevaile with the sword by force, then they deale with their deceiveable tongues; for faith and trueth they have none, neither will use any, unlesse it be to their owne advantage. And this I give you warning, that if you give them parle, they will betray us; and for my part, of all nations in the world it would grieve me most to be overtaken[1] by this nation and the Spaniards; and I am glad it was my fortune to pay them with one of their owne fetches[2], for I warrant you they understand me better then you thinke they do. And with this I pray you be satisfied; I hope it is for all our goods. For what shall be gaine by parle, when (by the helpe of God) we have gotten already that we came for? Should we venture that we have gotten with our swords, to see if they can take it from us by words and policy[3]? There were no wisedome in so doing. You know what it hath cost us, and how many men lie wounded that be not yet hole of this other nights hurts. And therefore from hencefoorth I give this commission, that if any be taken, he be sent away with this order (although he come as a friend), that if either he or any other approch us from henceforth, he shalbe hanged out of hand; and other course then this I will not take with them. Which course was followed; for within 3 or 4 days after, it was performed, by two taken in the night; and after that we were never troubled with spies. And although divers slaves came running from their men to us, by which we understood much of their working and pretences, yet the admirall would enterteine few of them.

In this meanetime that we began to worke, the Portugals, with the country people, were not idle; for, seeing us so busie, about sixe nights after our comming in, they privily in the night

---

[1] To 'overtake' was to get the better of a person.
[2] Tricks or stratagems.   [3] Craft.

cast up a trench in the sands, about a sacar shot from our ships, minding there to plant ordinance, which would have offended our ships greatly, and they would not have bene able to have rode there to take in their lading, which now began to go aboord of them. The admirall, hearing this, about 3 of the clocke in the afternoone marshalled our men, and he and all the rest of the captaines marched toward them. The Portugals and Indians, perceiving our comming, began to withdraw themselves within the trench, meaning (as it should appeare) to fight it out there. But we made no stand, neither did it behove us, but presently approched the trenches with our muskets and pikes, afore their trenches were thorowly finished; so that (by Gods helpe) we entered them. And the Portugals and Indians left the place, and left unto us 4 good peeces of brasse ordinance, with powder and shot and divers other necessaries; and among the rest 5 smal carts of that countrey, which to us were more worth then al the rest we tooke, for the lading of our goods from the towne to the waters side; for without them we could not have told what to have done, much of our goods being so heavie that without carts we were not able to weyld them. All these things we brought away, and destroyed al those platforms that they had made. And then we had rest with them for certaine dayes; in which we went forward, deviding our marchandize with Captaine Venner (according to our consort), and went daily lading them abord; every ships company according as their turnes fell out, but only the three Dutch ships; for, the goods being put into their boats, their owne companies laded themselves. And this farther good chance (or blessing of God) we had to helpe us, that as soone as we had taken our cartes, the next morning came in a ship with some 60 negros, 10 Portugall women, and 40 Portugals. The women and the negros we turned out of the towne; but the Portugals our admirall kept to draw the carts when they were laden, which to us was a very great ease; for the countrey is very hote and ill for our nation to take any great travell [i.e. labour] in.

In this towne there is no fresh water to be had, and therefore we were every 5 or 6 dayes compelled to passe over the river into the maineland to get fresh water; which after the first or second time the Portugals kept, and would have defended [i.e. prevented] our watering. So that we were driven to water of force, and at severall times some of our men were hurt, and onely two or three slaine; and with this danger we were forced to get our water.

And as they molested us in our watering, so they slept not in other devises, but put in practise to burne our ships or remove them out of the harbour. For within some 20 dayes after our comming in, they had prepared 5 caravels, and filled them with such things as would best take fire and burne. These they brought within a mile (or little more) of our ships, and there set them on fire, for neerer they could not well come, because of our watch of boates; for (as is above said) the admirall had alwaies 6 boates that kept watch above halfe a mile from the ships, for feare of such exploytes as these; which was the cause they could not fire them so neere the ships as they would have done. But these fired caravels had the tide with them, and also the little winde that blewe was in their favour; which caused them to come downe the streame the faster. Which our boats perceiving, made to them with as much expedition as conveniently they could; but, the tide and wind both serving them, they approched toward the ships with great expedition. Our men in the towne began to be in some feare of them; yet no man mooved or started from his quarter more then if there had bene nothing to doe. Also the masters, and such as were aboord, were somewhat amased to see 5 so great fires to be comming downe among their ships; but they prepared for to cleere them of it as well as they could, being provided aforehande and judging that some such stratagems would be there used, the river being very fit therefore. But (God be thanked, who was alwaies with us, and our best defence in this voyage; by whose assistance we performed this so great an attempt with so small forces) our companie in the boats so played the men, when they saw the fires come neere our ships, that, casting grapnels with yron chaines on them (as every boat had one for that purpose), some they towed aground, and some they brought to a bitter[1] or anker, where they rode till all

---

[1] Smyth, in his *Sailor's Word Book*, explains that 'a ship is "brought up to a bitter" when the cable is allowed to run out to that stop.' The expression 'to the bitter end' is thought to be derived from this.

their force was burned out; and so we were delivered (by Gods helpe) from this fearefull danger.

Within some 6 nights after this (which might be about the 26 day after our comming in and abode there) about 11 of the clocke at night came driving downe other 3 great raftes, burning with the hugest fires that I have seene. These were exceeding dangerous; for when our men approched them, thinking to clap their grapnels upon them, as they had done upon the caravels the night before, they were prevented; for there stooke out of the rafts many poles, which kept them from the body of the rafts, that they could not come to throw their grapnels into them. And yet they had this inconvenience, worse then al the rest, which most troubled us; there stooke out among the poles certaine hollow trunks, filled with such provision of fireworkes that they ceased not still[1] (as the fire came downe to those trunks to set them on fire) to spout out such sparkles that our boats, having powder in them for our mens use, durst not, for feare of fyring themselves with their owne powder, come neere those sparkles of the raftes. But seeing them to drive neerer and neerer our ships, they wet certain clothes and laid upon their flaskes and bandelers[2], and so ventured upon them, and with their grapnels tooke holde of them and so towed them on ground, where they stooke fast, and were not burnt out the next day in the morning. Diverse logs and timbers came driving along by our ships and burning, but with our boats we easily defended them. And thus (God be praysed) we escaped the second fires. A third firing was prepared, as a negro gave us to understand, but this we prevented by our departure. For this third firing were very great preparations; and we were credibly informed of certainetie that this firing should be such as we should never be able to prevent. And assuredly these fires be dangerous things, and not to be prevented upon the sudden, unlesse it be afore prepared for and foreseene; for when it commeth upon the sudden and unlooked for and unprovided for, it bringeth men into a great amazement and at their wits ende. And therefore let

[1] Continually.
[2] The bandolier was a broad belt worn over the shoulder and across the breast, carrying cases for musket charges.

all men riding in rivers in their enemies countrey be sure to looke to be provided beforehand; for against fire there is no resistance without preparation.

Also it is a practise in these hot countreys, where there be such expert swimmers, to cut the cables of ships; and one night it was practised to cut the admirals cable, and yet the boate rode by the cable, with two men in her, to watch all the night; and the bwoy onely was cut, but not the cable. But after that night, seeing then our good watch, they never after attempted it.

While all these things passed, our ships (God be thanked), thorow the industry of our governours and diligent labour of our men, began to be wholly laden, and all the best marchandize conveyed aboord our ships. So that our admirall ment to depart that night, which was the 31 day after our entrance, or else on the next day at the farthest; and so warning was given to all men to make themselves readie. Our admiral, being aboord his ship the same morning, espyed in the sands, right against the place where the ships rode, that there was a small banke of sand newly cast up, under which he perceived now and then some people to be. Presently [i.e. immediately] he tooke his boat and went to the towne, and called all the captaines together, declaring that the enemies were about some pretence right against the ships; consulting whether it were best to sally out and see what they were doing, or depart that evening according to the former determination. The admirall was of opinion to depart that night, saying it was but folly to seeke warres, since we had no neede to doe it. Other affirmed it were good to see what they did, least the winde might be contrarie and the ships not get out, and so our enemies may build upon us to our great disadvantage. Well, said the admiral, the matter is not great, for there can be no danger in this sally; for where they worke it is within falkon-shot[1] of the ships, and if any power should come against you, the ships may play upon them with 40 peeces of ordinance at the least, so that a bird cannot passe there but she must be slaine. I am somewhat unwilling you should go, for I have not bene well these two dayes and I am not strong to march upon those heavie sands. They answered all at once: You shall not neede to

---

[1] The falcon (named after a bird) was a small cannon.

trouble yourselfe for this service; for you see it is nothing and of no danger, being so neere the ships; doubt you not we will accomplish this service well ynough, and returne againe within this houre. The admirall answered: The danger cannot be great; but yet you shall goe out strong, for feare of the worst. And so the admirall marshalled them 275 men, French and English; which were under the conduct of Edmund Barker, Captaine Barker of Plimmouth (vice-admirall to Captaine Venner), Captaine Addy, and the three French captaines, all going out together. And they were to march upon a narrow peece of ground to the place whether they were sent unto. In the brodest part, betwixt the sea and the water on the other side, it is not above a stones cast, for it is a bank of sand lying betweene the river and the sea; so they needed not to feare any comming on their backs or on their sides, and before them could no man come but he must passe by all the ships, which no company of men were able to do without present death. The admirall commanded them at their departure to go no further then the place he sent them to; and so he himselfe went aboord the ships and made readie all the ordinance for feare of the worst, not knowing what might insue, although he saw no danger might follow.

Thus we marched quietly till we came to the place we were sent unto, being right over against the ships; out of which place came some dozen shot [i.e. musketeers], which, seeing us come, discharged and ranne their wayes, with such as were working within the said platforme; so that we came into it, and perceived they had begunne to lay plankes to plant ordinance upon. Our admiral commanded, if there were any such thing, to burne the plankes and returne in againe; which we might have done without hurting of any mans finger. But our leaders were not content to have performed the service committed them in charge, but would needes expresly and against their order march on further, to fight with certaine ensignes almost a mile off, cleane out of the reach of the ordinance of all our ships and where lay the strength of the whole countrey. When our men began to draw neere those ensigns of men, the ensignes seemed to retire with great speed; which our men followed with such great hast that, some outrunning other some, our order was broken; and those ensignes retyred themselves into the force of the whole countrey. So that our formost men were in the midst of their enemies yer [i.e. ere] they were aware; which were slaine yer the rest could come to succour them. The enemies, incouraged by this, came also upon the rest; which presently began to retire; and the enemies followed them til they came within the reach of the ordinance of our ships, where they were beaten off and left their pursuit. In this conflict were slaine Captain Barker (captaine of the *Salomon*), Captaine Cotton (the admirals lieutenant), Captaine John Noyer (a French captaine of Diepe) and another French captaine of Rochel, with M[aster] John Barker and other, to the number of 35; for these were the formost and hottest in the pursuit of the ensignes aforesaid, and by their forwardnes came all to perish. At our returne into the towne the admiral came to us, much bewayling the death of so many good men as were lost, wondering what we ment to passe the expresse order that was given us. With this losse our men were much danted; but our admirall began againe to encourage them, declaring that the fortune of the warres was sometimes to win and sometimes to loose; and therewithall he wished every man to prepare and make himselfe readie, for that night (God willing) he would depart, for all our ships were readie and laden and he would not stay any further fortune.

The evening being come, the ships began to wey and go forth of the harbour; and God be thanked of his goodnesse toward us, who sent us a faire wind to go foorth withall; so that by 11 of the clocke in the night we were all forth in safety. The enemies, perceiving our departing, planted a peece or two of ordinance and shot at us in the night, but did us no harme. We were at our comming foorth 15 sailes, that is, 3 sailes of Hollanders (the one of 450 tunnes, the other of 350 tunnes, and the third of 300 tunnes), foure sailes of French, and one ship which the admiral gave the French captain, 3 sailes of Captain Venners fleet of Plimmouth, and 4 sailes of our admirals fleete. All these were laden with marchandizes, and that of good worth. We stayed in this harbour, to passe all this businesse, but onely 31 dayes; and in this time we were occupied with skirmishes and attempts of the enemie 11 times; in all which skirmishes we had the better, onely this last excepted. To God be the honour and praise of all, &c.

The whole fleete being out in safety, the next day in the morning the admirall gave order to the whole fleete to saile toward Peranjew, a harbour lying some 40 leagues to the northward of Fernambucke, and there to take in fresh water and to refresh themselves. And to make provision for refreshing, our admirall had sent thither some 6 daies before, two Frenchmen in a smal pinnesse; which Frenchmen he had provided from Diepe before his comming out of England for that purpose. For both these two spake the Indians language very perfectly; for at this port of Peranjew and another called Potaju, some 6 leagues to the northward[1], the Frenchmen have had trade for brasill-wood, and have laden from hence by the Indians meanes, who have fet [i.e. fetched] it for them some 20 leagues into the country upon their backs, 3 or 4 ships every yere.

Thus we all sailed toward Peranjew; at which place we arrived in the night, so that we were forced to lie off and on with a stiffe gale of wind, in which we lost the most part of our fleete; and they, not knowing this coast, put off to the sea, and so went directly for England. Our admirall, and some 4 saile more with him, put into the harborow of Peranjew, and there watered and refreshed himselfe very well with hens, conies, hares, and potatos, with other things which the two Frenchmen had partly provided before his comming. This is a very good harborow, where ships may ride and refresh very well; but (as I am given to understand) since our comming from thence the Portugals have attempted the place and doe inhabite it, and have put the French from their accustomed trade.

Here having watered and refreshed ourselves, we put to the sea, plying after the rest of our fleete which were gone before; which we never heard of till our arrivall in England at the Downes in the moneth of July, where we understood the rest of our consorts to be passed up for London, Captaine Venner[2] and

---

[1] These cannot be identified with certainty; but it appears from Hakluyt and Purchas that in the district to the north of Pernambuco the French had for some time a regular trade for brazil-wood.

[2] On p. 69 it is stated that Venner died in Brazil.

his fleete to be at Plimmouth[1], and the French ships to be safe arrived at Diepe: which to us was very great comfort.

At our setting sayle from the Downes, according as the custome is, finding the Queenes ships there, we saluted them with certaine ordinance. The gunner, being carelesse, as they are many times of their powder, in discharging certain pieces in the gunner roome, set a barrel of powder on fire, which tooke fire in the gunner roome, blew up the admirals caben, slew the gunner, with 2 others, outright and hurt 20 more, of which 4 or 5 died. This powder made such a smoke in the ship with the fire that burnt in the gunner roome (among all the fireworkes) that no man at the first wist what to doe. But recalling backe their feare, they began to cast water into the gunner roome in such abundance (for the Queenes ships now, and also the other ships that were in our company, came presently to our helpe) that (God be praised) we put out the fire and saved all, and no great harme was done to the goods. By this may be seene that there is no sure safety of things in this world. For now we made account to be out of all danger, where behold a greater came upon us then we suffered all the whole voyage. But the Almightie be praysed for ever, which delivered us out of this and many other in this voyage. Our fire being well put out, and we taking in fresh men, (God be praysed) we came to Blackewall in safety.

---

[1] A letter from Sir Francis Drake and Sir John Hawkins at Plymouth, 21 July 1595, announced the arrival of two ships from Brazil, bringing 800 chests of sugar, 12 or 14 tons of pepper, and sundry other goods (*Cal. S.P. Dom.* 1595–97, p. 75).

II

LANCASTER HIS ALLARUMS[1]

HONORABLE ASSAULTES, AND SUPPRISING OF THE BLOCK-HOUSES AND STORE-HOUSES BELONGING TO FERNAND BUCKE IN BRASILL, WITH HIS BRAVE ATTEMPT IN LANDING IN THE MOUTH OF THE ORDINAUNCE THERE, WHICH WERE CANNONS CULVERING, CANNON PERIALL[2], AND SACRES OF BRASSE; WITH OTHER SUNDRY HIS MOST RESOLUTE AND BRAVE ATTEMPTS IN THAT COUNTRY, FROM WHENCE HE LADED OF THEIR SPOYLES AND RICH COMMODITIES HE THERE FOUND FIFTEENE GOOD SHIPS; WHICH WAS SINEMON, SUGAR, PEPPER, CLOVES, MACE, CALLOCO-CLOTH, AND BRASSEL-WOOD, WITH OTHER COMMODITIES.

WITH THE NAMES OF SUCH MEN OF WORTH, HAVING CHARGE, WITHIN[3] THIS MOST HONORABLE ATTEMPT LOST THEIR LIVES.

Published for their eternall honor by a Wellwiller[4].

Imprinted at London by A. I.[5] for W. Barley, and are to be solde at his shop in Gratious-Street[6], neer unto Leadenhall gate.

---

[1] Particulars of this pamphlet are given in the introduction.
[2] Possibly this should be cannon-perer, defined by Smyth as an ancient piece of ordnance which threw a stone shot.
[3] Apparently an error for 'which in.'
[4] The author of this pamphlet was Henry Roberts, who was a hanger-on at the courts of Elizabeth and James, and was ever ready to break out into panegyrics in prose and verse. In 1585 he wrote a 'Farewell' to Sir Francis Drake (signing himself, as here, 'a wellwiller') and in 1588 he published a 'Welcome' to Capt. Cavendish; while similar effusions appeared from time to time. All these are now very rare. The *Dict. of Nat. Biography* identifies him with the 'sworn esquire of Her Majesties person,' who was sent by Elizabeth on a mission to Morocco in 1585–89 (Hakluyt's *Voyages*, 1589, pp. 237–9).
[5] Abel Jeffes. The pamphlet was entered by him at Stationers' Hall on 29 July 1595 (Arber's *Transcripts*, vol. III, p. 46).
[6] Gracechurch Street.

[Dedication.]

To the moste resolute and valiant minded Captain James Lancaster all encrease of valour, with your most worthy harts desire and prosperous successe in all your attempts.

It hath beene, right woorthy captaine, their custome in elder times amongst some forraine nations, which held honor in regarde, by all signes and showes of joy to welcome home such adventurers that for their countreys honor and princes benefit had any way adventured, not only dooing them all the publicke honor they could, but invested them with titles of all honor. Such customes, albeit among the vulgar sorte it be denyed, yet doubtlesse those good mindes which honor armes and their countrey adventures attribute unto them honorable prayse, as they deserve.

Amongst many other, valorious capataine, that honor your woorthy deeds, desirous to register your noble actions amongst the best deserving, as they woorthily merit, though my slender skill be not such as may deserve to register so notable and woorthy exploite by you perfourmed: yet have I boldly attempted to set downe the same, that our countreymen, specially such as stand upon tearmes of being what they are not, envying the vertues and well deserving adventurer, might blush to beholde what you have perfourmed, through Gods sufferance and your politik and most valiaunt resolution, whilst they lye sweating one their easie beddes. Of which I humblye crave pardon, who intends well unto all men, but especiall bend my devotion unto such skilfull adventures at sea, for that my profession is such, who am and ever wilbe readie in all true zealous affection and [1] doe you all the best service I can or may, when and where it shall stand with your good pleasure for to commaund mee,

Your devoted wellwisher,

H. R.

[1] To?

To the Reader

No tale of Robinhood I sing,
Ne[1] olde wives stories write;
Nor idle toyes to mervaile at,
Vaine people to delight.
But woorkes of woorth most rare and true
To you I doe present;
Which to the bravest mindes may be
A worthy president,
Where Cavallers[2] of high esteeme
Doe Londiners contemne,
May know what worthy mindes they bear
and serve like valiant men.
As Lancaster his last attempt,
That hee in Brassill made,
May witnesse well unto his fame,
If you the same will read.
Rare are his acts. Peruse them then,
Whose manhood dooth excell.
His haughtie deeds doone to our foes
The same at large doth tell.
Recorde may wee his worthines,
And write but what is true.
And you that saw the welth he brought
Give Lancaster his due.
If London merchaunts dare to doe
Such actions as hee did,
Then why should not their acts be tolde?
Why should his fame be hid?
Amongst the cheifest Cavilers
Give Lancaster his place,
Who by his worthy pollicie
The foeman hath disgrast.
He is the man whose courage great
Was never seene to quaile.
He is the man that formost was,
Where wee did foes assaile.

---

[1] An archaic form of 'nor.' [2] Court gallants.

Brave Lancaster, for woorthines
In this attempt of thine,
The foeman dooth commend thy worth,
Whose vertues so dooth shine.
Then Cavaliers of highest prize
And citizens of fame,
Extoll his prayse, which hath deservde
And bravely gaind the same.
And gallant brutes, which yet are bound
Your masters to obay,
When time shall make you free againe,
Think then what I now say.
Learne by this man of woorth to guyde
Yourselves in everie place,
By land or sea to gaine renowne
And enemies to disgrace.
Your countrey then your[1] honor shall,
For prince doe service good;
And men, that see your woorthynes,
For you will spend their blood.
He is a lamp to light you one[2]
Fames pallace to attaine;
Wherby your names shall ever live,
If fame you seeke to gaine.
Learne by his woorth, that valiantly
Hath ventured life and limme,
To shame of dastard coward base,
In place where he hath beene.
His deeds at large doe but peruse,
And then you all shall say;
An act of more resolve hath not
Beene complisht at the sea.[3]

H. R.

Finis.

---

[1] You?   [2] On.
[3] The rhyme reminds us that the old pronunciation of 'sea' was 'say.'

The most honorable attempts and fortunate successe of our woorthy citizen and brave-minded generall, James Lancaster, and his associates.

That a prophet is not esteemed in his owne cuntrey it hath beene often saide, and not so commonly sayd but true sayd; as is manifest in our ungratefull cuntreymen, which holde honours champions in account [no?] longer then the present occasion of use serveth for them; which maketh us so common a bywoord amongst other nations for our ungratefullnes. If wee could as well imitate in good actions such noble straungers as have lived in elder time as follow their vanities and manners in all vicious exercises, wee might well be noted for the moste only people of the whole earth. Then might that most excellent histories which now declare the noble and bountifull mindes of the Romaines bee shut up, and our histories fill the eares of all nations with reportes of our now living and brave-minded adventure[r]s. But those times be past. Such men live not to recompence their worthines, nor those of learning to give them their due.

If Roome, the abject of earth now for her vice, hath beene furnished with such noble cittizens that gained, both for their valour and bountie, such eternall prayse, not only for hazarding in many perrills their goods but their owne persons, ayming at nothing but honor, esteeming the goodes gotten as thinges transitorie, why should not our thrise famous cittie of London, the only wounder of the earth for beautie, government, and welth, holde their honor in like account? The Romaines exalted all men of woorth for their vertues, not regarding their parentage, makeing the ignoble and baseborne tribunes, senatours, and vicerois in their territories, honoring them with all titles of nobilitie and honour, and after their victoryes caused them in tryumphs to ride throughout their citties, erecting trophies in memorie of their actions. Through which they encouraged the noble-minded, and moved the most basest groome to adventure.

Yf such were the manners and conditions of our minded cuntrymen, how florishing an estate might we boast of? But we, forgetting vertue, esteeme wealth, not vallor: not men before money, but money farre before men.

Yet are there some of worshippe, patrones of this famous and most renowned cittie, who, esteeming their cuntries benifit, have by their great charge enriched the commonwelth, and of the[i]r car[e]full love to their cuntry enlarged the navy of our land by their most bountifull exspences; so that, thorough a number of worshipfull cittizens our eneimies are weakned, our streingth increased, our eneimies impoverished, and our land enriched; all for our cuntryes honor, whereat they ayme, as is dayly seene, by the great adventures they make. And I could recite, but time causeth me to admit [omit?] them and their worshipes names in this place, not doubting but in time some of good learning, for honor of our land, will register their names to eternall honor. Unto such I commend them, to recount unto you this latest and most rare exploit of a most resolute and brave gentleman, a cittizen of this most famous cittie, uppon our enimies the Spaniards[1]; wherin, as he got fame by this most resolute and brave attempt, purchasing therby his cuntries honor and benifit of our commonweale, and that his vertues, beeing a cittizen of this famous cittie of London, though by birth of gentillity, might not be obscured, I have set downe his proceedings in this action, that our brave-minded youthes, in tyme to come, seeing what hath ben done by men of our time, may imitate the vertues, and endevoring to deserve, like him, honor in his cuntry, and remaine a terror to all enimies.

In September now last past, 1594, these worshipfull grave citizens and fathers of London and most faithfull subjectes to our prince and country, the Worshipfull John Wats, alderman, Master Paul Baning, alderman, Master Sute Salter, Master Boreman, and others of woorship in this most famous cittie, desirous for their cuntries honor and benefit to employ their substance, victualed and equiped, for all needfull things to so hard and daungerous a voyage appertaining, three good ships. videl., the *Consent*, of the burthen of 240 tunnes or thereabout: the *Salomon*, of 170 tunnes or thereabout: and the *Virgine*, [of]

---

[1] Really the Portuguese; but as both were subjects of Philip II, little distinction was made between them.

60 tunnes or thereabouts; appointing for commaunders in this voyage James Lancaster, of London, gentleman, generall of the fleete, Mun [i.e. Edmund] Barker, of London, viz-admirall, and John Awdley, of Popler, neer London, their reare-admirall; having in their company John Wats[1], the sonne of Alderman Wats, a proper and forward gentleman, full of resolution, and Symon Boreman, sonne of M[aster] Boreman, owner of the *Salomon*, a toward and likely youth.

These forenamed shippes, fully equipped and furnished with all needfull provision moste royally, departed from Blackwall-rood, neer London, in October last past, keeping our owne coast close abourd; where they met with fowle weather, such gusts and stormes that, the *Salomon* spending her mast not far from Darkmouth, they put into harbour; and by the care and earnest industrie of the generall and other having charge were shortly againe provided; which doone, the carefull generall, loth to make longer stay then was needfull, having a pleasing gale for their purpose, put from Darckmouth the last of November following, applying [i.e. plying], as winde served, for their desired place. But, contrary to our expect[2] (as God by many favours tryeth His people), not fiftie leauges from our owne coast wee lost the *Salomon* and the *Virgine*; yet, being alone, in hope to meet them about Graund Canaries or Cape Blanck, we kept our course for the place; and, as God sent us favourable windes, plyed untill we came to the Canaries; but could heare no tydinges of our consorts, which greatly cumbred us. Thence went wee bearing for Tinireef; where in the morning earely wee had sight of a sayle, who, being becalmnd under the shoare, was towing with their boate aheade, having one other at her stearne. For this sayle we mande our boate, apointing our men well for fight, if neede should serve them; but the cowardly Portugales[3], seeing our boate come, entred theirs and, leaving the ship, sought to save themselves by flight. But our men, being full of courage, hartned on with the brave, imboldning speach of our generall, and in hope of some better good by getting the men,

---

[1] The alderman had two sons of the name of John, but presumably the one here mentioned was the eldest son (afterwards knighted), who must have been under twenty at the time of the expedition.

[2] An old form of 'expectation.'   [3] Spaniards (see p. 33).

pursued them so fast and with such egar desire, that they
bourded them and brought them with their shippe to our
generall. This was laden with Canarie wine, which came not
unto us before it was well and better welcome. This shippe was
maned and kept.

Plying that day and the next night thereabouts, the very
next morning wee had sight of one other, but not so much
woorth as the first was, which had eightie tunnes of wine, the
other but fortie. To her in like manner wee sent our boat; but
their gunner (beeing a drunken Flemming) standding on his
tearmes, made a shotte at her and shot [off] a propper young
mans arme. It[1] wee enforced them to strike and to take that
part their countreymen did. A lamentable tale it were to
discover the pittiefull lookes of the poore Portugales, who,
trusting to Our Lady, had no hope of her sonne for comfort.
Well, weeing[2] possest with this good liquor, a substance which
must unite [sic] the life, praysed God for it and that other good
releif wee found amongst them, beeing therewith well refreshed.

The Portugales, having their free passage and an acquit-
tance for deliverie of their wines, were all set ashoare on Tene-
reefe; making a quick returne of their long voyage, who were
bound for Margareta[3], in the Indies.

The men having their discharge, and all thinges [taken?] out
that might doe us any good, we left the place, plying for Cape
Blanck. But before we came thether, wee met againe with the
Virgine, the reare-admyrall, who haling us tolde us for very
trueth the *Salomon* was gonne for England, enforced so to doe
by spending her mast; which wee found contrarie, for, comming
to Cape Blanck, wee met the *Salomon*, who had fished[4] with the
cane-hookes[5]; the best fish and other commodities hee found in
ryfling twentie-foure shippes and carvels. Of this good companie wee were all joyfull, and had great hope of the blessing of
God in performance of our intended voyage. And so, after

[1] Yet.   [2] Wee being?
[3] The island of Margarita, in the Caribbean Sea, off the north coast of
Venezuela.
[4] See p. 8.
[5] Smyth gives 'can-hook' (a contrivance for slinging casks on board) and
'camock' (a crooked piece of timber). The latter seems more likely here.

some parle and making frolick for joy of our meeting one with the other, praysing God for all, wee plyed for Mayeo; where comming to ancor, our generall and the rest of the captanes went ashoare to veiu the place where we might in best safetie set our gallie together; which frame we brought from England of purpose to land men in the cuntrey.

Heere we discharged our great pryze of wine, and set her on fire. But before our comming thether, you shall understand wee had sight of foure sayles, which was Captaine Venard [i.e. Venner], in his shippe the *Perugrine*, and a proper Biskane which he tooke at Cape Blanck, the *Welcome* of Plimmought, and her pynnes; all which stood with us. But they, seing our flagges, [not?] expecting such good fellowes as we, did beare from us all the[y] might; which our people tooke very unkindely, that, beeing all freinds, they would neither enquire nor tell us any newes of our freinds, but, without making any shew of kindnes, so to depart.

From Cape Blanck wee tooke likewise with us three shippes, viz. one daintie carvell and one canter[1], with one other bark, for to serve us in the cuntrey, drawing little water, for divers purposes.

As before I have sayd, the choice beeing made for the place to build the gallie, ashore it was brought; where the carpenters did their true intents and faithfully applyed their worke; still cheered unto it by the generalls good giftes bestowed amongst them, and kind usage of all the rest [of the] commaunders; not without great care of the captaine for the safetie of them all by keeping good watch. Yet one negligent fellow, which had no knowledge of the cuntry, straing from his companie, was by the Mooers taken, and very kindely used and brought againe unto us; for which good [service?] the generall rewarded them well with giftes very acceptabell, which they tooke as kindly.

While we were thus busily imployed about the foresayd gallie, we descryed at sea 4 sayles, which we had good hope woulde have proved Indiesmen or some to have brought us what we looked for; but they proved Captaine Venard with his fleet as aforesayde, who, seeing us at ancor, came in unto us

---

[1] A Spanish fishing-boat.

[and?] ancored also; where spending some time, and beeing acquainted with our generalls determination for landing, consorted with us, and their bills (according to the manner of the sea) were made, and signed of ether parte; whereby our strength was encreased, to all our comforts.

Three weekes or thereabouts we stayed in this place before the gally was finished; which done, putting men into her and fitting her with ores, having 14 bankes on a side, a maste and sayle, the commaundment of her was committed unto Master Wats, an honest, skilfull maryner.

From thence we put againe to sea, and[1] hope of like successe; and went for the ile Dett Bravo, where we watered; which done, we made no long stay after, but bent our course as derectly as we could for the place[2]. But before we came thither, we lost our carvell and one of the other pryzes; our owne shipps beeing all well and in good saftie, [for?] which thankes [be?] to God (the comforte of all that builde faythfully upon Him), by whose sufferance we recovered the place; making our first fall with the land to the southward of Cape Augustine; from whence we applyed still to our desired port of Farnand Bucke, and did so much that about midnight we came before the harbor; where some plyed up and downe, holding that the best pollicy to forbear the entring till day might give them light, the harbought [sic] being bard[3], and therfore the more perillous.

Our shippes being in saftie well arived, God was praysed, and the generall in his boat went from shippe to ship, willing them to make ready such men as they could spare, with muskets, pykes, bylles, bowes, arrowes, and what weapons they had, to follow him. Himself, with fourescore men from his owne shippe. embarqued himselfe in the gallie, which carryed in her prowe a good sacare.

The inhabitaunts, which saw so much shipping, dreading what did follow, were gathered togither, by estimation to the number of 1000 men; and from their platforme, beeing oppisite with the harboughts mouth, well planted with cannon periall and sacars of brasse, plyed upon us with them, our shippes ryding within sacar-shot in the very face of them; yet did they

---

[1] In?   [2] Pernambuco.   [3] Having a bar at the entrance.

not hurt any shippe. But our gunners borrowed little of them, but payd them well whatsoever they sent amongst us, and with such sound payment that two shot from the admyrall, by Gods help and the gunners good industrie, beat their watchhouse about their eares.

This beginning made the faintharted swades[1] to quaile, that their harts were in counsayle with ther heeles, which should be the best member. In the end, by generall consent, they agreed to see a littell more, intreating their heeles to be redy to make shifte for them.

But our generall otherwise imployed his men. Being shipped, [he?] rowed to the shore, all the nyght [sic] appoynted with his companies, and encouraging his men in the very face of the platforme and mouth of their ordinaunce landed, leaping to the waste in water, in the breach of the shoare; his men following him, leaving their gallye, which beate so on the shoare as shee did little other service (a notable pollicie of the generall, if hee had beene matcht with cowards); which the generall little regarded, making that a tryall, and encouraging his men, cryed stil: Saint George, brave gallants, this is our owne. The whitelivored cravins, as they be provde cowardes, not respecting the advantage they had of our people beeing so wette, which easely they might have foyled, like harmelesse honest men, trusting to their olde freindly heeles, their cheifest comfort, leaving the generall in possesion of all, saved themselves, some in boates (which lay ready at the backside [of?] the house), others for the best prize made our men judges who was the best footemen; flying so fast as a hare from the egar greyhound, having not so much kindenes to bid them welcome, nor honestie to bid them farwell. The day of our arrivall was their Good Fryday, when by custome they usuall[y] whippe themselves; but God sent us now for a generall scourge for them all, wherby that labour amongst them might be well spared, for small leasure they had to doe that fopperie.

The generall waved the shippes, willing them to waye and to come in, which they did with all speed; himself taking order with his associates of what they had in possession, and, turning

---

[1] More usually 'swads,' i.e. rustics or peasants.

the ordinance, bent them that way they expected any anoyance from the towneward, made choyce of a place convenient for to builde a baracado, which strongly they fortified, brought the ordinance from the fort and placed them in theirs, what they could best use; the rest they sent abourd, their shippes keeping good and carefull watch. Now it is to be remembered that in this harbour they found three great hulcks[1], which came thether from Spaine to bring those goodes home which was there left, now two yeares since, by a carick which was cast away.

Our generall having in possession the towne, with all the goodes in the storehouses, sent for the Flemings and demaunded what they did there. They answered: for those goods they came, sent from Spaine by the honors[2] for them; and so after some wordes betweene them agreed for their fraught home to England; unto which they yeelded.

When these thinges were thus to our comfort accomplisht, the generall thought it small pollicie to make longer stay then was needfull, and therfore tooke order from everie shippe one to woork, the other to watch for their securitie. The first service [that?] was done, we unladed our wine prize, giving to every ship equall portions. Then, making ready every shippes holde, they brake the prize, making it to serve for a lighter to lade, and with her the *Welcomes* pynnace for the more expedition in their lading. So earnestly applying themselves as no oportuniti[e] was lost in performaunce thereof; our willing mindes holding it no trouble, watching by night, nor hard labour by day. But so vigilaunt they were in all there actions as was requisite they should in so perillous a place; otherwise they had enjoyed their good fortunes but a small time, such was the pollicie [i.e. craft] of those base roges; who in the night at one time fyred iij carvills—a pollicie to their cost learned in England, but perfourmed like themselves; for the carvills with the fire taking, like harmelesse boates, a quite contrary way, ran ashore, consuming themselves without any annoyance to our ships, as they intended they should have done.

This device sorting to no better effect, they made rafts with olde masts, and grapling them together, and planting them full

---

[1] The Dutch ships.   [2] Owners.

of light wood, heath, and such, fired them and sent them amongst our shippes. For this devise our generall ordained from everie shippe two boates to be ready ahead each shippe, having in each one of them a graplet to throw on the rafts; which sunck them all, and [they?] never had any advantage to doe us harme. These devices qualing [i.e. failing] by sea, every night they gave us bravadoes one the shore, bringing some few naked men, with bowes and arrowes, before our sconce[1]; which shot often, without dooing harme. All which was to draw us within compasse of their ambushment which they had laid, in hope we should have pursued them flying; but our generalls [sic] and captaines had more foresight then to venture themselves and us against naked wretches.

When they saw that all their devise was by pollicie frustrate, thinking wee would be carclesse of their dooing, they began in the night to builde a new forte in such a place as would have greatly annoyed us, if they had gone forward with it. But our generall, having intelligence of the same by some of the cuntry people, would not seeme unto them any way discontent; but secretly in the evening, quietly gathering his companies, issued upon them, put them from their woorke, tooke foure peices of brasse ordinaunce, and, slaying threescore of their men, put the rest unto flight, and retourned with losse of one man, bringing with him to our forte their ordinaunce, which they intended should have doone us the mischief. This their devises sorting to such ill successe, ever pretending, but never accomplishing any thing that ever did hurt us, our men with such care imploied themselves as was joyfull to see them.

In this painfull travell of ours, we had sight of a small man of warre of Deep in Fraunce, who had plyed up and downe two monethes, yet durst not put in untill they had sight of Saint George, which continually we bare in our toppes. This little Frenchman, comming in, saluted our admyrall as he could, after the sea manner, and hoysing his boat came abourd to our generall, acquainting him with his extremitie, wanting victualls; who, like himself, pyttying his distresse and waying the want himself had indured in his last long voyage with that noble

[1] Redoubt, or earthwork.

gentleman, Captaine Raymond, gave him wine, bread, pease, and such victualls as he had, to their great releef.

This Frenchman reported that he, not long before, met with Captaine Abraham Cock, who, beeing distressed for water, hee releived with one hogshed, having but two in all, and brought him to a place where they both watered. Not long after his arryvall, wee had sight of three sayles more, which we hoped had beene Indiamen, but prooved Frenchmen. The generall of this fleet was that same which brought our generall from Mona, after the losse of his shippe. To our generall [he] was hartily welcome, as was moste manifest by the entertainment he gave both him and his whole companie; wherein showing himself a most brave and gratefull gentleman, farre unlike such shaving people which never think of freindship longer then they reape commoditie, catch by all meanes they can from such as carry gentle and willing mindes to deserve well to doe good unto them that seeke their favour. Such unthankfull wretches I have oftentimes seene to begge for releif, where their piteous moanes have beene scorned.

But to our matter. The generall in this time being possest with such welthie commodities as he could not tell where to bestowe, after he had fraughted his owne three men of war, three Flemish hulcks of great burthen, three western[1] ships, viz. the *Perygrine*, the *Welcome*, and their prize, with two Spanyards which hee found in the roade, gave franckly unto his good freind the captaine what he would take of all such commodities as they had, which was cloves, mace, pepper, sinemon, and Calocow cloth, sugar, and brassellwood (wherof they had such store that everie night during the keeping their forte ashoare they burnt, by estimation, above two tunnes). With these commodities the Frenchman lading his three shippes, and the Deep man one, and yet the generall, to showe his further thankfulnes unto him, gave him freely one other shippe, which came into the harbought full laden with negers and other commodities, of which he tooke his pleasure. This favour the Frenchman tooke in very thankfull manner, and with diligence purveyed [i.e. prepared] to be gone with the fleet. Who being near ready to leave the harbought,

---

[1] West Country.

intelligence was given them by some of the cuntrey people that the governor had provided for making a new forte, opposit of the mouth of the harbourt, where perrilles were most incident, and where men should be most busied in dooing their labour to keepe them from the danger of the bar; which tydings nothing plesed him nor any of his companie. Wherfore sommoning the cheif of each shippe, uppon conference had of the daungers so bad a guest might there breed, being there planted, it was concluded to make such power as they could and to drive them from their labour, so to raze their fortification. This being with advise platted,[1] and a generall likeing of the devise, care was likewise taken for perfourming the same, and everie thing for the purpose accordingly fitted. Which done, the generall, that had beene often by flags of truce sommoned to parle with their governour, which continually he refused, scorning to have familiaritie with any his princesse enemies, as well to avoyde suspect of evill tounges as for his owne reputation, was for this cause envyed of the generall[2] the more, which doubtlesse would gladly have beene better acquainted with him, if possibly he might; and for the better bringing his devilish practises to effect, he first began this new fortification, which he imagined our generall would not indure, nor suffer him to perfourme; but, woorking by pollicie, he ambusht his people, seeking therby his overthrow; whome God defended, in dispight of what he could or might doe, as the sequell shall manifest. For hee, whose hope was neither in Pope, saint, or help of man, determining (as you have heard) to effect this new resolved woorke, ranged his companies and in most warlick and brave manner (like a conqueror) marched on to their forte; where with such courage he assayled the defendants as made them beleeve there shoulde few escape; which made them play their olde parts and, trusting to their best freinds, their nymble heeles, tournned their backes and departed. Whose dastardly minds our men disdaining, with eger pursute followed, spoyling many. But they, that thought on no manhood but pollicie, convaide themselves into a wood, closely followed of our people; into which they were no sooner entered but in sight of our people was placed xvij ensignes, that

---

[1] Plotted, or planned.   [2] This seems a slip for 'governor.'

made on towards them; and looking behinde them, they were backed with so many, besides those runawaies in the wood. This sight caused our people to stand and better to consider for their safties what to doe; who knowing that delay bread daungers, desirous to show their resolution in maintaining that honor which most valiantly they had alreadie obtained, rather were desirous to adventure their good fortunes with the swoorde then to loose what they had so honorably gained; subjecting themselves unto so mercelesse enemies. And heeron, resolving like Englishmen, who was as yet never knowen to forsake the feildes where tenne hath beene to one, the enimie approching one both sides, there was no remedie but to looke to themselves; which our generall and his valiant associates seeing, placing their companies as they could best one such a suddaine, both for defending themselves and annoying the enemie, like men no whit discomforted, beholding their huge numbers, which were of horsse and foote, Spaniardes and the cuntrey people, 5000, bravely and with great courage began the assault, applying their small shot so long as their poulder lasted; which finished, throwing from them their shot, betooke him[1] to their hand weapons, with which they did such wundrous spoyle as the Spaniards perswaded them[selves?] that they fought, not against men, but some of a more borish condicion.

A sore and cruell battell was there heer begonne and continued, with so few to such a multitude as seldome hath beene seene in the enemies cuntrey; whose valiant harts were never dared [i.e. daunted], nor for no extremitie, although thorow their hot and earnest labor in such a broyle, and in a cuntrey so contagious, many were distrest for want of drink, yet minded they what they had in hand more then their bellies, playing the partes of men and brave Englishmen, defending and annoying the enemie with such corage that the enemies wundred therat; evermore cheering themselves, and the generall chearing all, crying out, to the terrour of the enemie: Saint George, God for S. George, Englands defence.

But in this glorie, when their hopes were such to escape all daungers, thorough the mightie hand of our God, which caused

---

[1] At this period 'him' or 'hem' is occasionally found in place of 'them.'

so many to fall before Sampson with the jawbone, beholde a mervelous terrour unto our men. The French captain, our generalls great amico[1], leading threescore of his cuntreymen, was slaine. At whose fall his followers, being discomforted, beganne to flye, shewing theirin right partes of themselves; which our men perceiving, and knowing no cause, made shift for themselves, as these cowards did, and recovered their botes and their shippes in good safetie, backed from the raging pursute of the enemie by our shippes.

In this conflict also was slaine Captaine Barker, Captaine Cotton, two moste brave and resolute gentlemen, and much lamented[2]. This battell finished, and all men come abourde that could come, our generall thought that he had done moste honorably, and generally the whole companye; bewayling the losse of his good freind, the French gentleman, slaine: cryed out of cowardice of those baser groomes[3], his followers, perswading himself that, if they had stood with them, the honor of this comrie[4] had beene theirs; so great was all their hopes in His mercie, that in so many perrils, since they came from their owne cuntry, had so mightily preserved them. Then laboured our men to cloy[5] that ordinaunce we left in our forte, which we ramd full of spykes, stones, and other trumperie, making them unservisable.

The generall, seeing what was done and that there was no meanes to withstand so great a multitude, least, armed with foolish hardines, he should endaunger the honor hee had gained (then which hee rather would choose to dye); seeing it would bee hot abyding there, the enemie planting so neere him, commaunded the whole fleet to make ready, bring their ancours abourd, and upon the first of the ebbe to goe out; which with such expedition was done that their was no show of any idle hands.

At this push, beholde one other most mervelous favour of God toward us. The windes, which long before blew great and vehemently into the harbought mouth, had altered her [i.e. their] place and fitted our turnes. So that, being ready to set sayle, we

---

[1] Friend (Italian).
[2] The extra leaf in the Huntington copy (see p. 72) is inserted here.
[3] Used as a general term of abuse for men of an inferior position.
[4] The *Oxford Eng. Dict.* has 'cumray' as a verb, meaning to overwhelm or rout.   [5] An old term for 'spike.'

had a fayre topsale gale, which caryed us cleare off the harbought and the barre, without receiving any domage from the enemie, which shot franckly [i.e. freely] at us a long time, never hitting any one hull but one of our Flemings, a great hulck which was as fair a marck as a church; which winde lasted not long, nor found wee the like in seven weekes after.

Thus being delivered from the hands of our enemies, having in our companies, of English, French, and Dutch, the number of fifteene sayles, laden all deep with their commodities, the generall commaunded the whole fleet to bear for Peren-Jew, where hee determined to water and to take such other provision as we could there gette; sending the little Frenchman of Deepe (which sayled well) to purvaie what hee could for us. With this place we fel about the midst of night. Our generall, comming to ancour in the offine, put out his lightes, that they might be therby advertised what to doe. Yet notwithstanding, some put into the harbought, others overshotte it, and wee in the admyrall, ryding a foule and most bitter rough[1], were faine to shift for ourselves and put into the sea, where wee lost our fleet and never met them after until our aryvall in the Downes; where it was sayde unto our generall (to his and all our comforts) that the *Salomon*, with one Flemish hulck, was come unto London; the *Perygrine*, the *Welcome*, with their pynace and one other hulck laden, were at Plimmouth; and one of the Spanish shippes, which we laded for our owne use, arrived at Breast in Brittaine [Brittany]; the other, by mischance comming foule of another shippe, was broken down to the water, which our men left in the sea. The Frenchmen, with their five shippes, are (as wee heare) all arryved in safetie. Our shippe, with the *Virgine* and one other hulck, being the last that came home, whose long stay made our freindes greatly to doubt of our well dooings. But prayse to His holie name, that hath so preserved us all and sent us with such happie fortune amongst our freinds, with no great losse; though some we had. Amongst which that lost their lives and most lamented was Captaine Venard [Venner], whome we buryed royally in the cuntry; the other our master chi[r]urgion, Randall Starkey, a man of singuler skil and as good government as may be required; who (of the disease called the flux) dyed and

---

[1] A spell of stormy weather.

was there buryed, and almost all our chiurgions, one only excepted of whose help (God be glorified) we had little neede untill our arrivall in the Downes; where a most sore and greevous mischance befell us, thorow the necligence of our master gunner, whose carelesse dooings made us all full heavie, after a most troublesome and hard adventures to be at our owne doores, when every man was reconing to sollace him with his freindes, then by such a casuall hap to be spoyled as we were; for the gunnor himself was slaine, with two others, and twentie others greivously hurt; a woorthy mirour for all men of government taking charge, how so carelessely they demaine themselves, looking with more care unto the charge unto them committed, especially such as have the commaund of poulder and suchlike substance, which is not to be jested withall. The proofe thereof hath beene to[o] often seene, to the great damage of the woorshipfull owners. God graunt this may be the last.

Thus, good reader, I have truly discoursed unto you the troubles of this our voyage; which, to the glorie of God and our cuntries woorthy deserved commendations, I have heere explayned, that you, which beholde the wunders God hath done for us and our cuntrey, may with us, and wee with you, prayse Him, and hartely desire that never woorsse succes befall any of our nation that, as wee have done, fight and adventure in such hassard for our prince and cuntrey; whose life and honor God ever maintaine, to the terrour of all domesticall enemies and the overthrowe of all those that wish her or us ill.

A commemoration of those woorthy and valiant gentlemen, Captaine Barker and his freind, Captaine Cotton, who in this moste honorable attempt lost their lives.

Gallants of England, Marses chosen pheres[1],
Brave men of worth, chaveleres[2] of fame,
Lay armes aside and poure forth brinish teares,
Wayling their losse whom cowarde foes hath slaine.
Barker, brave man, the honor of thy name,
Whose hautye deedes, yet ill successe in warre,
In cheifest mirth doth cause our tunes to jarre.

[1] Companions. It is usually spelt 'feres.'   [2] Cavaliers.

And courtious Cottonne, for his brave attempt
Didst well deserve a worthy captaines place.
Their valiant force these Spaniards proud have felt,
Which purchase fame unto thier great disgrace;
Pursuing foes like lions in their chase,
Fighting in right of cuntry and our Queene,
Like men of worth, most resolute and sterne.

In midst of broyles, where foes were ten to one,
Thier shot beeing spent, a wunder twas to see
How many Spaniards by them to death were brought,
Crying: S. George, sweete England, now for thee.
The warcke[1] of Spaine we have good hope to see.
This sayd those gallants, and even therewithall
A luckelesse strook causde Barker dead to fall,

Whose death fearce Cottonne requited so
That many a foe by him to hell was sent.
So shewed this man of worth his force gainst foe,
Whose hart with rigor to revenge was bent.
But chance of warre hath often wrong event,
In cheifest hope to have a joyfull day,
A cursed shot his life hath tane away.

Thus fought those men, like champions of our Queene,
Having at most in all three hundred men
Against five thousand, which armd in feilde was seene,
Ranged to fight, such cowardes still they benne.
Yet all their force they wayed not a pyn,
But bravely then the onset on them gave,
And by their valour from their fort them drave.

But dead they be, yea, dead are both our freinds,
Whose fames shall live eternized for ay,
That all may know how brave they made their endes,
Which, whilst they lived in this most hardy fray,
Did scourge these curres and held them at a bay.
Whose senceles truncks though loe enterd[2] they lye,
Their glorious soules both rest above the skye.

Finis   H. R.

---

[1] Wreck?   [2] Interred.

ADDENDUM[1]

But especially Captaine Randolph Cotton, whose courage in midst of all broyles never quailed. This brave and worthy minded gentleman, albeit he had endurde most hard and cruel crosses in his last adventure to the sea, accompaning that moste renowmed and forward gentleman, Thomas Candish [i.e. Cavendish], Esquire, who held him for his vertues in great account. The remembrance of whose death with greef he [Cotton] oftentimes bewayled, and the many cares and troubles of that most unfortunate voyage, not yet exiled out of his minde; desirous to make once againe tryall of his fortunes, arming his never conquered minde for the same, resolving ether to gaine fame, which before welth he pryzed; not like those peny fathers[2], which care not who loose, so they gaine; expecting but opportunitie and such companie as he wished, rested so, untill our generalls arrivall at Darckmouth (where hee made his abode); with whome having conference, and knowing his pretended voyage for these confines of Fernand Bucke, and that his determination was to land, thought this a time fitting his minde. Wherfore, without any desire to see his best freinds, kynne, or allyes, which commonly draw men from many attemptes, hee not only adventured his mony in the action but his bodye. With whose good companie the generall was well pleased, and all the rest of his compeeres[3]; having great hope of his valor, which not only showed in his manly countenance, but specially induced therunto by the rare reportes of his forward attempts in many other actions where hee had charge, as well by sea as by land. An instance of which was manifested by those that accompaned

---

[1] This is the extra leaf which appears in the Huntington copy only. It was intended for insertion between C 2 and C 3 (at the point shown on p. 68). Dr George Watson Cole, in his article on *Elizabethan Americana*, says (p. 168): 'This extra leaf contains a long commendatory notice of Captain Randolph Cotton, who was slain at Pernambuco. It would seem that, after the pamphlet had been printed, it was considered that not enough credit had been given him; so an extra leaf was added, to supply the omission. Unfortunately, the binder of the Huntington copy mistook this leaf for a cancel and destroyed leaf C 3.'

[2] Penurious persons.   [3] Associates.

that most rare and famous captaine and navigator, John Vames[1], where, by his good counsaile in times of extremities and valiant corage in all times of service, hee gayned by curtesie the sole love and generall likeing of all the companie.

All which good partes, conjoyning in this woorth[y] gentleman, mooved the generall, with consent of his freinds and compheres, to elect him for their principall leader for their land service; as one whose skill and moste woorthy resolution they wholely (under God) relyed uppon; which was every way answerable to what they expected, so that therein they were not deceived at all, as his great care in perfourming that charge [which] was unto him committed did manifest. For what many men accounted great paine and moste troublesome labour hee held and esteemed as meere pleasure; such diligent care he had in keeping on shore such vigilaunt watch and warde, bothe for his companies securit[i]e as his owne, as was necessary and most convenient to be used in a place of such daunger; besides his hard labour in buylding three baracadoes, where he framed[2] his hands, which in such labours had [not?] beene usually accoustomed, to toyle and take paine, whereby he might drawe on others, and the better to encorage them to their busines and careful industrie; ever and in everie attem[p]t showing both valour and resolution in his actions as [i]s well seene at the supprizing of their enemies first begunne forte; where giving a most couragious onset, [he] put them from their woorke and supprizing [sic] their ordinaunce, and with no small honor most valiantly brought it unto their forte.

This woorthy and most valiant gentleman, as hee was forward to acomplish those actions which to such valiant and resolute exploites belonged, so was he unto his followers, as well of resolute assaults as of carefull industrie, a spectacle[3] in his enterprises, never daunted or receiving foyle, untill the fatall time of his death, which honorably he received. Thus showing himself a most woorthy leader and faithfull subject to his prince and cuntrey; leading his companies to this venterous and rare

---

[1] Davis is intended. He and Cotton were great friends, and were together in Cavendish's last voyage.
[2] An old sense of 'frame' is 'to adapt.'
[3] In the obsolete sense of 'example.'

exploite, invironed with the extremitie of these base and cowardly peasants, who takeing him at a vantage, was most butcherly murthered, without regarde either of his vertues or valour.

But the cruell tyranny of those detestable wretches shall [not?] nor can blemish his deserved fame, nor oblivion extinguish his resolute actions, wherby he woorthyly deserved such memorie as tung or pen can or may render, for requitall as well of his vertuous behaviour, carefull industrey, and resolution in all his actions.

With whome there dyed that valiant captaine, Mun Barker; bothe which, as long as they lived, so encouraged our people that there was no feare amongst them, but everie one resolved to fight it out; whose death was greatly lamented amongst us all.

This battle finished, and all men come abourd the shippes [*continue as on p. 68, line 12.*]

THE THIRD VOYAGE
1601–03

I

THE ACCOUNT IN *PURCHAS*[1]

The first voyage made to East-India by Master James Lancaster (now Knight) for the Merchants of London, anno 1600 [*i.e.* 1601], *with foure tall shippes, to wit, the* Dragon, *the* Hector, *the* Ascension, *and* Susan, *and a victualler called the* Guest[2].

§ 1

The preparation to this voyage, and what befell them in the way till they departed from Saldania.

THE merchants of London, in the yeare of Our Lord 1600, joyned together and made a stocke of seventie-two thousand pounds, to bee imployed in ships and merchandizes, for the discovery of a trade in the East-India, to bring into this realme spices and other commodities. They bought foure great ships, to be imployed in this voyage: the *Dragon*, of the burthen of six hundred tunne; the *Hector*, of the burthen of three hundred tunnes; the *Ascension*, of the burthen of two hundred and three score tunnes[3]. These ships they furnished with men, victuals, and munition for twentie monethes; and sent in them, in merchandise and Spanish money, to the value of seven and twentie thousand pounds. All the rest of their stocke was spent and consumed about the shippes and other necessaries apper-

---

[1] From *Purchas His Pilgrimes*, lib. III, cap. iii (p. 147). There is, unfortunately, no clue to the name of the writer; but he was evidently on terms of familiarity with Lancaster, and this suggests that he was one of the merchants on board the *Dragon*.

[2] Entries in the Court Minutes (see *The Dawn of British Trade*, pp. 147, 154, 264) show that the vessel was really named the *Guift* (i.e. *Gift*). She is so termed in the other two accounts of the voyage.

[3] The *Susan* has been omitted in error.

tayning to them, with money lent to the mariners and saylers beforehand that went upon the voyage.

The merchants were suters to Her Majestie, who gave them her friendly letters of commendation, written to divers princes of India [i.e. the East Indies], offering to enter into a league of peace and amitie with them, the copies of which letters shall hereafter appeare in their places[1]. And because no great action can well be carryed and accomplished without an absolute authoritie of justice, shee granted to the generall of their fleet, Master James Lancaster, for his better command and government, a commission of martiall law[2].

The said Master James Lancaster, the generall, was placed in the *Dragon*, the greatest shippe, being admirall; Master John Middleton, captaine in the *Hector*, the vice-admirall; Master William Brand[3], chiefe governour in the *Ascention*; and Master John Heyward in the *Susan*. And more, in every of the said ships three merchants to succeed one the other, if any of them should be taken away by death.

These ships were readie and departed from Wolwich, in the river of Thames, the thirteenth of February, after the English accompt, 1600 [i.e. 1601], with foure hundred and fourescore men in them: in the *Dragon* two hundred and two men; in the *Hector* an hundred and eight; in the *Ascention* fourescore and two; and in the *Susan* fourescore and eight. The *Guest*, a ship of a hundred and thirtie tunnes[4], was added as a victualler. These ships stayed so long in the river of Thames and in the Downes, for want of wind, that it was Easter Day[5] before they arrived at Dartmouth, where they spent five or sixe dayes in taking in their bread and certaine other provisions appointed for them. From thence they departed the eighteenth of Aprill 1601, and road in

---

[1] This promise was only fulfilled in the case of the letter to the king of Achin (see p. 94), which appears to have been specially drawn. Five or six others were taken out in the voyage, with blanks for the names and titles of the respective princes. The text of these circular letters is given in *The First Letter Book*, p. 19, and in Bruce's *Annals*, vol. I, p. 147.

[2] This commission is printed in *The First Letter Book*, p. 2.

[3] In the Court Minutes the name is generally spelt Brund, and he is described as 'a grave and discreet merchaunt and one which hath the Arabyann, Spanish, and Portugall languages' (*The Dawn*, p. 93).

[4] According to the Court Minutes, this should be 120 tons (*The Dawn*, p. 147).   [5] 12 April.

Tor Bay till the twentieth in the morning. While wee roade there, the generall sent aboord all the shippes instructions for their better company-keeping, at their comming to the seas; and further gave directions, if any of the fleet should bee separated the one from the other by stormes of wind, tempests, or other casualties, what places to repair unto for their meeting together again[1].

The second[2] of Aprill 1601 the wind came faire and we hoysed our anchors and departed out of Tor Bay, directing our course towards the ilands of the Canaria. The wind holding faire, the fift of May in the morning we had sight of Alegranza, the northermost iland of the Canarias, and directed our course betweene Forteventura and the Grand Canaria. And comming to the south part of the Grand Canaria, thinking to water there, wee fell into the calmes, which proceed by reason of the high land that lyeth so neere the sea side.

The seventh of May, about three of the clocke in the afternoone, wee departed from the Grand Canaria, having the wind at north-east; and we directed our course south-west by south and south-south-west, till we came into $21\frac{1}{2}$ degrees. From the eleventh to the twentieth our course was for the most part south, till we came into eight degrees, the wind being alwayes northerly and north-east. In this heigth we found the calmes and contrarie winds which, upon this coast of Ginney at this time of the yeare, are very familiar, with many sudden gustes of wind, stormes, thunder and lightening, very fearefull to be seene, and dangerous to the shippes, unlesse a diligent care be had that all sayles be stricken downe upon the sudden, perceiving the ayre never so little to change or alter; and yet many times, although the masters of ships were carefull and looked unto it with great diligence, the suddennesse was such that it could hardly be prevented.

---

[1] 'These places were the calmes of Canarie, and, if weaknesse permitted not to double the Cape, Soldania; the third, Cape Saint Roman in Madagascar; to Cirne; and so to Sumatra, their first place of trade' (note in *Purchas*). Cape St Roman (or Cape Romania), now called Cape Andavaka, is on the south-eastern coast of Madagascar. Cerne or Cirne was the name given by the Portuguese to the island afterwards re-christened (by the Dutch) Mauritius. Evidently a decision had already been taken to go outside Madagascar instead of through the Mozambique Channel (as in Lancaster's first voyage).

[2] An error for 20 April.

From the twentieth of May till the one and twentieth of June wee lay the most part becalmed, and with contrarie winds at south. And turning up and downe with this contrary wind, with much adoe we got into two degrees of the north side of the Line. Where wee espyed a ship, to the which the generall gave chase, commanding all the rest of the ships to follow him; and by two of the clocke in the afternoone we had set her up[1] and tooke her. She was of the citie of Viana[2] in Portugall, and came from Lisbone in the companie of two carrackes and three gallions bound for the East India, which ships she had lost at sea. The three gallions were ships of warre, and went to keepe the coast of the East-India from being traded with [by?] other nations. We tooke out of her an hundred, sixe and fortie buts of wine. an hundred, threescore and sixteene jarres of oyle, twelve barrels of oyle, and five and fiftie hogsheads and fats [i.e. vats] of meale; which was a great helpe to us in the whole voyage after. The generall divided these victualls indifferently to all the ships; to every one his proportion without partialitie.

The last of June, about midnight, we doubled [i.e. passed] the Line and lost the sight of the north star; having the wind at south-east. And we held our course south-south-west, and doubled the Cape of Saint Augustine[3] some sixe and twentie leagues to the eastwards. The twentieth of July we were shot into nineteene degrees, fortie minutes to the southward of the Line, the wind inlargeing daily to the eastward. Here wee discharged the *Guest*, the ship that went along with us to carry the provisions that our foure ships could not take in in England. After wee had discharged her, we tooke her masts, sayles, and yards, and brake downe her higher buildings for firewood; and so left her floting in the sea, and followed our course to the southward.

The foure and twentieth of July we passed the Tropick of Capricorne, the wind being north-east by north, we holding our course east-south-east. Now by reason of our long being under the Line (which proceeded of our late comming out of England,

---

[1] A hunting expression, for 'brought her to bay.'
[2] Vianna do Castello, about forty miles north of Oporto.
[3] In Brazil (see p. 36).

for the time of the yeare was too farre spent by six or seven weekes to make a quicke navigation), many of our men fell sicke. Therefore, the nine and twentieth of July, being in 28½ degrees, hee [i.e. Lancaster] wrote a remembrance to the governour of each ship, either to fetch Saldania or Saint Helena for refreshing.

Thus following on our course, the first of August we came into the height of thirtie degrees south of the Line; at which time we met the south-west wind, to the great comfort of all our people. For by this time very many of our men were fallen sicke of the scurvey in all our ships, and unlesse it were in the generals ship only, the other three were so weake of men that they could hardly handle the sayles. This wind held faire till wee came within two hundred and fiftie leagues of the Cape Buena Esperanza, and then came cleane contrarie against us to the east, and so held some fifteene or sixteene dayes, to the great discomfort of our men. For now the few whole men we had beganne also to fall sicke; so that our weaknesse of men was so great that in some of the ships the merchants tooke their turnes at the helme, and went into the top to take in the topsayles, as the common mariners did. But God (who sheweth mercy in all distresses) sent us a faire wind againe, so that, the ninth of September, wee came to Saldania; where the generall before the rest bare in and came to an anchor, and hoysed out his boats to helpe the reste of the ships, for now the state of the other three was such that they were hardly able to let fall an anchor to save themselves withall. The generall went aboord of them and carried good store of men and hoysed out their boats for them, which they were not able to doe of themselves. And the reason why the generals men stood better in health then the men of other ships was this; he brought to sea with him certaine bottles of the juice of limons, which hee gave to each one, as long as it would last, three spoonfuls every morning, fasting; not suffering them to eate anything after it till noone. This juice worketh much the better if the partie keepe a short dyet and wholly refraine salt meate; which salt meate, and long being at the sea, is the only cause of the breeding of this disease. By this meanes the generall cured many of his men and preserved the rest; so that in his ship (having the double of men that was in the rest of the ships) he had not so many sicke nor lost so many men as they did (which was the mercie of God to us all).

After the generall had holpen the rest of the ships to hoyse out their boats, they began all to be greatly comforted. Then he himselfe went presently aland to seeke some refreshing for our sicke and weake men; where hee met with certaine of the countrey people, and gave them divers trifles, as knives and peeces of old iron and such like, and made signes to them to bring him downe sheepe and oxen; for he spake to them in the cattels language (which was never changed at the confusion of Babell), which was *moath* for oxen and kine, and *baa* for sheepe; which language the people understood very well without any interpreter. After hee had sent the people away, very well contented with their presents and kind usage, order was presently given that certaine of every ships companie should bring their sayles aland, and build tents with them for their sicke men; and also to make fortifications of defence, if by any occasion the people should take any conceit of offence against us, and thereby offer us any violence. And the generall prescribed an order for buying and selling with the people, which was that at such times as they should come downe with the cattell, only five or sixe men, appointed for that purpose, should goe to deale with them; and the rest (which should never bee under thirtie muskets and pikes) should not come neere the market by eight or ten score [paces] at the neerest; and always to stand in their ranke in a readiness, with their muskets in their rests[1], what occasion sooner should befall. And this order was most strictly observed and kept, that no man durst once goe to speake with any of the people without speciall leave. And I take this to be the cause why we lived in so great friendship and amitie with them, contrary to that which lately had befallen the Hollanders, which had five or six of their men slaine by their treacherie[2].

The third day after our comming into this bay of Saldania, the

---

[1] At this period a musket was fired while resting upon a wooden support, forked at the top and spiked at the bottom.

[2] This had occurred three years before. The Dutch fleet was commanded by Conelisz. Houtman. John Davis, who was with him, recounts the incident and says that thirteen Dutchmen were killed (*Purchas*, vol. 1, bk. iii, p. 118).

people brought downe beefes and muttons, which we bought of them for pieces of old iron hoopes, as two pieces (of eight inches apiece) for an oxe and one piece (of eight inches) for a sheepe; with which they seemed to be well contented. Within ten or twelve dayes we bought of them a thousand sheepe and two and fortie oxen; and might have bought many more if wee would.

Now within twelve dayes they ceased to bring us any more cattell. But the people many times came downe to us afterward; and when we made them signes for more sheepe, they would point us to those wee had bought, which the generall caused to be kept grazing upon the hilles about our tents, and was the cause (as we judged) they thought we would have inhabited there, and therefore brought us no more. But (God be thanked) we were well stored to satisfie our need, and might then very well forbeare buying. These oxen are full as bigge as ours, and were very fat; and the sheepe many of them much bigger, but of a very hairie wooll, yet of exceeding good flesh, fat and sweet, and (to our thinking) much better then our sheepe in England.

The people of this place are all of a tawnie colour, of a reasonable stature, swift of foot, and much given to picke and steale. Their speech is wholly uttered through the throate, and they clocke with their tongues in such sort that, in seven weekes which we remained heere in this place, the sharpest wit among us could not learne one word of their language. And yet the people would soone understand any signe wee made to them.

While wee stayed heere in this bay we had so royall refreshing that all our men recovered their health and strength, onely foure or five excepted. But before our comming in, and in this place, wee lost out of all our ships one hundred and five men. And yet wee made account wee were stronger at our departure out of this bay then wee were at our comming out of England, our men were so well inured to the southerne climates.

§ 2

Their departure from Saldania and proceeding in their voyage to Achen, in Sumatra; with their trading at Saint Maries, Antongill, Nicubar, the strange plant of Sombrero, and other occurrents.

The foure and twentieth of October the generall caused all our tents to bee taken downe, and our men to repaire aboord the ships. And being fitted both of wood and fresh water, the nine and twentieth of October wee put to sea, and went out by a small iland[1] that lieth in the mouth of the said bay, which is exceeding full of seales and pengwines, so that, if there were no more refreshing, one might very well refresh there. Over the bay of Saldania standeth a very high hill, flat like a table, and is called the Table. Such another plaine marke to find an harbour in is not in all that coast, for it is easie to be seene seventeen or eighteene leagues into the sea.

Sunday, the first of November, in the morning, we doubled the Cape of Buena Esperança, having the wind west-north-west, a great gale.

The sixe and twentieth of November wee fell with the headland of the iland of Saint Laurence, somewhat to the east of Cape Sebastian[2]. And being within five miles of the shoare, wee sounded, and found twenty-five fathome; the variation of the compasse being (little more or lesse) sixteene degrees. For in an east and west course the variation of the compasse helpeth much, and especially in this voyage.

From the sixe and twentieth of November till the fifteenth of December wee plyed to the eastward, the neerest our course wee could lie; always striving to have gotten to the iland of Cirne[3], which in some cardes is called Diego Rodriques. But wee found the wind alwaies, after our comming to the iland of Saint Laurence, at east and east-south-east and east-north-east, so that wee could not obtaine it. And to strive long, in hope of change of windes, wee could not, for now our men began againe to fall sicke of the scurvy. Then the captaine of the vice-

---

[1] Robben Island (see p. 3).   [2] Now Faux Cap.
[3] See note on p. 77.

admirall[1] called to the generall and thought it best to beare into the bay of Antongile[2], and there to refresh our men with oranges and limons, to cleere ourselves of this disease; which was by him and the whole counsell (called for that purpose) well approoved.

The seventeenth of December wee had sight of the southermost part of the iland of Saint Mary[3]; and the next day wee anchored betweene Saint Mary and the great iland of Saint Laurence, and sent our boats aland to Saint Maries, where wee had some store of limons and oranges, which were precious for our diseased men, to purge their bodies of the scurvy. Now, as we roade heere, buying oranges and limons, there arose upon us a very great storme, so that three of our ships were put from their anchors; but within some sixteen houres the storme ceased, and the ships returned and weighed their anchors againe. The generall thought it not good to make any longer stay there, seeing the uncertaintie of the weather and that there was upon this iland so little refreshing to be had; only these oranges and limons, a little goates milke, and some small quantitie of rice. We saw onely one cow, and that they drave away as soone as they saw us come on land. Seeing this place so dangerous to ride in, the generall gave present order to sayle toward the bay of Antongile; the time of the yeere being spent, the easterly winds come against us, and our men sicke.

This iland of S. Mary is high land and full of woods. The people are blacke, very handsome and tall men, and of curled haire; onely before in their foreheads they stroke it up, as the women doe here in England, so that it standeth some three inches upright. They are wholly without apparell; onely their privy parts covered. They are very tractable to converse [i.e. deal] withall, yet seeme to be very valiant. The most of their food is rice and some fish; yet at our being there wee could buy but small store of rice, for the time of their store was farre spent and their harvest was at hand. There are two or three watering places on the north part of this iland, but none of them

[1] John Middleton.
[2] Antongil, a spacious bay on the north-eastern coast of Madagascar, in about lat. 16° S.
[3] Eleven leagues south of Antongil Bay. Later it became notorious as the resort of European pirates.

very commodious; yet with some travell [i.e. labour] there is water enough to be had.

The twentie-third of December we departed from this iland of S. Mary; and the twentie-fift (being Christmas Day) we came into the baye of Antongill, and came to an anchor in eight fatham water betweene a small iland and the mayne; lying in the bottome of the baye, a very good and a safe roade. But the best riding is neerest under a small iland, for the defence of the winde that bloweth there. For while we abode in this baye there blew an exceeding great storme, and those of our shippes that road neerest the small iland, beeing under the wind, sped best; for two of our ships drove with three anchors ahead, the ground being ozy and not firme. At our going aland in the little iland we perceived, by writing upon the rockes[1], of five Holland ships which had beene there and were departed about two monethes before our comming in, and had had some sicknesse among their men and had lost (as we perceived) betweene one hundred and fiftie and two hundred men while they roade in that place[2].

The next day after our comming to an anchor we went aland to the mayne iland, where the people presently repaired to us and made us signes of the five Holland ships departed, and that they had bought the most part of their provision. Yet they entred into barter with us for rice and hennes, oranges and limons, and another fruit called plantans; and held all at high rates and brought but a pedlars quantitie. Our market was neere to a great river, into which we went with our boats, and some men which were appointed to be buyers went ashore. The rest remained in the boates, alwaies readie with their weapons in their hands, and the boates some fifteene or twentie yardes off into the water, where the people could not wade to them, and

[1] It was a common practice to carve upon rocks at a roadstead the dates of arrival and departure of ships, for the information of later comers. Some of those carved at Table Bay are now in the Cape Town Museum; and similar ones are preserved at St Helena.
[2] This was part of the fleet of thirteen vessels which left Holland in April 1601, under Jacob van Heemskerck and Wolphert Harmensz. At the Azores it divided, part going (under Heemskerck) to the Moluccas and part (under Harmensz.) to Mauritius and Bantam. Heemskerck's ships stayed twelve days in Antongil Bay, leaving again on 29 August.

were readie at all times (if they ashore had had any need) to take them in. So we trifled off some daies before (as aforesaid) we could bring them to any reall trade, for all these people of the south and east parts are very subtill and craftie in their bartering, buying, and selling, that, unlesse you hold a neere hand with them, you shall hardly bring them to trade in any plaine sort. For they will sift you continually to give a little more, and then no man will sell without that price; so that you must not inlarge to anyone more then another, for in so doing all will have that price or none. The generall, seeing this, commanded measures to be made of almost a quart, and appointed how many glasse beades should be given for every measure, and he that would not deale in this manner should not deale at all. The like order was set downe for oranges, limons, and plantans, how many for every beade, or else not. Our merchants, after a little holding off, consented, and our dealing was francke and round, without any contradiction or words. So that, while we abode heere, we bought[1] $15\frac{1}{4}$ tunnes of rice, fortie or fiftie bushels of their pease and beanes, great store of oranges, limons, and plantans, and eight beeves [i.e. oxen], with many hennes.

While we roade in this baye we reared a pinnace, which we brought in peeces in our shippes out of England, and cut downe trees, of which there were very great (and great store); which trees we sawed out in boordes, and sheathed her. This pinnace was of some eighteene tunnes, and very necessary, and fit to goe before our shippes at our comming into India [i.e. the Indies].

In the time we stayed heere, there died out of the generalls shippe the masters mate[2], the preacher[3], and the surgeon, with some tenne other common men; and out of the vice-admirall there died the master[4], with some other two. And out of the *Ascention*, by a very great mischance, were slaine the captaine[5] and the boatswaines mate[6]. For, as the masters mate out of the generalls shippe was carried aland to be buried, the captaine of the *Ascention* tooke his boate to goe aland to his buriall; and, as it is the order of the sea to shoote off certaine peeces of ordnance

---

[1] Purchas has 'brought.'
[2] William Winter.
[3] The Rev. Thomas Pullen (or Pulleyn).
[4] Henry Napper. [5] William Brund. [6] John Parker.

at the buriall of any officer, the gunner of the ordnance shotte off three peeces, and, the bullets being in them¹, one stroke the *Ascentions* boate, and slue the captaine and the boatswaines mate starke dead; so that they that went to see the buriall of another were both buried there themselves. Those that died heere died most of the flux; which (in our opinion) came with the waters which we drunke, for it was the time of winter, when it rained very much, which caused great flouds to overflowe the countrie; so that the waters were not wholsome, as in most places in these hot countries they are not, in the times of their raines. This disease also of the flux is often taken by going open, and cold in the stomacke, which our men would often doe when they were hot².

We set saile out of this baye the sixth of March, and held our course toward the India. And the sixteenth we fell with an iland called Rogue-Pize³, which lyeth in 10½ degrees to the south of the Equinoctiall Line. To this iland the generall sent his boate, to see whether there were any safe riding for the shippes; but the boate (for the most part) found deepe water, where the shippes could not safely ride. As we coasted along this iland, it seemed very faire and pleasant, exceeding full of foule and coconut trees; and there came from the land such a pleasant smell, as if it had beene a garden of flowers. And surely, if there be any good riding for shippes in this iland, it must needes be a place of very great refreshing; for as our boates went neere the land, they saw great store of fish; and the foules came wondering about them in such sort that with the oares, wherewith the

---

¹ At this period blank charges were never fired, and such accidents were not uncommon, with at times troublesome results, if natives were the victims.

² John Davis of Limehouse, in his 'Ruter' (*Purchas*, vol. I, p. 448), says that Antongil Bay is 'a place of very uncertaine and contagious weather, for raine, thunder, and lightning, as ever I came in, and very unwholsome, for we lost many men here.'

³ An island of this name appears in contemporary maps, but not in the position indicated; and the supposed island of Roquepez, mentioned in the first edition (p. 69), has been proved to be non-existent. I suggest that the island seen by the fleet was really Agalega (or Galega) Island, which lies in about lat. 10° 25′ S. and long. 56° 36′ E. It is about eleven miles long, and consists of two portions connected by a ridge of sand submerged at high tide. It is described as flat, but covered with coconut palms and high Casuarina trees. There is little or no anchorage available.

mariners rowed, they killed many, which were the fattest and the best that we tasted all the voyage. And of these there was such exceeding great abundance that many more shippes then we had with us might have refreshed themselves therewith.

The thirtieth of March 1602, being in sixe degrees to the south of the Line, wee happened upon a ledge of rockes[1]; and looking overboord and seeing them under the shippe about five fathome deepe, it much amazed us, falling upon the sudden and unexpected. Then, as wee were presently casting about the ship, wee found eight fathome, and so held on our course east. One of our men, being in the top, saw an iland south-east of us, some five or sixe leagues off, being but low land. This we judged to be the iland of Cardu[2], although in our course we could not (by computation) find ourselves so farre shot to the eastward. Bearing on our course some thirteene or fourteene leagues, we fell upon another flat of rockes. Then wee cast about to the southward and, sayling some twelve leagues, found other rockes. So that, proving divers wayes, wee found flats of rockes round about us, and twentie and thirtie, and in some places, forty and fiftie fathome, water in the middest of the flats. Here we were for two dayes and an halfe in exceeding danger, and could find no way to get out. But at last wee resolved to seeke to the northward, and in sixe degrees, fortie-three minutes (God bee thanked) wee found sixe fathome water; the pinnasse always going before us and sounding, with commandement to make signes what depth she had, that thereby we might follow her. Thus (thankes be to God) being delivered out of this pound, we followed our course, with variable windes, till the ninth of May, about foure of the clocke in the afternoone; at which time we had sight of the ilands of Nicubar, and bare in and anchored on the north side of the channell. But the wind changing to the south-west, wee were forced to hoyse our anchors and to beare over to the south side of the channell, and so come to an anchor under a small iland that lyeth on the said shore. Here wee had

---

[1] They had come upon the Chagos Islands, as appears from the 'Ruter' of John Davis of Limehouse, who calls them the *Baixos das Chagas*, and adds: 'these shoalds are very dangerous.... We were twenty houres upon and among these shoalds.'

[2] This was a mistake. Cardu is one of the Maldive group.

fresh water and some coconuts; other refreshing wee had little. Yet the people came aboord our shippes in long canoas, which would hold twentie men and above in one of them; and brought gummes to sell instead of amber, and therewithall deceived divers of our men; for these people of the east are wholly given to deceit. They brought also hennes and coconuts to sell, but held them very deare; so that we bought few of them. We stayed here ten dayes, placing of our ordnance and trimming of our ships, because we would be in all readinesse at our arrivall at our first port, which we were not now farre from.

The twentieth of Aprill[1], in the morning, we set saile to goe toward Sumatra; but the wind blew so hard at south-southwest, and the currant was against us, that we could not proceed. But beating up and downe, our ships fell into two leakes, so that wee were forced to goe to the iland of Sombrero[2], some ten or twelve leagues to the northward of Nicubar. Heere we in the admirall lost an anchor; for the ground is foule and groweth full of counterfeit corrall and some rockes, which cut our cable asunder, so that we could not recover our anchor.

The people of these ilands goe naked, having only the privities bound up in a peece of linnen cloth, which commeth about their middles like a girdle, and so betweene their twist[3]. They are all of a tauny colour, and annoint their faces with divers colours. They are well limmed, but very fearefull; for none of them would come aboord our shippes or enter into our boates. The generall reported that he had seene some of their priests or sacrificers, all apparelled, but close to their bodies, as if they had beene sewed in it; and upon their heads a paire of hornes turning backward, with their faces painted greene, blacke, and yellow, and their hornes also painted with the same colour; and behind them, upon their buttocks, a taile hanging downe, very much like the manner as in some painted cloathes we paint the divell in our countrey. He demaunding wherefore they went in

[1] An error for 'May.'
[2] The Sombreiro Channel separates Little Nicobar from the more northerly group of the Nicobar Islands. Sir Clements Markham concluded that 'Sombrero Island must be Nancowry.' John Davis of Limehouse, in his 'Ruter,' says the 'Ilha de Sombrero' is so called 'because upon the souther side the land is like a hat.'
[3] Defined by Cotgrave (1611) as 'that part of the bodie from whence the thighes doe part.'

that attire, answer was made him that in such forme the divell appeared to them in their sacrifices, and therefore the priests, his servants, were so apparelled.

In this iland grow trees, which for their talnesse, greatnesse, and straightnesse, will serve the biggest shippe in all our fleete for a mainemast; and this iland is full of those trees. Heere likewise we found upon the sands by the sea-side a small twigge growing up to a young tree; and offering to plucke up the same, it shru[n]ke downe into the ground, and sinketh, unlesse you hold very hard. And being plucked up, a great worme is the roote of it. And looke, how the tree groweth in greatnesse, the worme diminisheth. Now as soone as the worme is wholly turned into the tree, it rooteth in the ground, and so groweth to be great. This transformation was one of the strangest wonders that I saw in all my travailes. For this tree being plucked up little, the leaves stripped off, and the pill [i.e. peel], by that time it was dry, turned into an hard stone, much like to white corrall. So that this worme was twice transformed into different natures. Of these we gathered and brought home many[1].

[1] To this passage in the previous edition Sir Clements Markham appended the following note:
'Mr Homfray, the officer in charge of the Nicobar Islands, informs me that the curious animal described in the text is common at the Nicobar [and] Andaman Islands. It is found in the sand, between high and low water mark, and is, he thinks, one of the coralliferous polyps (*Virgularia mirabilis*). It protrudes from its hole as the tide rises, disappearing almost completely when it falls, or on being touched, unless it is clutched very firmly. With much perseverance it is dug out of the ground, while being held by one hand; during which operation it sustains some injury. The so-called leaves break off, owing to the animal having constantly to seek shelter below the sand; and are supposed to be really seaweed or fungus parasites. Out of fifty specimens collected for Mr Homfray only four had leaves.
'Mr Warneford, the chaplain at Port Blair (Andaman Islands), tells me that they are found in great variety, sometimes in sand but more frequently in mud. Some of them, at the top or part projecting above the surface, do branch out just like a small tree. They vary in colour, in length, and in shape. Mr Warneford has some specimens in spirits, and numbers of dried ones, white, mauve, and yellow. Some are rough, some smooth; and Mr Warneford says that the description in the text is true, though rather enlarged. When pulled up, they have a large fleshy bottom, which is really the intestines of the animal, not a separate worm. They have the power of drawing themselves down into the mud when touched.'
It is interesting to note that, long afterwards, the Royal Society, in a series of questions addressed to Sir Philberto Vernatti, Resident in Batavia, included one concerning this strange phenomenon. The answer was: 'I cannot meet with any that ever heard of such a vegetable' (Sprat's *History of the Royal Society*, 1722, p. 160).

§ 3
Their entertainement and trade at Achem.

The nine and twentieth of May we set saile from this iland of Sombrero; and the second of June we had sight of the land of Sumatra; and the fifth of June we came to anchor in the roade of Achem, some two miles off the citie; where we found sixteene or eighteene saile of shippes of divers nations, some Goserats[1], some of Bengala, some of Calicut (called Malabares), some Pegues, and some Patanyes[2], which came to trade there.

There came aboord of us two Holland merchants, which had beene left there behind their shippes, to learne the language and manners of the country. These told us we should be very welcome to the king, who was desirous to intertaine strangers; and that the Queene of England was very famous in those parts, by reason of the warres and great victories which she had gotten against the king of Spaine[3]. The same day the generall sent Captaine John Middleton, captaine of the vice-admirall, with foure or five gentlemen to attend upon him, to the king, to declare unto him that he was sent from the generall of those shippes, who had a message and a letter from the most famous Queene of England to the most worthy King of Achem and Sumatra; and that it would please his royall majesty to give to the said messenger audience to deliver his message and letter, with a sufficient warrant for the safety of him and his people, according to the law of nations holden in that behalfe. This messenger was very kindly intertained by the king, who, when he had delivered his message, gladly granted his request, and communed with him about many questions; and after caused a royall banquet to be made him, and at his departure gave [him] a robe and a tucke[4] of calico wrought with gold; which is the

---

[1] Vessels from Gujarāt, in western India.
[2] From Patani, on the east side of the Malay Peninsula.
[3] John Davis, in his account of his visit to Achin in 1599 in Houtman's fleet (*Purchas*, vol. i, bk. iii, p. 118), says that the king inquired whether there were any Englishmen in the fleet, and insisted upon their production. He treated Davis with favour, and 'enquired much of England, of the Queene, of her basha's, and how she could hold warres with so great a king as the Spaniards (for he thinketh that Europe is all Spanish).'
[4] A 'tuck' is a turban.

manner of the king of this place to those he will grace with his speciall favour[1]; and withall sent his commendations to the generall, willing him to stay one day aboord his ships, to rest himselfe after his comming from the disquiet seas, and the next day to come aland and have kind audience and franke leave, with as great assurance as if he were in the kingdome of the Queene his mistris. And if he doubted of anything of this his royall word, such honourable pledges should be sent him for his further assurance as he should rest very well satisfied therewith.

The third day, the generall went aland, very well accompanied, with some thirtie men or more to attend upon him. And first at his landing the Holland merchants met him, and carried him home to their house, as it was appointed; for as yet the generall would make choyce of no house of his owne, till he had spoken with the king; but stayed at the Hollanders house, till a nobleman came from the king, who saluted the generall very kindly, and declared that he came from His Majestie and represented his person. Then he demaunded the Queenes letter of the generall; which he refused to deliver, saying he would deliver it to the king himselfe; for it was the order of embassadours, in those parts of the world from whence he came, to deliver their letters to the princes owne hands, and not to any that did represent the kings person. So he demaunded to see the superscription; which the generall shewed him, and he read the same, and looked very earnestly upon the seale, tooke a note of the superscription, and did likewise write Her Majesties name; and then with courtesie tooke his leave and repaired to the court to tell the king what had passed; who presently sent six great elephants, with many trumpets, drums, and streamers, with much people, to accompany the generall to the court, so that the presse was exceeding great. The biggest of these elephants was about thirteene or fourteene foote high; which had a small castle (like a coach) upon his back, covered with crimson velvet. In the middle thereof was a great bason of gold, and a peece of silke exceeding richly wrought to cover it, under which Her Majesties letter was put. The generall was mounted upon

---

[1] On the contrary the king was merely following a practice very general in the East of presenting a dress of honour to a favoured visitor.

another of the elephants. Some of his attendants rode; others went afoote. But when he came to the court gate, there a nobleman stayed the generall, till he had gone in to know the kings further pleasure; but presently the said nobleman returned and willed the generall to enter in. And when the generall came to the kings presence, he made his obeysance after the manner of the country, declaring that hee was sent from the most mightie Queene of England to congratulate with His Highnesse, and treat with him concerning a peace and amitie with His Majestie, if it pleased him to entertaine the same. And therewithall began to enter into further discourse, which the king[1] brake off, saying: I am sure you are weary of the long travaile you have taken; I would have you to sit downe and refresh yourselfe: you are very welcome, and heere you shall have whatsoever you will in any reasonable conditions demaund, for your princesse sake; for she is worthy of all kindnesse and franke conditions, being a princesse of great noblenesse, for fame speaketh so much of her. The generall, perceiving the kings mind, delivered him the Queenes letter; which he willingly received, and delivered the same to a nobleman standing by him. Then the generall proceeded to deliver him his present; which was a bason of silver, with a fountaine in the middest of it, weighing two hundred and five ounces, a great standing cup of silver, a rich looking-glasse, an headpeece with a plume of feathers, a case of very faire dagges[2], a rich wrought embroidered belt to hang a sword in, and a fan of feathers[3]. All these were received in the kings

---

[1] The king (or Sultān, as he styled himself) of Achin at this time bore the title of Alā-uddīn Riāyat Shāh. Davis (in *Purchas*, vol. I, bk. iii, p. 121) describes him as 'a lustie man, but exceeding grosse and fat,' aged one hundred years ('as they say'). Martin puts his age at the more moderate figure of sixty-three. According to Davis (whose story is accepted by Marsden), he had originally followed the humble calling of a fisherman, but, having displayed great skill and daring in the wars, was raised to the chief command of both the navy and the army and married to a near kinswoman of the reigning monarch. Marsden says that the latter (Mansur Shāh) was murdered in 1585 by the man he had thus honoured, who thereupon placed on the throne the infant grandson of the dead king and installed himself as Protector. Three years later the child was put to death, and the Protector assumed the throne himself. He died in 1604.

[2] Pistols.

[3] Particulars of some of these presents will be found in the Court Minutes (see *The Dawn*, pp. 118, 141, etc.).

presence by a nobleman of the court. Onely he tooke into his owne hand the fanne of feathers, and caused one of his women to fanne him therewithall, as a thing that most pleased him of all the rest. The generall was commanded to sit downe in the kings presence, as the manner is, upon the ground; where was a very great banquet provided. All the dishes in which the meate was served in, were either of pure gold or of another mettall, which among them is of great estimation, called tambaycke, which groweth of gold and brasse together[1]. In this banquet the king, as he sate aloft in a gallery (about a fathome from the ground) dranke oft to the generall in their wine, which they call racke [i.e. arrack]. This wine is made of rice, and is as strong as any of our aquavitae; a little will serve to bring one asleepe. The generall, after the first draught, dranke either water mingled therewithall, or pure water. The king gave him leave so to doe; for the generall craved his pardon, as not able to drinke so strong drinke. After this feast was done, the king caused his damosels to come forth and dance, and his women to play musicke unto them. And these women were richly attired, and adorned with bracelets and jewels; and this they account a great favour, for these are not usually seene of any but such as the king will greatly honour. The king also gave unto the generall a fine white robe of calico, richly wrought with gold, and a very faire girdle of Turkey worke, and two creses[2], which are a kind of daggers; all which a nobleman put on [him?] in the kings presence. And in this manner he was dismissed the court, with very great curtesies; and one sent along with him to make choyce of an house in the citie, where the generall thought most meete. But at this time he refused this kindnesse, and rather chose to goe aboord his ships; and left the king to consider of the Queenes letter, the tenor whereof hereafter followeth.

[1] Malay *tāmbaga*. It was a mixture of copper and zinc, and hence a form of brass. The reference may, however, be to the alloy called *suasa*, described as 'a mettall halfe copper, halfe gold' (Best, p. 210).
[2] The well-known Malay *kris* or dagger.

Elizabeth, by the grace of God Queene of England, France, and Ireland, Defendresse of the Christian Faith and Religion, to the great and mightie King of Achem etc., in the iland of Sumatra, our loving brother, greeting.

The eternall God, of His divine knowledge and providence, hath so disposed His blessings and good things of His creation for the use and nourishment of mankind, in such sort that, notwithstanding they growe in divers kingdomes and regions of the world, yet by the industrie of man (stirred up by the inspiration of the said omnipotent Creator) they are dispersed into the most remote places of the universall world, to the end that even therein may appeare unto all nations His marvelous workes, Hee having so ordained that the one land may have need of the other, and thereby not only breed intercourse and exchange of their merchandise and fruits, which doe superabound in some countries and want in others, but also ingender love and frendship betwixt all men, a thing naturally divine.

Whereunto wee having respect, right noble king, and also to the honourable and truly royall fame which hath hither stretched of Your Highnesse humane and noble usage of strangers which repaire into that your kingdome, in love and peace, in the trade of merchandise, paying your due customes, wee have beene mooved to give licence unto these our subjects, who, with commendable and good desires, saile to visite that your kingdome, notwithstanding the dangers and miseries of the sea naturall to such a voyage which (by the grace of God) they will make, beeing the greatest that is to be made in the world, and to present trafficke unto your subjects. Which their offer, if it shall bee accepted by Your Highnesse, with such love and grace as wee hope for of so great and magnanimious a prince, wee for them doe promise that in no time hereafter you shall have cause to repent thereof, but rather to rejoyce much; for their dealing shall be true and their conversation sure, and wee hope that they will give so good proofe thereof that this beginning shall be a perpetuall confirmation of love betwixt our subjects on both parts, by carrying from us such things and merchandise as you have need of there. So that Your Highnesse shall be very well served, and better contented then you have heretofore beene with the Portugals and Spaniards, our enemies, who only, and none else of these regions, have frequented those your and the other kingdomes of the East, not suffering that the other nations should doe it; pretending themselves to be monarchs and absolute lords of all these kingdomes and provinces as their owne conquest and inheritance, as appeareth by their loftie title in their writings; the contrarie whereof hath very lately appeared unto us, and that Your Highnesse and your royall familie, fathers and grandfathers, have, by the grace of God and their valour, knowne not onely to defend your owne kingdomes, but also to give warres unto the Portugals in the lands which they possesse, as namely[1] in Malaca, in the yeere of the humane redemption 1575, under the conduct of your valiant captaine Ragamacota[2], with their great losse and the perpetuall honour of Your Highnesse crowne and kingdome.

And now if Your Highnesse shall be pleased to accept into your favour and grace and under your royall protection and defence these our subjects, that they may freely doe their businesse now and continue yeerely hereafter, this bearer, who goeth chiefe of this fleet of foure ships, hath order (with Your Highnesse licence) to leave certaine factors, with a setled house of factorie, in your kingdome, untill the going thither of another fleet, which shall goe thither upon the returne of this; which left factors shall learne the language and customes of your subjects, whereby the better and more lovingly to converse with them. And the better to confirme this confederacie and friendship betwixt us, wee are contented, if Your Highnesse be so pleased, that you cause capitulations reasonable to be made, and that this bearer doe the like in our name; which wee promise to performe royally and entirely, as well herein as in other agreements and arguments which he will communicate unto you; to whom we doe greatly desire Your Highnesse to give intire faith and credite, and that you will receive him and the rest of his companie under your royal protection, favouring them in what

---

[1] Used in the obsolete sense of 'especially.'
[2] Marsden takes this as referring to the expedition of Mansur Shāh against Malacca and Johore in 1582, and supposes that the name of the commander was Raja Makuta.

shall be reason and justice. And we promise on our behalfe to re-answere in like degree in all that Your Highnesse shall have need out of these our kingdomes. And wee desire that Your Highnesse would be pleased to send us answere by this bearer of this our letter, that wee may thereby understand of your royall acceptance of the friendship and league which wee offer, and greatly desire may have an happie beginning, with long yeares to continue.

At his [i.e. the general's] next going to the court, hee had long conference with the king concerning the effect of the Queenes letter, wherewith the king seemed to be very well pleased, and said, if the contents of that letter came from the heart, he had good cause to thinke well thereof. And for the league Her Majestie was desirous to hold with him, hee was well pleased therewith. And for the further demands the generall made from her, in respect of the merchants trafficke, he had committed all those points to two of his noblemen, to conferre with him; and promised what Her Majestie had requested should by all good meanes bee granted. With this contented answer, after another banquet appointed for the general, he departed the court. And the next day he sent to those noblemen the king had named to him, to know their appointed time when they would sit upon this conference. The one of these noblemen was the chiefe bishope[1] of the realme, a man of great estimation with the king and all the people; and so he well deserved, for he was a man very wise and temperate. The other was one of the most ancient nobilitie, a man of very good gravitie, but not so fit to enter into those conferences as the bishop was. A day and a meeting was appointed, where many questions passed betwixt them. And all the conferences passed in the Arabicke tongue, which both the bishop and the other nobleman well understood. Now the

[1] Islam has no hierarchy; but evidently it was the practice at Achin for one ecclesiastic to be in authority over the rest. Davis (*Purchas*, vol. I, bk. iii, p. 122) says that 'they have an archbishop and spirituall dignities.' In 1615 we find a present given by the English to the 'Bishop of Achin' (*Letters Received*, vol. III, p. 97); and Bowrey, who was there in 1675, relates (*Countries round the Bay of Bengal*, p. 314) an incident in which 'the Siddy or Bishop of Achin' set free a *mulla* who had been condemned to death. By 'Siddy' is here meant *sayyid*, a title given to one claiming descent from the family of the Prophet, through his grandson Hasan.

generall, before his going out of England, intertained a Jew, who spake that language perfectly; which stood him in good steed at that time[1]. About many demands the generall made touching freedomes for the merchants, the bishop said unto him: Sir, what reasons shall we show to the king from you, whereby he may the more willingly grant these things which you have demanded to be granted by him? To whom the generall answered with these reasons following: Her Majesties mutuall love. Her worthinesse in protecting others against the King of Spaine, the common enemie of these parts. Her noble mind, which refused the offer of those countries. Nor will shee suffer any prince to exceed her in kindnesse. Whose forces have exceeded the Spaniards in many victories. And hindred the Portugals

---

[1] During his enforced stay in the Maldives (1602–7) Pyrard made the acquaintance of this Jew, of whom he gives (vol. I, p. 283) the following unflattering account: 'About the same time came to Malé a man who was a Jew in faith and race, and knew a large number of languages; among others, he spoke Arabic and the Indian tongues well. He was a man of Barbary, and the greatest scoundrel in the world. The English had taken him to England, where he had learnt English well. About the same time that we left France four ships also left England, and the general took this fellow as his body-servant; and he was with him in the Indies. He was already at Achen when our general arrived there, and he it was who informed me that the general had been poisoned by the Portuguese. As for the English general, when he saw that he could not load with pepper at Achen, he went to Bantan in Java, where this Jew robbed him of twelve or fifteen hundred pieces of forty sols Spanish, and made his escape. With the English he was of their religion; with the Mahometans, of theirs; whereas he was all the while a Jew. He married a wife wherever he happened to be, and thus he had four or five wives in India. He embarked at Achen in a ship of Surrate, which had lately passed by the head of the Maldives, and was so ill-advised as to land with all his goods. He had still left about one hundred and fifty crowns, for he had spent all the rest. After stealing the money he had gone to Surrate, where he married. At length, on this last voyage, being arrived at Malé, he came to make offer of his services to the king, under the pretext that he was a good gunner; but he knew nothing about it. He was well received at first, but when it was seen that he was a liar, no further notice was taken of him. Soon after he fell sick, and begged me to get his leave of the king; and I, making the request through the lord with whom I resided, obtained it with great difficulty. He said that he was married in Guzeratte, and had a child there, which was partly the cause why his leave was granted; though after he got it he remained three or four months longer, and spent the remainder of his money, and then embarked with the richest merchant of Cananor, a Malabar Mahometan....His name was Poccaca. So the Jew went with him to Cananor.'

In view of what Pyrard says concerning the readiness of the Jew to apostatize, it can hardly be doubted that it was he who was baptized at the Cape, with Lancaster as godfather, as described at p. 124 below.

attempts against these parts. The Grand Signor of Turkie hath alreadie entred into league with Her Majestie on honorable conditions. *Reasons of another kind.* Moreover, it is not unknowne to the king what prosperetie trade of merchandise bringeth to all lands, with increase of their revenues, by the custome of these commerces. Also, princes grow into the more renowme and strength, and are the more feared, for the wealth of their subjects, which by the concurse of merchandises grow and increase. And the more kindly that strangers are entertained, the more the trade doth grow. The prince is thereby much enriched also. And for Achem in particular, this port lieth well to answere to the trade of all Bengala, Java, and the Moluccas, and all China. And these places, having vent of their merchandise, will not let [i.e. fail] to resort hither with them. So that by this meanes the royaltie of the kings crowne will greatly increase, to the decrease and diminishing of all the Portugals trade and their great forces in the Indies. And if it shall happen that His Majestie wanteth any artificers, hee may have them out of our kingdome, giving them content for their travaile, and free course to goe, as they have good will to come. And any other necessarie that our countrie bringeth forth, and may spare, shall be at the kings command and service. But I hope His Majestie will not urge any demands more then Her Majestie may willingly consent unto, or that shall be contrarie to her honour and lawes and the league she hath made with all Christian princes her neighbours.

Further the generall demanded that His Majestie would cause present proclamation to be made for our safetie, and that none of his people should abuse any of ours, but that they might doe their businesse quietly. And this last request was so well performed that, although there were a strict order that none of their owne people might walke by night, yet ours might goe both night and day without impeachment of any. Onely, if they found any of ours abroad at unlawfull houres, the justice brought them home to the generals house and there delivered them.

After these conferences ended, the bishop demanded of the generall notes of his reasons in writing, as also of his demands of the priviledges he demanded in Her Majesties name for the merchants, and hee would shew them to the king, and within few dayes he should have His Majesties answere to them. And with these conferences and much gratulation, and with some other talke of the affaires of Christendome, they broke up for that time. The generall was not negligent to send his demands to the noblemen, which for the most part were drawne out beforehand; for he was not unreadie for these businesses before he came aland in the kingdome.

At his next going to the court and sitting before the king, beholding the cock-fighting (which is one of the greatest sports this king delighteth in), hee sent his interpreter with his obeisance to the king, desiring him to be mindfull of the businesse whereof hee had conferred with his noblemen. Whereupon he called the generall unto him, and told him that hee was carefull of his dispatch, and would willingly enter into peace and league with Her Majestie, and for his part would hold it truely. And for those demands and articles he had set downe in writing, they should all bee written againe by one of his secretaries, and should have them authorized by him. Which, within five or six dayes, were delivered the generall by the kings owne hands, with many good and gracious words; the tenor of which league and articles of peace are too long to be inserted[1]. According to their desires was to the English granted: first, free entry and trade; secondly, custome free, whatsoever they brought in or carried forth, and assistance with their vessels and shipping to save our ships, goods, and men from wracke in any dangers; thirdly, libertie of testament to bequeath their goods to whom they please[2]; fourthly, stability of bargaines and orders for payment by the subjects of Achen, etc.; fiftly, authority to execute justice on their owne men offending; sixtly, justice against injuries from the natives; seventhly, not to arrest or stay our goods or set prizes [i.e. prices] on them; eightly, freedome of conscience.

This league of peace and amitie being setled, the merchants continually went forward providing pepper for the lading of the

---

[1] The document will be found among the appendices.
[2] This was a very necessary stipulation, as in many kingdoms the goods of strangers dying there were deemed to belong to the king.

ships; but there came in but small store, in respect of the last yeeres sterility. So by some of them he [i.e. the general] understood of a port, about an hundred and fiftie leagues from thence in the south part of the same iland, called Priaman[1], where he might lade one of his smaller ships. Then he prepared the *Susan*, and placed for captaine and chiefe merchant in her, M[aster] Henry Middleton[2].

He was also not a little grieved that Captaine John Davis, his principall pilot, had told the marchants, before our comming from London, that pepper was to be had here for foure Spanish royals of eight the hundred[weight][3]; and it cost us almost twentie.

The generall daily grew full of thought how to lade his shippes to save his owne credit, the merchants estimation that set him aworke, and the reputation of his countrey; considering what a foule blot it would be to them all, in regard of the nations about us, seeing there were merchandise enough to bee bought in the Indies, yet he should be likely to returne home with empty ships.

Besides, the Portugall embassador[4] had a diligent eye over

---

[1] On the west coast of Sumatra, in lat. 0° 40′ S.

[2] Henry Middleton was the youngest of three brothers who formed part of the family of fifteen children, born to John Middleton, merchant, of Chester (see Myddelton's *Pedigree*). John, the eldest of the three, was the captain of the *Hector* in the present voyage and died at Bantam. David, the next, took part in the Company's Second Voyage, commanded the *Consent* in the Third (1607) and the *Expedition* in the Fifth (1609); in 1614 he went out again as general of a fresh fleet, and died on his way home in the following year. Henry, the youngest, after taking home the *Susan* in the present voyage, was sent out in command of the Second Voyage and was knighted on his return. He afterwards commanded the fleet of the Sixth Voyage, and died at Bantam on 24 May 1613.

On the present occasion he took with him to Priaman a permit from the king of Achin. The original of this, bearing the stamp of Sultān Alā-uddīn Shāh, is now in the Bodleian (*Douce MSS*. Or. e. 4), and the Malay text (with an English translation) is given by the Rev. W. G. Shellabear in his article on 'The oldest Malay MSS. now extant,' published in the *Journal of the Straits Branch of the Royal Asiatic Society*, July 1898, p. 110.

[3] Davis says that in 1599 the Dutch paid 64s. per bahar, i.e. about 18s. per 100 lb. (*Purchas*, vol. 1, bk. iii, p. 123). Evidently the English now paid at a high rate for their pepper, owing to its scarcity and the competition of the French.

[4] If, as is probable, this was the envoy from Malacca whom the Dutch found there in June 1599, his name was Alfonso Vincent (Davis, *ut supra*).

every steppe we trode; but was no whit accepted of the king. For the last day of his beeing at the court he had demanded of the king to settle a factorie in his countrey and to build a fort at the comming in of the harbour. His reason was, for the more securitie of the marchants goods, because the city was subject to fire. But the king, perceiving what he meant, gave him this answer backe againe: Hath your master (saith he) a daughter to give unto my sonne, that he is so carefull of the preservation of my countrey? He shall not neede to be at so great a charge as the building of a fort; for I have a fit house about two leagues from this citie, within the land, which I will spare him to supply his factorie withall, where they shall not need to fear either enemies or fire, for I will protect him. Hereupon the king was much displeased at this insolent demand, and the embassadour went from the court much discontented.

§ 4

Portugall wiles discovered. A prize taken neere Malacca.

Shortly after this, there came to our house an Indian (to sell hennes) which was appertaining to a Portugall captaine who came to that port with a ship laden with rice, out of the port of Bengala. This captaine lay in the embassadors house; and the generall mistrusted he [i.e. the Indian] came only for a spy to see and perceive what we did. And yet he gave commandement he should be well intreated, and they should alwayes buy his hennes and give him a reasonable price for them. At last he himselfe tooke occasion pleasantly to commune with the Indian, whence hee was and of what countrey; saying a young man of his presence merited some better meannes then buying and selling of hennes. Sir, said he, I serve this Portugall captaine, yet am neither bound nor free; but being free borne, I have beene with him so long time that now he partly esteemeth me as his owne; and so great they are that wee cannot strive with them. Then said the generall unto him: If thy liberty be precious unto thee, thy person meriteth it; but what wouldst thou doe for him that would give thee thy libertie, without pleading with thy master for it? Sir, said the Indian, freedome is as precious as life, and my life I would adventure for him that should do it. Proove me therefore in any service that I can doe for you, and my willingnesse shall soone make good what I have said. Well, said the generall, thou hast willed me to proove whether thou meanest truely or no; I would aske of thee what the embassador saith of me and my shipping which I have in this place, and what pretences [i.e. intentions] he hath. Sir, said the Indian, he hath had a spie aboord of all your ships, a Chinese, who is continually conversant with your people; so that he hath a draught drawne, not onely of your ships and their greatnesse, but also of every piece of ordnance that each ship hath, and how they are placed, and the number of your men that are in them. And he findeth your ships strong and well appointed; but by reason of the sickenesse that hath been in them they are but weake of men and easie to be taken, if any force come upon them on the suddaine; and within few dayes he meaneth to send his draughts to Malacca, for force to attempt your ships as they ride. The general laughed pleasantly to heare these things, saying the embassador was not so idle as he thought him. For hee well knoweth (said he) that I care little for all the forces of these parts; it is but to make thee, and the rest that are about him, beleeve that you are stronger then you be. But goe thy way, and be here once in a day or twaine, and tell me whether the embassadour goe forward in his proceedings, and when those messengers shall depart with the plots thou speakest of; and although it will benefit me little to know these things, yet I will give thee thy libertie, for thy goodwill thou shewest therein, as I have promised thee to doe. This Indian went away very well contented, as any man might easily perceive by his countenance and the lightnesse of his pace. Now when he was gone, the generall turned about and said to me: We have met with a fit man to betray his master, if we can make any benefit of the treason. And surely he was not deceived in his opinion; for by this meanes whatsoever the embassadour did all the day, we had it either that night or (at the furthest) the next day in the morning. And this fellow carried the matter so warily that he was neither mistrusted of any of the ambassadors house nor knowne to any of ours what businesse he went about; for he had the right conditions of a spie, being wily, fearefull, carefull, subtill, and never trusting any to heare what conference he had with the generall, but delivered his minde unto him alone; and that in such carelesse sort as if hee had answered the generall idlely whatsoever he demanded of him. For he stood in feare of our owne people, least they would bewray the selling of his hennes, which covered all his comming and going to our house.

The next day the generall was sent for to the court, and the king had conference with him about an embassage that the king of Siam had sent him, touching the conquest of Malacca, and with what force he would assist him by sea, if he undertooke that service. For this king of Sumatra is able to put a very great force of gallies to sea, if he may have but some fourre or five moneths warning beforehand to make them ready. This conference the generall furthered with many reasons, and tooke an occasion to enter into talke of the Spanish[1] embassadour: how insolently proud he carried himself, and that his comming into His Majesties kingdome and court was for no other purpose but onely as a spie to see and discover the strength of his kingdome. I know it well (said the king), for they are enemies of mine, as I have beene to them; but what causeth thee to see this? The generall answered him that he could take nothing in hand but his spies attended upon him to marke what he went about and to what ende. And among other things (saith he) he hath taken a draught of his ships and meaneth to send it to Malacca, and to procure forces to set upon him at unawares. The king smiled to heare the generall mention these things, and said: Thou needest not feare any strength that shall come from Malacca, for all the strength they have there is able to doe thee no harme. The generall answered: I doe not (said he) feare their strength what they can doe to me; but it may be much to my hinderance that, they understanding the time I meane to goe to sea, they shall thereby bee advised to keepe themselves withing their ports, so that I shall not be able to offend them. Is it so? said the king. Yea, said the generall, and therefore I would intreate Your Majestie to make stay of two of the embassadors servants that

[1] Portuguese.

are now going to Malacca within these few dayes; who take not their passage from hence, but will goe to another port of yours, and there hire a barke to transport them thence, because they will be sure not to be intercepted; and if Your Majestie intercept them there, you shall be privy to some of their plots and pretences. Well, said the king, let me understand of their departure from hence, and thou shalt see what I will doe for thee. So the generall took his leave of the king well contented, and had daily conference with his merchant that sold hennes; so that there was not anything done or said in the embassadors house but he was privy to it.

Now the time was come that the embassadors two servants were to depart with their plots and their masters letters; and they went downe to a port[1] about five and twentie leagues from Achen. But the generall was not slacke to advise the king thereof; who had given order before. So that at their comming thither, and when they had hired their passage and had imbarked themselves with all their letters and were going over the barre, a mile from the citie, a frigget went after them and caused the barke to strike sayle, that the justice might see what their lading was. And when the justice came aboord and saw two Portugals there, he asked them from whence they came and whither they were going. They answered they came from Achem, and belonged to the Portugall embassadour. Nay, said the justice, but you have robbed your master and runne away like theeves with his goods; and therefore I will returne you againe to him from whom you are fled, and there you shall answer it. But in this hurly-burly and searching of them they lost their plots and their letters, and their trunkes were broken open, and they sent to Achem, bound backe againe to the court, to be delivered to the embassador, if they did belong unto him. The generall had some intelligence of these things; and the next time he came to the court the king called him unto him and said: Now what sayest thou? Art thou contented? The generall made him obeisance, and gave him humble and heartie thanks for his clemencie and kindnesse towards him. And with some other conference the generall departed for that time. The marchant of

---

[1] Probably Pedir, on the north coast of the island, in long. 96° E.

hennes came daily following his merchandize, and (as the generall suspected and he himselfe afterward confessed) not without his masters consent, to advise from us as well as he advised from his master.

But now the summer was past and September came, the time that the generall meant to goe to sea, to seeke meanes to supply his necessities. And now fell out the greatest crosse of all to his pretence. The embassador himselfe had his dispatch from the king to be gone. Which the generall knowing went to the court, and where the king sate seeing the sports that were made before him, he sent his interpreter to him, desiring him that it would please him to heare a certain request which he had unto His Majestie. Whereupon the king immediately called for him, and demanded what he would have him to doe. It hath pleased Your Highnesse, said the generall, to doe me many curtesies, and therefore I am further imboldened to proceed to request one kindnesse more at Your Majesties hands. What is that? (said the king, smiling) Are there more Portugals going to Malacca to hinder thy pretences? Yea, said the generall, the embassadour himselfe, as I am given to understand, hath Your Majesties dispatch to be gone at his pleasure, and is determined to depart within five dayes. And what wouldst thou have me to doe? said the king. Only stay him but tenne dayes, till I be gone forth with my ships. Well, said the king (and laughed), thou must bring me a faire Portugall maiden when thou returnest, and then I am pleased. With this answer the generall took his leave and departed, and hasted all that he could to be gone. For he had left the merchants behind him and under the protection of the king till his returne, and in the meanetime to buy what pepper they could to helpe to furnish the *Ascentions* lading, which was now more then three parts laden; but the generall would not leave her behind him, riding in the port, but tooke her in his company, for she road but in an open place. All the three ships were made readie; and there was a captaine[1] of a Dutch ship in the road, who desired the generall that he might goe to sea in his company and take part of his adventure. His ship was above two

---

[1] 'This was the captaine of a ship of Holland, called Speilberge' (note in *Purchas*). For Speilbergen's voyage see note on p. 133.

hundred tunnes, but had as little money to lade himself as we, and therefore refused no consort. So the generall was contented to give him $\frac{1}{8}$ of what should be taken, and hee rested therewith contented. The generall having taken his leave of the king and presented two of the chiefe merchants unto him, M[aster] Starkie and M[aster] Styles, the king graciously tooke them into his protection and safeguard; for these merchants, with some others, were left behind (as I said before) for the providing of such pepper as was there to be had, against the returne of the ships from the sea. The ships being ready, we set sayle the eleventh of September toward the Straights of Malacca.

Now let me tell you how the king dealt with the embassadour of Portugall after our departure; which every day urged his dispatch to be gone, but still, upon one occasion or other, his passage was deferred. At last, foure and twentie daies after our departure, the king said unto him: I marvaile you are so hasty to be gone, seeing the English embassadour is abroad at sea with his shipping: if he meete you, he will be able to wrong you and doe you violence. I care little for him, said the embassadour, for my friget is so nimble with saile and oares that, if I have but her length from him, I will escape all his force. Well, said the king, I am the more willing you should depart, because I see you rest assured of your owne safety. And so he had his dispatch to be gone. This service came well to passe for us; for if he had gone away in time, such advice would have beene given from Malacca by frigots into the Straights that all shippes would have had warning of us; but by this meanes we lay within five and twentie leagues of Malacca itselfe and were never descryed, whereby to be prevented.

The third day of October, we being in the Straights of Malacca, laying off and on, the *Hector* espyed a sayle; and calling to the rest of the shippes, we all discried her. And being toward night, a present direction was given that we should all spread ourselves a mile and a halfe one from another, that she might not passe us in the night. The shippe fell with the *Hector*, that first espied her; and presently she called unto her, and shot off two or three peeces of ordnance; so that the rest of the shippes had intelligence and drew all about her, and began to attempt her with their great ordnance, and she returned shot againe. But when the admirals ship came up, he discharged sixe peeces together out of his prow; and then her maine-yard fell downe. After that she shot no more, nor any of our shippes, fearing least some unfortunate shot might light betweene wind and water and so sinke her (for the generall was very carefull). So the fight ceased till the morning. At the breake of day the captaine, with some of the rest, entred their boate, and the *Hector*, being next her, called them to come aboord him; and Maister John Middleton, the captaine, being vice-admirall, brought the boate and captaine aboord the generall; to whom they rendered their shippe and goods. The generall presently caused all the chiefe men of the prize to be placed aboord our shippes, and onely placed but foure of our men aboord the prize, for feare of rifling and pillaging the good things that were within her; and those foure suffered none other to come aboord, and their charge was, if anything should be missing, to answer the same out of their wages and shares. For when the shippe was unladen, the boateswaine and the marriners of the same shippe did wholly unlade her, and none of ours came within her to doe any labour. Onely they received the goods into their boates, and carried them aboord such shippes as the generall apointed them to doe. So that by this order there was neither rifling, theeving, pillaging, or spoiling; which otherwise would hardly have been avoyded in such businesse as this. Within five or sixe daies we had unladen her of nine hundred and fiftie packes of calicoes and pintados, besides many packets of merchandize. She had in her much rice and other goods, whereof we made small account. Now a storme arising, all their men were set aboord, and we left her riding at an anchor[1].

This shippe came from a place called St. Thoma, that lyeth in the Bay of Bengala, and was going for Malaca[2]. When we intercepted her, she had in her above sixe hundred persons, men, women, and children. Her burthen was nine hundred tuns. The generall would never goe aboord to see her; and his reason was to

---

[1] According to Speilbergen this was on 10 October.

[2] As stated later, her name was *Santo Antonio*. According to a letter from Goa, given in *Archivo Portuguez-Oriental*, Fasc. 1, pt. ii, p. 110, her cargo was worth over 300,000 cruzados.

take away suspicion, both from the mariners that were there and the merchants that were at London, least they might charge or suspect him for any dishonest dealing by helping himselfe thereby. He was very glad of this good hap, and very thankfull to God for it; and (as he told me) he was much bound to God, that had eased him of a very heavy care, and that hee could not be thankfull enough to Him for this blessing given him. For, saith he, He hath not onely supplied my necessities to lade these ships I have, but hath given me as much as will lade as many more shippes as I have, if I had them to lade; so that now my care is, not for money, but rather where I shall leave these goods that I have, more then enough, in safety, till the returne of the ships out of England.

The one and twentieth of October our shippes returned out of the Straights of Malaca for Achen; where by the way a great spout of water came powring out of the heavens and fell not farre from our ship; which we feared much. For these spouts come powring downe like a river of water; so that, if they should light in any ship, she were in danger to be presently sunck downe into the sea. It falleth with such an extreame violence, all whole together as one drop, or as water powred out of a vessell; and sometimes dureth [i.e. lasts] a quarter of an howre together, so that the sea boyleth with froth of an exceeding height, by the violence of the fall of the spoute.

§ 5

Their present to and from the king. His letters to Queene Elizabeth. Their departure for Priaman and Bantam, and setling a trade there.

The foure and twentieth of October we cast our anchors in the port of Achen in Sumatra, where the generall went ashore and found all the merchants well and in safety; who gave great commendations of their good and kind entertainment received from the king in the generals absence. Wherefore the generall, willing to gratifie the king with such things as he had taken in the prize, sorted out a present of divers things that he thought might be most to his liking; and at his first going to the court presented them unto him. The king received the present, and welcomed the generall, and seemed to be very joyfull for the good successe he had against the Portugall; and jestingly said hee had forgotten the most important businesse that he requested at his hands, which was the faire Portugall maiden he desired him to bring with him at his returne. To whom the generall answered that there was none so worthy that merited to be so presented. Therewithall the king smiled and said: If there be anything heere in my kingdome may pleasure thee, I would be glad to gratifie thy goodwill.

After this the generall commaunded the merchants to put aboord the *Ascension* all such pepper, cinnamon, and cloves as they had bought in his absence; which was scarcely the ships full lading, but at that time there was no more to be had, nor that yeare to be hoped for. And therefore he willed the merchants to put all their things aboord the ships, for his resolution was to depart from thence and goe for Bantam, in Java Major; where he understood both of good sale for his commodities and great returne of pepper to be had, and at a much more reasonable price then they could buy it at Achen. This determination once knowne, all men hasten to put their things aboord. So the generall made the king privy to his departure, and went to the court and had long conference with him; who delivered him a letter for Her Majestie, written in the Arabian tongue, the tenor whereof is as followeth:

The letter of the King of Achen to the Queene of England[1].

Glorie be to God, who hath magnified Himselfe in His workes, glorified His dominion, ordained kings and kingdomes, exalted Himselfe alone in power and majestie. He is not to be uttered by word of mouth, nor to be conceived by imagination of the heart. He is no vaine phantasme; no bound may containe Him, nor any similitude expresse Him. His blessing and His peace is over all His goodnesse in the creature. He hath beene

---

[1] The fate of the original letter is not known; but a copy of the concluding portion is among the *Douce MSS.* (Or. e. 5) in the Bodleian: see the article by the Rev. W. G. Shellabear noted on p. 100.

proclaimed by His Prophet heretofore, and since that often, and now againe by this writing at this present, inferiour unto none. For this citie, which is not slacke to shew their love, hath manifested it in the entertainment of that societie which filleth the horizons with joy, and hath confirmed it to the eye by a signe which bringeth knowledge of remembrance of it generally and particularly. And for that their request is just, with purpose for exchange, and they themselves of honest carriage, and their kindnesse great in doing good in generall to the creatures, helping the creature in prosperitie and adversitie joyntly, giving liberally unto the poore and such as stand in neede of their abundance, preserving the creature to their uttermost with a willing mind, which for them is now extended unto India[1] and Arach[2], sending forth the chiefest men of discretion and note, calling also the best of the creatures to counsaile therein.

This is the Sultana which doth rule in the kingdome of England, France, Ireland, Holland, and Friseland[3]. God continue that kingdome and that empire long in prosperitie. And because that he which hath obtained the writing of these letters from the king of the kingdome of Ashey[4], who doth rule there with an absolute power; and for that there came unto us a good report of you, decleired and spread very joyfully by the mouth of Captaine James Lancaster (God continue his welfare long), and for that you doe record that in your letters there are commendations unto us and that your letters are patent priviledges, Almightie God advance the purpose of this honourable consociation and confirme this worthy league. And for that you doe affirme in them that the Sultan of Afrangie[5] is your enemy

[1] The East Indies.
[2] 'Or Carmania' (note in *Purchas*). This is nonsense, for Carmania denotes a part of Persia. Possibly it was due to a misreading by the translator, i.e. the word in the original may have been Acheh, the Malay name for Achin. The Arabic characters for 'Acheh' and 'Arach' bear a somewhat close resemblance.
[3] This manifest exaggeration may have been due to Lancaster's having, in his talks with the king, boasted of the help given by Elizabeth to the Dutch in their struggle against the Spaniards. With the same intention of belittling commercial rivals, Sir Thomas Roe told Prince Shāh Jahān in 1618 that the Dutch were 'a nation depending on the King of England' (*Embassy*, p. 427).
[4] 'Or Achen' (note in *Purchas*).
[5] 'Or Spaine' (note in *Purchas*). It is the Arabic *Ifranji*, generally applied to Europe, though in Northern Africa it would often mean Spain.

and an enemy to your people, in what place soever he be, from the first untill now, and for that he hath lift up himselfe proudly and set himselfe as king of the world (yet what is he besides his exceeding pride and haughtie mind?), in this therefore is our joy increased and our societie confirmed, for that he and his company are enemies in this world and in the world to come; so that we shall cause them to die, in what place soever we shall meete them, a publicke death.

And moreover you doe affirme that you desire peace and friendship with us. To God be praise and thankes for the greatnesse of His grace. This therefore is our serious will and honourable purpose truely in this writing, that you may send from your people unto our ports[1] to trade and to traffique; and that whosoever shall be sent unto us in Your Highnesse name, and to whomsoever you shall prescribe the time, they shall be of a joynt company and of common priviledges. For this captaine and his company, so soone as they came unto us, we have made them of an absolute societie, and we have incorporated them into one corporation and common dignities, and we have graunted them liberties and we have shewed them the best course of traffique.

And to manifest unto men the love and brotherhood betweene us and you in this world, there is sent, by the hands of this captaine (according to the custome) unto the famous citie[2], a ring of gold, beautified with a ruby richly placed in his sete, [and] two vestures woven with gold, embroidered with gold, inclosed in a red boxe of Tzin[3].

Written in Tarish[4] of the yeere 1011 of Mahomet.

Peace be unto you.

Translated out of the Arabick by William Bedwel[5].

---

[1] 'Or bandar' (note in *Purchas*). *Bandar* is the Persian word for 'harbour.'
[2] 'Of London' (note in *Purchas*).
[3] 'Or China' (note in *Purchas*). The box was probably of red lacquer.
[4] 'That is, by computation of time' (note in *Purchas*). The word is *tarīkh*, 'date.' A.H. 1011 commenced in June 1602.
[5] The Rev. William Bedwell, rector of St Ethelburga's, Bishopsgate Street, and one of the translators of the Bible. He was well known as an Arabic scholar. He seems to have found his task difficult, for his version is far from clear.

For a present to Her Majestie he sent three [*sic*] faire cloathes richly wrought with gold, of very cunning worke, and a very faire rubie in a ring; and gave to the generall another ring and a rubie in it. And when the generall tooke his leave, the king said unto him: Have you the Psalmes of David extant among you? The generall answered: Yea, and wee sing them daily[1]. Then said the king: I and the rest of these nobles about me will sing a psalme to God for your prosperitie; and so they did, very solemnly. And after it was ended, the king said: I would heare you sing another psalme, although in your owne language. So, there being in the company some twelve of us, we sung another psalme. And after the psalme ended, the generall tooke his leave of the king. The king shewed him much kindnesse at his departure; desiring God to blesse us in our journey and to guide us safely into our owne countrey; saying: If hereafter your ships returne to this port, you shall find as good usage as you have done.

All our men being shipped, we departed the ninth of November; being three ships, the *Dragon*, the *Hector*, and the *Ascention*. We kept company two days, in which time the generall dispatched his letters for England and sent away the *Ascention*; she setting her course homeward toward the Cape of Buena Esperanza, and we along the coast of Sumatra toward Bantam, to see if we could meete with the *Susan*, which had order to lade upon that coast.

As we sayled along the coast of Sumatra, we sodainly fell among certaine ilands in the night; and the day approching, wee marvelled how wee came in among them without seeing any of them. They were all low landed and full of flattes and rockes; so that wee were in great danger before we could cleere ourselves of them. But thankes be to God, who delivered us from many other dangers, as He did also deliver us from these. So holding on our course from[2] Priaman, we passed the Equinoctiall Line the third time, and came thither the sixe and twentieth of November, and found the *Susan* there, which the generall had sent before from Achen to lade there. Now when they saw us,

---

[1] It was the practice on board ships to sing a psalm at the changing of the watch.   [2] 'For' is intended.

they were very glad of our comming; and had provided toward their lading some six hundred bahars of pepper and sixtie-sixe bahars of cloves. Heere our pepper cost us lesse then at Achen; but there is none growing about this port, but is brought some eight or ten leagues out of the countrey, from a place called Manangcabo[1]. This place [i.e. Priaman] hath no other merchandise growing there; only there is good store of gold, in dust and small graines, which they wash out of the sands of rivers, after the great flouds of raine that fall from the mountaines, from whence it is brought. This is a place of good refreshing, and is very wholsome and healthfull; and yet it lyeth within fifteene minutes of the Line. At this port, having refreshed ourselves with the good ayre, fresh victuals, and water, the generall gave commission to the captaine[2] of the *Susan* to make what haste he could for his lading, which would bee accomplished with some hundred bahars of pepper, and so to depart for England. And the fourth day of December we took our course toward Bantam, in the iland of Java Major; and we entred the Straights of Sunda the fifteenth of December, and came to an anchor under an iland three leagues from Bantam, called Pulopansa[3].

The next day, in the morning, we entred the road of Bantam, and shot off a very great peale of ordnance out of the *Dragon* (being our admirall) and out of the *Hector*: such an one as had never beene rung there before that day. The next day, in the morning, the generall sent his vice-admirall, Captaine John Middleton, aland with a message to the king, declaring that he was sent by the Queene of England, and had both a message and a letter to deliver to His Majestie from her; and required His Majesties safeconduct and warrant to come aland to deliver the same. The king returned him word that he was very glad of his comming, and sent backe a nobleman with Captaine Middleton, to welcome the generall and to accompany him aland. The generall tooke some sixteene men in his company and went aland with the nobleman to the court; where he found the king

---

[1] Manangkabo, a mountainous district in the interior of the island.
[2] Henry Middleton.
[3] Pulo Panjang lies at the entrance of the Bay of Bantam.

(being but a child of ten or eleven yeares of age) sitting in a round-house, with some sixteene or eighteen noblemen of the countrey about him in some reasonable estate. The generall did his obeysance, and the king welcommed him very kindly. And after the generall had had some conference about his message, hee delivered to the kings hand Her Majesties letter, with a present of plate and some other things withall; which the king received with a smiling countenance, and referred the generall, for further conference, to one of his nobles, who was then Protector. After some houre and an halfes conference had of many things, the said nobleman (as from the king) received the generall under the kings protection, and all his company; willing him to come aland, and buy and sell without any kinde of molestation, for there he should be as safe as if he were in his owne countrey; and to this all the nobles agreed with one consent. There passed many speeches of divers things, which, for brevities sake, I omit to trouble the reader withall; for my purpose is to shew the effect of this first setling of the trade in the East-Indies, rather then to particularize of them.

The generall, after his kind welcome and conference had, tooke his leave of the king and the rest of the nobles, and presently gave order for the providing of housing, whereof the king willed him to make his best choice, wheresoever he would. So within two dayes the merchants brought goods ashore and beganne to sell. But one of the kings nobles came to the generall, and said it was the custome of that place that the king should buy and furnishe himselfe before the subjects should buy anything. The generall was well contented, for he was advised that he would give a reasonable price and pay very well. The king being served, the merchants went forward in their sales; so that within some five weekes much more was sold there in goods then would have laden our two shippes; and yet they brought away from thence two hundred and seventie-sixe bagges of pepper. These contayned sixtie-two pound waight apiece, and cost at first penny $5\frac{1}{2}$ rials of eight[1] the piece, beside our anchorage and the kings custome; which anchorage, for our two ships, cost us, by agreement the generall made with the

---

[1] 'A riall of 8 is foure shillings six pence sterling' (note in *Purchas*).

Savender[1] (or Governour of the citie) fifteene hundred rials of eight, and one riall of eight upon every bagge of custome.

Wee traded heere very peaceably, although the Javians be reckoned among the greatest pickers and theeves of the world. But the generall had commission from the king (after hee had received an abuse or two) that whosoever he tooke about his house in the night, he should kill them; so, after foure or five were thus slaine, we lived in reasonable peace and quiet. But continually all night wee kept a carefull watch.

As we went buying pepper we sent it aboord; so that by the tenth of February our ships were fully laden and readie to depart. But in this meanetime the captaine of the *Hector*, Master John Middleton, fell sicke aboord his ship in the roade (for the generall observed this, from the beginning of the voyage, that if he himselfe were ashore, the captaine of the vice-admirall kept aboord, because both should not be from their charge at one time). The generall, hearing of his sicknesse, went aboord to visit him, and found him weaker then hee himselfe felt; which experience had taught him to know in these hot countries. And so it happened with Captaine Middleton, then walking up and downe; who dyed about two of the clocke next morning.

Now the generall began to put all things in order and hasten his departure. And appointed a pinnasse of about fortie tunnes, which he had, to bee laden with commodities, and put in her twelve men, with certaine merchants, and sent her for the Moluccas, to trade there and settle a factorie, against the returne of the next shipping out of England[2]. Moreover, he left eight men and three factors in Bantam; the chief of which factors was Master William Starkey, whom he appointed to sell such commodities as were left there, and to provide lading for the shippes against the next returne[3]. Also the generall went to the court to take his leave of the king; where he received a letter for Her

---

[1] *Shāhbandar*, a title usually given to an official charged with the supervision of a port.

[2] The pinnace (which was the one bought from the Dutch at Achin) sailed early in March 1603, but, after battling for nearly two months against contrary winds, was forced to return to Bantam. The factors then resold her to the Dutch.

[3] See the instructions given on a later page.

Majestie, and a present for her of certaine bezar-stones[1], very faire. And to the generall he gave a very faire Java dagger (which they much esteeme there) and a good bezar-stone, with some other things. And thus the generall tooke his leave of the king, with many kind countenances and good words.

§ 6

Their departure for England, and occurrents in the way.

The twentieth day of Februarie we went all aboord our ships, shot off our ordnance, and set sayle to the sea toward England; with thankes to God and glad hearts, for His blessings towards us. The two and twentieth and three and twentieth of the same moneth wee were in the Straights of Sunda; and the sixe and twentieth wee were cleere of all the iles that lye in those straights, and cleere of all the land; holding our course south-west, so that the eight and twentieth wee were in eight degrees and fortie minutes to the south of the Line. Upon Sunday, the thirteenth of March, wee were past the Tropicke of Capricorne, holding our course for the most parte south-west, with a stiffe gale of wind at south-east. The fourteenth day of Aprill wee were in thirtie-foure degrees; judging the land of Madagascar to be north of us. The eight and twentieth day we had a very great and a furious storme; so that we were forced to take in all our sayles. This storme continued a day and a night, with an exceeding great and raging sea, so that, in the reason of man, no shippe was able to live in them. But God, in His mercie, ceased the violence thereof and gave us time to breath and to repaire all the distresses and harmes we had received. But our ships were so shaken that they were leakie all the voyage after.

The third of May wee had another very sore storme, which continued all the night; and the seas did so beate upon the ships quarter that it shooke all the ironworke of her rother [i.e. rudder], and the next day, in the morning, our rother brake cleane from the sterne of our shippe, and presently [i.e. at once] sunke into the sea. This strooke a present feare into the hearts of

---

[1] Bezoar stones, calcareous concretions found in the bodies of certain animals (especially goats), and valued as antidotes to poisons.

all men; so that the best of us and most experienced knew not
what to doe. And specially seeing ourselves in such a tempestuous sea and so stormie a place, so that I thinke there bee few
worse in all the world. Now our ship drave up and downe in the
sea like a wracke, which way soever the wind carried her. So
that sometimes we were within three or four leagues of the Cape
Buena Esperanza; then commeth a contrary wind and driveth
us almost to fortie degrees to the southward, into the hayle and
snow and sleetie cold weather; and this was another great miserie
unto us, that pinched us exceeding sore, so that our case was
miserable and very desperate. Yet all this while the *Hector* kept
by us carefully (the company whereof was some comfort unto
us), and many times the master of the *Hector* came aboord our
shippe. So at the last it was concluded to take our misenmast
and put it forth at the sterne port, to prove if wee could steere
our shippe into some place where we might make another rother,
to hang it to serve our turnes home. But this device was to small
purpose; for when we had fitted it and put it forth (the seas
being somewhat growne), with lifting up the mast it did shake
the sterne and put all in such danger that it was needfull to make
all convenient haste to get the mast into the ship againe; which
we were very glad when we had brought it to passe. Now we
were without all remedie, unlesse we made a new rother, and
could bring it to passe to hang it in the sea; which to performe,
let every man judge how easie a thing it was, our ship being of
seven or eight hundred tunnes, and in so dangerous a sea as this
was; but necessitie compelleth to proove all meanes. Then the
generall commanded the carpenter to make a rother of the said
misenmast, to proove what wee could doe. But this barre fell in
our way, that, at such time as wee lost our rother, wee lost also
the most of our rother irons, wherewith to fasten the rother.
But yet wee went forward and made all the haste we could, and
one of our men dived to search what rother irons remayned;
who found but two, and one that was broken, to helpe us withall.
Yet, by Gods helpe, finding a faire day, wee made fast the
said rother, and sailed on our course homewards. But within
three or foure houres the sea tooke it off againe, and wee had
much adoe to save it. And with the saving of it wee lost another

of our irons, so that now wee had but two to hang it by; and our men began to be desirous to leave the ship and goe into the *Hector* to save themselves. Nay, said the generall, wee will yet abide Gods leasure, to see what mercie He will shew us; for I despaire not to save ourselves, the ship, and the goods, by one meanes or other, as God shall appoint us. And with that he went into his cabbin, and wrote a letter for England. purposing to send it by the *Hector*; commanding her to depart and leave him there (but not one of the companie knew of this command). The letter was very briefe, and the tenour litle more or lesse as followeth:

Right Worshipfull,

What hath passed in this voyage, and what trades I have settled for this Companie, and what other events have befallen us, you shall understand by the bearers hereof, to whom (as occasion hath fallen) I must referre you. I will strive with all diligence to save my ship and her goods, as you may perceive by the course I take in venturing mine owne life and those that are with mee. I cannot tell where you should looke for mee, if you send out any pinnace to seeke mee; because I live at the devotion of the winds and seas. And thus fare you well; desiring God to send us a merrie meeting in this world, if it be His good will and pleasure.

The passage to the East-India lieth in $62\frac{1}{2}$ degrees by the north-west on the America side.

Your very loving friend,

JAMES LANCASTER.

This letter being delivered, the generall thought they would have beene gone in the night, according to their commission; but when he espied the ship in the morning, he said to me: These men regard no commission. Now the ship kept some two or three leagues from us, and came no neerer[1]; for the master was an honest and a good man, and loved the generall well, and was loth to leave him in so great distresse.

And now it was time for us to seeke all meanes that could be

---

[1] Lest the sailors of the *Dragon* should be tempted to desert her and make for the *Hector*.

to save ourselves and the ship. Then the carpenter mended the rother we had saved; and within two or three dayes the weather began to bee somewhat faire and the sea smooth. So we put out a signe to the *Hector* to come neere us; out of which the master, Master Sander Cole[1], came and brought the best swimmers and divers that he had in his ship, who helped us not a little in the businesse wee had to doe. Thus, by Gods good blessing, we hung our rother againe upon the two hookes that were left; so that we had some goode hope to obtaine one port or other to relieve ourselves withall. Now wee had beene beaten to and fro in these mightie seas, and had many more stormes of weather then are here expressed (sometimes for one whole moneth together); so that our men began to fall sicke and diseased. And the wind fell so short that wee could fetch no part of the coast of Africa, which was neerest to us. Committing ourselves therefore to God, we set saile straight for the iland of Saint Helena; for we knew we had doubled the Cape of Buena Esperanza, by the height wee were in to the northward [*sic*]. As we were in our course, the maineyard fell downe, and strooke one of our men into the sea, and he was drowned.

This was the end (God be thanked) of all our hard fortunes. The fift day of June wee passed the Tropicke of Capricorne; and the sixteenth, in the morning, wee had sight of the iland of Saint Helena; at the sight wereof there was no smale rejoycing among us. Wee bare close along by the shoare, the better to get the best of the road in the harbour; where wee came to an anchor, right against a small chappell, which the Portugals had built there long since. Our ships rode in twelve fatham water, which is the best of the harbor. At our going ashoare, we found by many writings that the carrackes of Portugall had departed from thence but eight dayes before our comming.

In this iland there is very good refreshing of water and wild goats; but they are hard to come by, unlesse good direction be given for the getting of them. And this course our generall tooke. He appointed foure lusty men and of the best shot he had, to goe into the iland and make their abode in the middest of it; and to every shot he appointed foure men to attend him, to

---

[1] I.e. Alexander Cole (see p. 126). He went out again in the same capacity in the Second Voyage and was drowned in Table Bay on the outward voyage.

carrie the goats that hee killed to the rendevous. Thither went every day twentie men, to fetch home to the ships what was killed. So there was no hoyting[1] or rumour in the iland to feare the goats withall. And by this meanes the ships were plentifully relieved, and every man contented. While wee stayed here wee fitted our shipping and searched[2] our rother, which wee hoped would last us home. All our sicke men recovered their health, through the store of goats and hogs wherewith wee had refreshed ourselves; having great need of good refreshing, for in three moneths wee had seene no land, but were continually beaten in the sea.

The fift day of July we set saile from this iland, our course being north-west. The thirteenth day wee passed by an iland called the Ascension, which standeth in eight degrees. No ships touch at this iland, for it is altogether barraine and without water. Onely it hath good store of fish about it; but deepe water and ill riding for ships. From hence wee held our course still north-west (the wind being south and south-east) till the nineteenth day, and then wee passed the Æquinoctiall Line. The foure and twentieth day wee were six leagues to the northward; at which time wee judged ourselves to be an hundred and fiftie leagues from the coast of Ginney. Then wee steered away north and by west and north till the nine and twentieth, at which time wee had sight of the iland of Fogo[3]. Here wee were becalmed five dayes, striving to passe to the eastward of this iland, but could not, for the wind changed and came to the north-east; so we stood west-north-west. The seventh day of August wee were in sixteene degrees, and the twelfth day wee passed the Tropicke of Cancer, that lieth in $23\frac{1}{2}$ degrees; holding our course northerly. But the three and twentieth the wind came westerly. The nine and twentieth wee passed the iland of Saint Marie[4]; the wind faire.

The seventh day of September wee tooke sounding, judging the Lands End of England to be fortie leagues from us. The eleventh day wee came to the Downes, well and safe to an anchor; for the which thanked be Almightie God, who hath delivered us from infinite perils and dangers in this long and tedious navigation.

---

[1] Riotous shouting.   [2] Examined.   [3] One of the Cape Verd Islands.
[4] Santa Maria, the easternmost island of the Azores.

II

A TRUE AND LARGE DISCOURSE[1]

OF THE VOYAGE OF THE WHOLE FLEETE OF SHIPS SET FORTH THE 20 OF APRILL 1601 BY THE GOVERNOURS [sic] AND ASSISTANTS OF THE EAST INDIAN MARCHANTS IN LONDON TO THE EAST INDIES; WHEREIN IS SET DOWNE THE ORDER AND MANNER OF THEIR TRAFFICKE, THE DISCRIPTION OF THE COUNTRIES, THE NATURE OF THE PEOPLE AND THEIR LANGUAGE, AND THE NAMES OF ALL THE MEN DEAD IN THE VOYAGE.

At London.

Imprinted for Thomas Thorpe, and are to be solde by William Aspley.

1603.

A true and large discourse of the East India Voyage, departing out of England the 20 day of Aprill 1601.

The 20 of Aprill 1601 we wayed anchor and set saile out of Torbay, by Dartmouth.

The 2 of May one of our admiralles men fell overboord from the maineyard and was drowned.

The 7 of May we came to the Canares, where the generall determined to renew our water; but altering his purpose, we wayed our anchors and departed with a faire winde.

The 10 of May, being Sunday, the generall, captaines, and maisters dined aboord the *Hector*; where the generall delivered

---

[1] Reprinted from a pamphlet now in the Bodleian Library, Oxford (Art. 40, C. 16, BS). Only one other copy is known, viz. that in the Marsh Library, Dublin (Pollard and Redgrave's *Short-Title Catalogue of Books printed*, 1475–1640). The pamphlet, which was obviously based on a journal kept aboard the *Ascension*, was registered at Stationers' Hall by William Aspley on 25 June 1603 (Arber's *Transcripts*, vol. III, p. 98), i.e. soon after the arrival of that vessel. The identity of the writer is not known; but he was evidently a person of some culture, and the choice seems to lie among the merchants on board, with the possible addition of the purser.

them articles to be observed and kept, both by sea and land, and what punishment should be inflicted upon the offenders.

The 12 of May wee passed the Tropicke, with a fresh gaile.

The 24 we had a great storme.

The 25 we had a storme, with great store of raine.

The 27 we had another storme, continuing two houres.

The 21 of June we tooke a Portingall, whose lading was wine, oyle, and meale, being about the burthen of 100 tunne; who, not resisting, was discharged of his marchandise in foure dayes, to every ship according to his proportion.

The 29 of June we passed the Equinoctiall, with a fresh gale of winde.

The 12 of July our maister gunner of the *Ascention* dyed; who was the first that dyed in that ship. Here we tooke many flying fishes in the aire.

The 16 of July we doubled the shoales of Braseele; and for joy thereof every messe had a canne of wine to supper.

The 20 of July we cast off the *Guift*, being about 18 degrees to the south of the Equinoctiall. Here we tooke more fish then we could eate.

About the first of August many of our men in every ship fell sicke of the scurvy. So that many died, and few were free of the infection throughout the fleete. So that there died 80 men in the fleete before we came to land.

The 9 of September it pleased God, after our long distresses, to send us to the sight of land at Soldania, 16 leagues from the Cape de Bona Esperance. And because it was in the night, and all our men very weake, we were in great danger, beeing very neare the shoare. But God strengthned us; so that by His helpe, and the helpe of some of our admiralles men (when they had mored their ship), we were preserved, not being able to helpe ourselves.

The 10 day our generall went ashoare, to see if he could get some fresh victuals. And after hee had talked with the countrey people, they made signes that they would bring oxen and sheepe within two or three sleepes.

The 14 day every ship sent provision on shoare for the building of tents. And this day the inhabitantes of the country brought bullockes and sheep; and so continued daylie for 12 dayes togeather. So that there were bought about 900 or 1000 sheep and bullockes in that time. The price of a bullock was two peeces of yron hoopes of 6 inches long apeece, and the price of a sheepe one peece of the same length; provided that the oxen and sheepe were fat, or else we would not buy them. The people are blacke, and goe naked, saving that they weare short coates of seales skinne, and a peece of the same skinne about their members. They are tall of stature, flat-nosed, swift in running. They will picke and steale, although you looke on them. Their language is very hard to be pronounced, by reason of a kinde of clacking with the tongue; so that we could not learne one worde of their language. The country is full of pleasant rivers. There is also deare, quailes, and partriges. In this baye there is a small iland, not inhabited, nor any good thing groweth. Thither did the general send 6 sheep and two rammes, for the reliefe of strangers that might come thither; which shortly after was found there by certaine Flemmings, to their reliefe, because they could get no cattell of the country people. In this iland there is great aboundance of seales and penguines, in such number as is almost incredible. The seales, some are russet and some are blacke; both ugly and fearefull to looke on. The olde ones, which are as big almost as a beare, cry like a beare, and the young ones crie like unto lambes. They have but two feete; yet they use their hinder partes in going, by which meanes they will goe or clime up any rocke a great pace. Some of these we killed, and made oyle of them; and some of the youngest we did eate, which to us seemed good meate. They lay partly on land and partly in the water; for there is their refuge. The penguine is as strange as the other; being a bird which hath a strange and a proude kinde of going. They are of the bignesse of a ducke. They have finny wings, with which they swim a great pace but cannot flie. And these are in such aboundance that you may take them up with your hands, as many as you will. The egges of these penguines was there in such aboundance as we could not almost go for them; so that we laded our boat with seales, penguines, and egges in two houres. In this bay likewise (as it is credibly reported by the Flemmings) there is another iland of conies, in as great aboundance as the other of seales and penguines[1].

Before our departure from hence we had a sermon and a communion, one a Sunday in the forenoone. And after noone one of our men, which was a Jew, was christened and called John; our generall being his godfather[2].

The 29 of October we wayed our anchors and set saile. There being dead in the whole fleete at this time 107; and others that were sicke recovered to health.

The first of November we doubled the Cape de Bona Esperance, with great store of winde, raine, and haile.

The 26 we saw Saint Laurence.

The 2 of December we had so many huge and great grampoyses[3] about our shippe as was strange and wonderfull.

The 4 of December we had great stormes, which continued al day and the same night; so that we were in danger to loose some of our company.

The 16 we saw the land of Madagascar and the iland of Saint Marie. And the next day we cast an anchor betweene both landes, and sent our boats to Saint Maries to see what was to be gotten; but could get nothing there but oringes and lemmans, of which we made good stoare of water, which is the best remedy against the scurvy.

Here we continued 3 or 4 dayes, but could get no other things but lemmons, some honycombes, some milke, and some rice; which we bought for beades. We saw but only one cow, which they drave away as soone as they saw us; whereby we imagined they had small store. The people of this iland are of a tal stature and very well limmed and proportioned, such as we have not seene in these parts of the world. They go naked, saving about their members they weare cloath made of the barkes of trees; and the women weare of the same stuffe, from their breasts to their feete.

---

[1] This island lies thirty-five miles to the northward of Table Bay. The English christened it Cony Island, on account of the abundance of those animals; while the Dutch gave it its present name of Dassen (which has the same meaning).

[2] See note on p. 97.

[3] The grampus is a cetacean of the dolphin family.

The 21 we had a mighty storme, both of winde and raine; so that our ship lost an anchor, the *Hector* let slip her anchor, and the *Susan* broake her bowsprit. And here we were in great danger, by reason we were in such a straight betweene two landes. Here our ship was almost aboord the admirall, but God delivered us. This storme continued 12 houres very forcible; in which time two of our admirals men fell from the maineyarde, whereof one was saved and the other drowned. And as the winde was vehement, so the aire was very thicke and misty; which made it the more dangerous.

The 26 day we anchored in the baye of Antogill. And the next daye our boates were sent on shoare and, meeting with the people of the countrie, we bought of them rice, lemmons, and plantons, in great quantitie and number; for we bought a measure of rice, which wayed two pounds and a halfe, for a bloudstone or a blew bead, and twentie lemmons or twentie plantons for a bead. In this place they have small store of cattell; but they went with us unto another baye, where there was more store; of whome we bought two or three, giving five and thirtie christall beads for a bullocke. And afterwards, because they would sell us no more, wee went and tooke some from them perforce, giving them in beads as we paide for the other, to the valew of ten shillings.

The first of January wee began to build our pinnace.

The 7 of January five of the *Susans* companie, being some boyes and some youthes, stoale away the boate from the ships stearne, thinking to have gone to the maine to have lived there; but by chaunce were espyed, so that they were faine to put themselves on shoare uppon a small iland not inhabited; where they continued two or three dayes and, beeing weary of their faire and lodging, came againe aboorde, and were punished for their offences.

The 17 of January one Christopher Newchurch, our surgeon of the *Ascention*, poysoned himselfe. But it did not worke his death, yet was he greevously tormented for three or foure dayes; for which cause he was dismissed of his place, and should have beene left in this place ashoare, had not Maister Havers[1] in-

---

[1] Hayward, captain of the *Susan*.

treated for him; who tooke him into his shippe, to live as an ordynary man.

The 4 day of February we had a great storme of winde and raine, which continued all day and the same night.

The 20 day Maister Brodbancke, maister of the admirall, died.

The 23 day of February Maister Pullin, our preacher, died.

The 23[1] day Maister Napper, maister of the vice-admirall, died. And the same day one of our admirals men, being sicke of the calanture[2], leaped overboord and was no more seene.

The 27 day, being Saterday, the lamentablest accident happened that happened since wee departed England; and thus it was. Maister Winter, the maisters mate of the admiral, dying, the rest of the captaines and maisters went to his burial; and according to the order of the sea, there was 2 or 3 great ordinances discharged at his going ashoare. But the maister gunner of the admirall, being not so carefull as he should have beene, unfortunately killed Maister Brand, captaine of the *Ascension*, and the boatswaines mate of the same ship, to the great danger of the maister, his mate, and another marchant, who were hurt and besprinckled with the bloud of these massacred men. So these men, going to the buriall of another, were themselves carryed to their owne graves. Thus did we loose a man religious, wise, and provident; such a one as the whole fleete will misse, both for good husbandry, care, and good advice.

Upon these alterations Roger Hankin[3] was made maister of the admirall; Maister Indeck[4] maister of the vice-admirall (for Maister Napper was dead); Maister Coale[5] maister of the *Ascension*. Maister Pope[6] was made captaine of the *Ascension*; and some of the other marchants remooved, some to one ship, some to another.

The 4 day of March wee set saile out of this tempestuous and unfortunate baye; where there was many men died of the flixe[7]

---

[1] Probably an error for '25.'
[2] A tropical disease characterized by fever and delirium.
[3] Master of the *Ascension*.
[4] John Indeck. He died before the fleet left Achin.
[5] Alexander Cole, who was afterwards master of the *Hector* (see p. 119).
[6] Robert Pope was one of the factors on board the *Dragon*.
[7] Dysentery. The more usual spelling is 'flux.'

out of the admirall. So that wee continued here two monethes and eight dayes, having for the most part every daye fearefull thunder, raine, and lightenning, as the like is not heard in our countrey. For they have many slaine with the thunder[1]; which maketh them make hast to gette home before night. The people are very industrious, and take great paines, both in setting of rice (which groweth there in great quantytie, so that there is whole stackes thereof), as also in beating and winnowing the same. They weave such thinges as they weare about their bodyes, beeing made of the barke of trees. Their houses are but meane; standing halfe a yarde from the ground and covered with leaves, with a hoale at one ende of the same house to creepe in at on their knees. They love wine exceedingly, with which they will bee very drunke. As there is many small townes, so there is many governours; which are knowne from the other, both by the reverence [that] is given them of the people and their ornaments of brasse rings and beades. They are marvelous nimble with their lawnces and targets [i.e. shields], but very fearefull of our peeces [i.e. muskets]. The chiefe governour came aboord of us with his wife to dinner; where we might perceive their manner of feeding to be very homely. And for their assurance of safetie, there was so many sent ashoare as came aboord. And after dinner Captaine Middleton gave the principall man a thinne shute of Manchester stuffe; which pleased him well.

Certaine words of their language[2]

Taughu, wine. *Rano*, water. *Herinco*, fish. *Bedehang*, beades. *Kissow*, a knife. *Totombar*, rice. *Lemona*, lemons. *Eeno*, full. *Semissu*, no more left. *Matty*, thunder. *Sungo Funsho*, ripe plantons. *Essa*, one. *Roe*, two. *Tellu*, three. *Effa*, foure. *Demi*, five. *Ena*, six. *Ceto*, seven. *Vallo*, eight. *Civi*, nine. *Foolo*, ten. *Beginning againe, and reckoning to ten.*

The 17 day of Aprill we passed the Equinoctiall Line; which is the second time that we passed it.

[1] See note on p. 5.
[2] Many of these words may be identified in the Malagasy vocabulary appended to Capt. Pasfield Oliver's edition (1890) of Robert Drury's journal of his stay in Madagascar.

The 30 day of March[1] we were on the shoales of Adu[2], which is nine degrees to the south of the Equinoctiall. And at the first sight of ground (being full of rockes) our ship had but 4 fadome and a halfe. Here we were in great danger, being inclosed and compassed round with rocks as in a pound. And having spent 2 dayes and nights in turning and returning, but could finde no way out, at the length the pinnace was sent before, to finde where there was least danger. And having found 7 or 8 fadom, we all followed her. And having passed this danger, we gave God the praise, which had mercifully delivered us.

The 7 day of May we had sight of Nicombar, which is about 40 leagues from Sumatra. This night following, we had a great storme. And in this storme, if God had not delivered us wonderfully, our ship or the *Hector*, or both, had suncke in the sea, being almost aboord of one another, in lying of[f] those ilands. This night also we lost company with the pinnace; but within 2 or 3 dayes she came to us in that ha[r]bor. Here we stayed 9 or 10 dayes, to water and ballast our shippes and to mount our ordinance. The people of the country brought us aboord coakernuts, cassado[3] rootes, pounceatrons[4], and lemmons, and some hens. But they made dainty of their hens, for they would not sell them under two counters[5] apeece (taking them for gould), although they solde other things for olde peeces of linnen and small peeces of yron hoopes. Some of these people speake Portugale; who tolde us that the Portugales use to put into this harbor as they goe to Mallacca, and that two gallions were there two moneths before our comming thether, which had bought all the ambergreese was to be gotten.

The 18 day we set saile from hence. But, by reason of fowle weather and contrary windes, our admirall lost his boate and sprung a leake; and therefore would have fetched that harbor againe, but could not. So wee went to other ilands, called Sombrai, 10 or 12 leagues to leeward [of] Nicombar. Heere our admirall lost an ancker, for the ground is rockie and full of counterfeit currall.

---

[1] An obvious error for April. [2] The Chagos archipelago (see p. 87).
[3] A form of 'cassava.'   [4] 'Pome-citrons,' the fruit of the citrus tree.
[5] Imitation brass coins.

The people of this iland goe naked, having onely their privities bound up in a narrow peece of linnen cloath, which commeth about their middle like a girdell, and so betweene their twist. They are of a tawnie couler. They annoint their faces with divers coullers. They are well limmed, but very fearefull; for they would neither come aboord our ships, nor come into our boates.

There groweth in this iland trees that, for the talenesse, greatnesse, and straightnesse thereof, they will serve the biggest shippe in our fleete for a mainemaste; and the iland is full of these trees. Heere likewise we did finde upon the sandes a small twigge, growing up greene like a young tree. And offering to pull the same up, it shrinketh into the ground and sincketh, unlesse you holde very harde. But beeing pulled up, a great worme groweth about the roote thereof, very strange to see. Of these I gathered many.

We departed from hence the 29 of this moneth. The 2 of June wee anckored in the roade of Dachen[1], where wee had [some] of the countrie people came aboorde of us with their canows, greater then any wee had seene before; having rafters [i.e. logs] of eache side of them, so that they cannot sincke.

The next day there came some of the factors for the Flemmings aboorde of us, to welcome us into that countrey. And the same daye our vize-admirall went ashoare to the king with a message from our generall, accompanied with Maister Salter[2], Maister Januerme[3], and Maister Grove[4]. Who, [i.e. the king] hearing of their landing, sent them elephants to ride to his court, being about a mile from the landingplace; where they were kindlie entertained, and giving to the vize-admirall a roabe and a tucke of callico, imbrodered with golde.

The 4 of June, being Saterday, the generall went on shoare, accompanied with Captaine Havers, Captaine Pope, and many other marchants, to deliver the Queenes letter, and to give him

---

[1] Achin was sometimes termed Dachen or Dachem, a corruption due to the adhesion of the Portuguese genitive. The Malay name is Acheh.
[2] Thomas Salter, a factor aboard the *Ascension*.
[3] Nathaniel Gamrym, Gamram, or Jamryn, a factor in the *Dragon*.
[4] Philip Grove, a Dutch pilot; sometimes called Philip de Grave. He was master of the *Dragon* in the Second Voyage. In 1608 he went out to India as master of the *Ascension*, and was held responsible for the loss of that vessel in the Gulf of Cambay. He died in India in 1610.

[i.e. the king] presents, which were a bason and ewer of silver, a standing cup of silver, a headpeece, a paire of hangers, a fanne of fethers, and a looking-glasse. These being delivered by the marchants, none pleased him so well as the fanne of feathers, with which hee caused his women to fanne him. First at the generals landing, the Flemmings mette him and carried him to their house, where he stayed untill the king sent for him. In the meanewhile there came a nobleman called Curcon[1], who would have received Her Majesties letter, to have delivered it to the king; but our generall refused to deliver it to any but to the king himselfe. Then did the king send sixe elephants for the generall and his attendants; whereof there was one elephant, which was the greatest, that carried a canopie covered with redde cloath; in which canopie was a peece of silke and a peece of cloath of gold to carrie Her Majesties letter in; and upon this elephant none did ride but he that carried the letter. The generall ridde upon another, with a guide before him; and uppon the rest some did ride and some did not. For it is very uneasie riding uppon them; their backes are so broade, and they so great and tall.

The king did likewise send his trumpets and other musicke; which played before the generall to the courte. And there was twentie other that carried streamers of silke of divers coulours, according to that countrie manner. So the generall, entering into the first gate of the court, rested himselfe there, untill the king had notice of his comming; who presently sent for him and foure other of the principall men about the generall; who, when they had brought him to the king, came backe for the presents, which were carryed in by the marchants appointed for that purpose. And after they had passed three courtes, they came into a place covered with cannopies, adjoyning to the kings gallerie, where the king satte. And after they had given Doulat[2]

---

[1] A secretary or registrar (*kārkun*). Davis mentions a 'secretary, named Corcoun,' as one of the principal officials.

[2] Persian *daulat*, prosperity, felicity. Davis says (*Purchas*, vol. I, bk. iii, p. 122): 'Before any man can come to the kings presence, he must put of his hose and shooes and come before him bare-legged and bare-footed, holding the palmes of the handes together and, heaving them up above his head, bowing with the bodie, must say Doulat; which done, dutie is discharged, and so hee sitteth downe, crosse-legged, in the kings presence.'

to the king, and the king resaluted them, according to their countrie fashion, which is by lifting both their handes above their heads, they satte downe to dinner; where they had great cheere, and to the number of two or three hundreth severall dishes of meate, baked, roasted, and boyled. The dishes and cuppes wherein they were served were most of goulde and of a mettall much like to bell mettall, which is dearer then goulde; every dishe covered, some with purslain of China. Their drinke is called aracke, and is verye strong, and is not to bee drunke without water. Yet that which is generally drunke in the countrie is nothing so strong, nor so wholesome.

The king asked our generall if our Queene were married and how long she had raigned; which when the generall had answered by his interpretor, the king wondred. The king likewise told the generall, if the words in Her Majesties letter came from the hart, he had cause to thinke well thereof. Dinner being ended, the king caused his damsels to daunce and his women to play musicke unto them; who were richly adorned with bracelets and jewels, and this was a great favour, for hee dooth not usually let them be seene to any. The king did likewise give unto our generall a fine white roabe and a tucke, imbrodered with gold very ritchly; also a great girdell and two crises [see p. 93]; all which one of his noblemen put on in the kings presence. And in this manner hee departed the court and went aboord. And the king sent him aboorde a bullocke and great store of fresh fish. So that, to conclude, he did receive Hir Majesties letter with great kindnesse, and entertained our generall with greater state then hee is accustomed to doe to other nations; as wee might perceive by divers embassadors that came thether whilest we were there.

The 5 of June Captaine Pope went ashoare for one of our men which was left in the towne all night by his owne negligence; for the generall did feare because hee spoake Portugale and that there were Portingalls in the towne, that hee might make knowne unto them something which might bee prejudiciall to the fleete. Maister Pope dined this day with the king; who gave him a heyffer [i.e. heifer] to carrie aboorde with him.

The 7 day of June, after the generall had licence under the

kings hand, both for the safe landing of all our marchandise without paying any custome or toale, as also that we might buy and sell of the country people without let or molestation; then did Captaine Havers, Maister Pope, Henry Middleton, and Maister Starkey take a house, wherin to lay their marchandise.

The 8 day of June the generall went ashoare, to lodge there.

The 11 day of June the king did annoint the generall with ritch oyntment, and called him his sonne.

About this time one Thorougood, in our admirall, was araigned and found guiltie of mutiny and comtempe, and therefore was condemned to bee hanged, but by great intreaty he was forgiven.

The 13 day the generall went to the young prince, which dwelleth halfe a mile from his father; and the generall gave him a peece of plate, a paire of hangers, and a sworde. The Prince entertained him kindely, gave him a roabe and a crises [sic]; and gave unto them which came in with him tuckes of callico lawne [i.e. muslin].

The 17 day of June, one Curcon, a principall man in that countrie, and divers others came aboord our ships to see them, but especially to see the *Susan*, whom the generall had offered to the king to sell for a certaine quantity of pepper, but could not agree. So after they had banqueted aboord the admirall and dyned aboorde the vice-admirall, they departed, with a peale of ordinance.

The 19 day the admirall received a boates lading of pepper, which was the first was bought. The price was 64 rialles of eight the bahar, which is of our waight, reckoning two hundred catties to a bahar and every catty thirty-one ounces, is three hundred, eighty-seven pound and a halfe[1], five score to the hundred [i.e. cwt.].

During the time we were at Dachem, the king desired to have our pinnace goe to Pedeir, accompanyed with a Portugalles frigat, to take (if they might) rovers at sea, which did rob his subjectes; and did send to the valew of 100 markes in golde for those that should be imployed in that businesse. And because the general sent the pinnace, with 14 or 15 men (of whome

[1] Best (p. 257) reckoned the *bahar* as equivalent to 386 lb. Croft (*ibid*. p. 175) made it 385 lb. Davis estimated it at 360 lb. which is obviously too low.

Gabriel Towerson[1] was captaine), but did no service, therefore the generall would have given the king that mony againe; but hee would not receive it by any meanes, saying what hee gave he gave and would not take againe.

And at the same time there was seven or eight hundred houses burnt at sundry times in Dachem while we were there. Therefore the generall bought an oulde stone house, builte it and covered it with slate, and at our comming awaye gave it to the king; the ground and house cost almost one hundred pound starling[2].

The generall, having intelligence of the price and goodnesse of pepper at Priaman, and seeing the smal quantity that was to be gotten at Dachem, sent the *Susan* thether (with our small pinnace to bring news of her successe). And because Captaine Haverd was lately dead, Henry Middleton was appointed cape marchant in his place.

The 24 daye of June there came into the road of Dachem a Flemmish pinnace, which had lost her admiral; of which fleete one Spilbacke, of Middlebourough [Middelburg], was generall[3]. Shee was of the burthen of fifty tunne, and had but three men and two boyes in her; which pinnace our general bought, for they mistrusted they should not heare of their generall againe.

There came also into the roade of Dachem a great shippe of Saint Mallos in Fraunce, of the burthen of foure hundred tunne[4].

---

[1] He had subsequently a long period of service under the Company, and was principal factor of the Moluccas when he was put to death by the Dutch in the 'Massacre of Amboyna.'

[2] Probably, at the time of purchase, Lancaster intended to leave some merchants at Achin. As stated, on his departure he presented the house to the king, who subsequently gave it to the Dutch (Speilbergen, p. 57).

[3] This was the fleet of Joris van Speilbergen, which left Holland in April 1601. It consisted of the *Schaep*, the *Ram*, and the *Lam* (the pinnace here referred to). The voyage (described in Speilbergen's *Journael*) was rendered memorable by a visit to Ceylon, during which the leader went up to Kandy and had a cordial interview with the king. The *Lam* had lost company near the Comoros and made her way to Achin, where she was promptly bought from her commander by Lancaster. The other two ships arrived on 6 September (according to Speilbergen), and the English general at once sent Philip Grove (himself a Dutchman) on board to greet them.

[4] The *Croissant* and *Corbin* sailed in May 1601, under the command of Michel Frotet, Sieur de la Bardelière. The *Corbin* was wrecked on the Maldives in June 1602, as described by François Pyrard de Laval, who was on board (see his narrative). A general account of the voyage was written by François Martin, and this states that the *Croissant* reached Achin on 14 July

The generall his name was Mounser de Bardeler. They lost their vice-admirall by shipwracke uppon the Maldevs; and departed from Dachem for France with about 14 tunne of pepper, some smale quantity of sinamon, and some indico; so that he had not halfe of his lading.

The 8 day of September came into this roade two Flemish ships from Seylon, with sinamon; unto whome did belong the pinnace that our generall bought. And because our generall had resolved to goe for Malacca, he did take the admirall of the Flemmings[1] with him, being about 200 tunne and very well manned; and in consideration thereof to have the 8 part of what was taken. And for our owne fleete the general had compounded that the company[2] should have the sixt part.

The 11 day of September our admiral, vice-admirall, rear-admirall, and the Flemish ship and pinnace[3] departed hence for the Straightes of Malacca; our generall dangerously sicke. Captaine Pope dyed. During the time of the generalles absence the Frenchmen had raised the price of pepper from 24 tayes[4] the bahar to 27 and 30 and 32; so that we were forced to buy some of that price.

The 3 day of October, being in the Straites of Mallacca, the *Hector* espyed a great ship towardes evening, which came from

[o.s.]. After procuring a small quantity of pepper, she sailed for France on 10 November. De la Bardelière died eleven days later, after an illness of about four months.

[1] The *Schaep*. The *Ram* was left at Achin to buy pepper.

[2] Meaning the crews of the vessels taking part in the enterprise. The men of the *Susan* (then at Priaman) were indignant at being excluded from the compact; and on their return to England they submitted a petition to King James, setting forth their grievance. The East India Company, in its reply to this representation, declared that all its sailors were engaged for a trading voyage only and their wages were fixed accordingly. Lancaster, it was stated, had therefore, before leaving Achin, made a special 'contract with all the marriners of the *Redd Dragon*, the *Hectour*, and the *Assention*, what shares they should have in such prize as should be taken by them then in consortshipp together;' and after their arrival in England the men were duly paid all that was owing to them on that account (*The First Letter Book*, pp. 25–7). How the controversy ended is not known.

It may be noted that the Company had also to pay to the Lord High Admiral (the Earl of Nottingham) the usual tenth levied by him on all prize goods (*The Dawn*, p. 246).

[3] The *Lam*, bought from the Dutch.

[4] The Chinese *tael* (ounce of silver), equal to about 5s. It seems here to be taken as the equivalent of the rial of eight.

S. Thoma and was bound for Malacca, and the next morning yeelded themselves without any resistance or so much as any one man hurt. This day we beganne to unlade her, and had out of hir 950 packes of calico and pentadoes, besides many great chestes with marchandise; all which was upon her orlops[1]. But her hould was full of rice. And because of a storme that did arise, we were forced to leave hir with that great aboundance of rice and with store of victuals, as porke, butter, cheese, ruske[2], conserves, suckets, hens in pickle, hens preserved, with store of sinamon water[3] and palmeto wine. The name of this ship was the *Saint Anthony*, and of the burthen of 700 tun. And it was strange to see the number of men, women, and children that were in her (not so few as 600 persons); whereof there was but a few Portingalles, the rest passengers and people of these countries. And in 6 dayes we had discharged her of the best of her lading, and would have taken more if we had had time and place.

Thus our fleete returning to Dachin the 28 of October, our generall gave order for the shipping, as well of such marchandise as came out of England and was unsould, as also all such pepper and sinnamon as was bought in the absence of the fleete; and made what speede possible might bee for our departures thence. At this time came our pinnace from Priaman with letters to our generall; where was good newes, both for the price and quantity of pepper. Uppon the receite whereof the generall sent the pinnace which we bought of the Flemmings to Priaman, with some of the prised goodes and other commodities.

The king of this countrey is very ritch in treasure and strong in the number of men. He hath great store of ordinance of brasse, and those verye great and massey. Their lawes are severely inflicted upon them that offend, either by delivering them to the elephantes to be devoured[4], or cutting of[f] their noses and eares, according to the haynousnesse of the offence. They bury their dead with great solemnitie, and mourne over their graves certaine dayes; setting up at each ende of their graves either one or two stones, carved according to the abilitie [i.e. means] of the person; and they are buryed together in families.

[1] The lowest deck, at the bottom of the ship.   [2] Biscuit.
[3] An aromatic drink prepared from cinnamon.
This is of course wrong. The elephant trampled upon the victim.

The people are verye subtill and cunning in bargaining, and unconstant in all their wordes; for they will sell one thing to divers men and take earnest of them all, and if another will give anything more, he shall have it. Their coyne is goulde and lead. That of goulde they call masse[1]; sixe of them for a royall of eight. Those of lead they call cashe; whereof 2100 maketh a masse. So that a copaine[2] is the fourth part of a masse, being 525 cashe; for which you may buye hearbes and fruites and fishe. Every daye in the weeke is a market day for victualls; not so much as Friday (which they call their good day)[3]; but they keepe no shoppes open for marchandize on that daye. There is great store of hennes, buffles, and bullockes, yet very deare; a henne at nine pence or twelve pence, buffels at two tayes[4] and a halfe (which is thirtie shillings starling), egges, eighteene or twentie for nine pence, and, at our comming away, foureteene for nine pence. Rice is brought from other places thether as good marchandize, and is sold by the bambue, sixe or seaven bambues for nine pence; every bambue being an ale quarte[5]. So that in this place there is neither marchandize nor anything else good cheape of itselfe.

The countrie is very unwholsome; that almost it may be said of it as it is said of Malacca: fewe come thether, but eyther loose hide or hayre. Heere we lost ten or twelve men out of our ship.

There are elephants in greater number and bigger stature then in any of those parts; which are the chiefe strength of this land. The greatest is ruled with a little boye, having a sticke with a hooke at the end; and is of the greatest understanding of any beast living. As for their strength, I did see one drawe the kings frigat (laden with pepper), which was aground, being ten or

---

[1] The *mas* was reckoned by John Davis (*Purchas*, vol. I, p. 117) at about 9½d. Croft (in *Voyage of Thomas Best*, p. 175) says that it was worth 9d. and in the text it is evidently taken at that value. Davis describes the cash as 'like a little leaden token, such as the vintners of London use;' he reckons 1600 of them to the *mas* (*Purchas*, vol. I, p. 123). Martin (p. 55) agrees with the number given in the text. Doubtless the value varied from time to time.

[2] Malay *kupang*.

[3] Friday is the Muhammadan equivalent of the Christian Sunday.

[4] The gold *tael* (of sixteen *mas*) is here valued at 12s. It was an imaginary coin.

[5] A section of a large bamboo, cut off just below one joint and below the next, has long been used in the East to carry dry goods or liquids.

twelve tunne, very easilie. The king taketh pleasure to see them fight, as likewise in cockfighting; at which game they lay a hundred pound, or a hundred and fiftie pound, starling on a cockes head.

Their shippes, sayles, mastes, anchors, and cables are all of wood[1].

Malies speech, such as is used in these Indies[2].

1, *Satu.* 2, *Dua.* 3, *Tiga.* 4, *Umpat.* 5, *Lema.* 6, *Nam.* 7, *Toufeurs.* 8, *Delapan.* 9, *Simbalan.* 10, *Sapula.* 11, *Sablas.* 12, *Duo blas.* 13, *Tiga blas.* 14, *Umpat blas, &c.* 100, *Saratus.* 1000, *Sariba. Pege,* goe. *Marre,* come hether. *Barapa,* how sell you? *Jam,* a henne. *Tellor,* egges. *Deduc,* sit downe. *Mana pege,* whether go you? *Harry,* a day. *Campan,* a ship. *Praw,* a boate. *Barass,* rice. *Ladda,* pepper. *Ladda sula,* white pepper. *Tanna,* earth. *Roma,* a house. *Macan,* eate. *Babbe,* porcke. *Pedang,* a sworde. *Cheremin,* a glasse. *Baick,* good. *Teda baick,* not good. *Carron,* a bagge. *Tally,* a corde. *Suda,* quickly. *Isuc,* tomorrow. *Bree,* give me. *Rotan,* that which they bind their houses with. *Cring,* drye. *Aire,* water. *Appe,* fire. *Attowan,* Sir. *Roge, Sultan,* the king. *Taw,* I understand you. *Tidatau,* I doe not understand. *Gyngo,* a Jews harpe. *Sussu,* milke.

When we were ready to depart this roade, we had a hundred and fourescore men dead in the whole fleete.

The 11 of November we wayed anchor altogether. And the 13 of the same moneth we parted with our generall and vize-admirall. They went to Priaman, where the *Susan* did lade, and from thence to Bantam (for there is the best saile for such commodities as were taken in the prise, of any place in all the Indies), and we for England. *Deus vortat bene*[3].

---

[1] The sails were of matting, and the cables of coir; but the general meaning is plain.
[2] This Malay vocabulary, Dr Blagden tells me, is fairly correct, though 'seven' is properly translated by *tujoh*, and 'campan' should be *sampan*, with the meaning of 'a boat.' 'Attowan' seems to represent *ya, tuan* ('yes, Sir); and 'gyngo' is for *genggong*.
[3] The classical *Di vortant bene* (May the gods prosper the plan) is here given a Christian turn.

The 11 of December we had the moonsoon, or trade winde; and so continued sayling before the winde unto the first of Januarie; after which time wee found the winde variable, being in the height of 20 degrees to the south of the Line.

The 11 of January, having a storme in the night, we had sixe *corpus sanctus*[1] (so called by the Portingals); whereof three were upon our mainetopmastehead, two on our foretop, and one upon our flagge staffe. They seemed to us to be as bigge as the biggest starres, and are never seene but in stormes, and vanish away before the storme endeth. If they be seene in the cheanes or shrowds of the ship, it is a signe the storme is of longer continuance; if in the highest toppes, it is likewise a signe the storme is ended. And so we found it for certaine.

About this time our maister gunner and another of the gunner roome dyed.

The 13 day we saw two marmaides. And (as we judged them) they were male and female, because the moste of one of their heads was longer then the other. Their heades are very round, and their hinder parts are devided like two legges. They say they are signes of stormy weather; and so we found it, for the 17 day following we had a great storme, with a contrary winde, which continued 4 dayes.

The 22 the French ship which we left at Dachem[2] overtooke us, being in the height of 33 and a halfe, and about 250 or 300 leagues from Cape de Bona Esperance; who was glad of our company, both in regard their ship was so leake that they were faine to pumpe almost continually, as also they had hope to be releeved of us with victualles; for they had nothing but rice and water. We caught daylie for sixe weekes space great store of fish (more then wee coulde eate), as of albecores, bonitos, and dolphins.

From the 22 to the 30 we had a faire winde at E.S.E. On which day, being in 34 and a halfe, we had a great storme; and as it was great, so it was suddaine, before we could take in our

---

[1] More usually *corpo santo*, or St Elmo's light—an electrical phenomenon, resembling balls of light, flickering about masts or spars during a storm of thunder and lightning.

[2] The *Croissant* (see p. 133). Martin does not mention her encounter with the *Ascension*.

sailes (which maketh them dangerous). Wee laye at hull two dayes; after which time we had a faire winde at E. and by S. (being about 60 leagues from Cape de Bona Esperance).

The 3 of February one of our men going to the toppemasthead espied the Cape de Bona &c.; as also two Holland shippes[1] (to our great joye and comfort), for whome we stayed. And whereas, before, the French and we had resolved to goe into Soldania Road the next morning, by reason of their company we shapte our course for S. Hellena. These two ships had beene at Patania, where they laded pepper, and at the Molucos, where they had cloves, and upon the coast of China, where they bought silkes, both raw and twisted; so that their lading was very rich; the admiral being of the burthen of 600 tun and the other 200 tun, both well appointed with men and ordinance, saving that some of their men were sicke. And when we had toulde them that our admirall and vice-admirall were gone to Bantam, they tould us of a certaine they should soone be laden, and at a low price. For they came from thence; and at their first comming thether the countrey thought they had come thither to buy pepper; but when they sawe they were laden already, they would have soulde it for any price. So that, in regarde of the marchandise our gennerall carryeth with him (which is the prize goods) and the great quantytie of peper which they have no meanes to utter, there is no doubt (by the grace of God) but they shall bee laden good cheape and in verye short time. Amen.

The 20 daye of Februarye wee had sight of Sainte Hellena. And the twentye one daye wee anchored in the roade; where wee delivered unto the Frenchmen and unto the Hollanders such victualles to relieve them as we could spare; which was six hogsheades of porke, two hundreth [i.e. cwt.] of stockfish, one hogshead of beanes, and five hundred of bread, whereof the Hollanders were in great want.

This iland is not an earthly Paradice, as it is reported; but it is a place of good water and some lemmon trees and fig trees, planted by the Portingalles, and great stoare of goats and hogges

---

[1] Identified on a later page as the *Amsterdam* and *Dergoes*, under Jacob Cornelisz. van Neck. See the account of his (second) voyage in *Begin*, p. 26.

and partridges, but not to be gotten without great labour and paines, for they are wilde and the iland full of great high hilles. The greatest refreshing in this place is fish in great aboundance; so that all our shippes have taken in one day foure hundred fish.

Here did one Moore die, which was one of our maister his mates. He was sicke ever since we came from Dachin.

The 9 day of March the Frenchmen departed this roade[1].

The 14 day of March the generall of the Flemmings anchor came home; which caused us to depart thence the same day, for their men were well recovered and refreshed.

The 21 day of March we had sight of the Ascention Iland; which lyeth in eight degrees to the south of the Equinoctiall.

The 28 and 29, very little winde.

The 30 day of March we passed the Equinoctiall Line, with a fine gale; which is the fourth time we passed it.

The first of Aprill, calme.

The 3, 4 and 5, very calme, much raine, and the winde verye mutable; beeing in two degrees to the northward of the Line.

The 6, 7, 8, and 9, a fresh gaile.

The 21 day of Aprill we entred the Saragoss Sea, being in 19 degrees.

The 25 day we passed the Tropickes [sic]. The same day one of our men died.

The last of Aprill wee were in 30 degrees, and the next day we had a great gaile with some raine.

The 15 day of May we were in 40 degrees and in the height of Flore and Corves[2]. Heere the windes were variable and very colde.

The 25 day we saw a small ship, but could not speake with her.

---

[1] Taking with them the letters mentioned on p. 144. The *Croissant* struggled on until, when nearing the coast of Spain, she met three Dutch ships coming from Venice. Her captain, finding his own vessel ready to founder, begged the Dutchmen to take on board her goods and crew, offering a share of the cargo in return. The Dutch, however, refused this arrangement, and in the end the Frenchmen had to be content with being received on board, with their private possessions, leaving the cargo to be pillaged by their preservers. The *Croissant* sank immediately after. The Dutch ships reached Plymouth on 3 June, and the letters for the English Company were at once forwarded to London.

[2] Flores is the westernmost of the Azores group; while Corvo is to the north of Flores.

The first of June we were in 44 degrees; having a good gaile of winde at the south-west, we holding our course north-east.

The 5 day we sounded, and found ground at 94 fadome.

The eight day of May[1] we had sight of the Lizard; and so without stay to the Downes, and from thence into the river to Woolwich[2]. God be praysed for it, and send the rest home in safety.

Certaine words of Pegu language[3].

Mugaru, what call you it? *Kidnan tiuan*, give mee bread. *Fegoe*, a carte. *Boon*, a knife. *Tobacu*, a pen. *Slappoit*, a booke. *Pappoit*, a table booke. *Memura*, what is your name? *Talla*, a chest. *Tene*, a pillow. *Tayongabalon*, a maste. *Pomeé*, breeches. *Cheochum*, stockins. *Botoway*, a thombe. *Toway*, a fist. *Cadup*, a head. *Suck*, haire of the head. *Slagota*, the eare. *Yu, Yu*, I, I [aye, aye]. *Moat*, eyes. *Tegla*, by and by. *Ciniaut*, let me see. *Catu*, the moone. *Shenon*, a starre. *Yacata*, the morning. *Keka*, good. *Kecho*, sit downe. *Cacadòe*, the palme of the head [hand?]. *Sanimbodoway*, the naile of the hand. *Nepóe*, Sir. *Mucherow*, how sell you? *Cabang*, a ship. *Aw, aw*, what say you? *Braw*, a woman. *True*, a man. *Fekeé*, a whoore. *Oiara*, I will goe. *Tamonra*, farewell. *Keag*, God. *Cling, clang*, much. *Nung, nung*, come hither. *Cleá*, dogge. *Cle*, bite. *Kleg*, a hogge. *Togatu*, noone. *Daick*, water. *Carrowtoway*, wash hands. *Ksole*, to spit. *Steake*, sleepe. *Notada*, arise. *Tarangcatu*, a doore. *Poctarang*, open the dore. *Dotarang*, shut the dore. *Chulay*, let [set?] it downe. *Downang*, take up.

A note of the mens names deceased out of the Dragon[4].

1. William Thomson. 2. Job Harket. 3. William Allin. 4. Raphe Arden. 5. Christopher Scot. 6. Edward Major. 7. Thomas May. 8. John Pegoune. 9. John Johnson. 10. Philip Salisbury. 11. Edmund Davies. 12. Richard

---

[1] A mistake for 'June.'

[2] The ship's arrival in the river was announced at a general court held on 16 June (*The Dawn*, p. 244).

[3] Dr Blagden has kindly examined this list, and has informed me that the language is Mon (Talaing), and that most of the words are recognizable.

[4] An entry on p. 137 shows that these lists include only the deaths up to the time of the departure from Achin.

Joanes. 13. Daniell Richardson. 14. John Clarkson. 15. Robert Poppe. 16. John Webbe. 17. John Humber. 18. William Burrowes. 19. Mathew Perchet. 20. Edward Keall. 21. Nicholas Williams. 22. Peter Bennet. 23. Leonard Nichols. 24. Robert Dame. 25. John Judson. 26. William Barker. 27. William Barret. 28. William Ridge. 29. Ralphe Salter. 30. Jeremy Gaufe. 31. Henry Thickpenny. 32. Henry Brigges. 33. Rice Williams. 34. Martine Topsaile. 35. M[aister] Willi[am] Bradbanke. 36. Richard Androwes. 37. M[aister] Tho[mas] Pullen, preach[er]. 38. Jeames Fullar. 39. William Winter. 40. William Hall. 41. John Hankin. 42. Richard Exame. 43. Robert Hill. 44. John Woodall. 45. John Jeane. 46. Robert Keachinman. 47. Jeames Caverly. 48. John Hope. 49. John Trincall. 50. John Duke. 51. Martaine Cornelison. 52. Launslet Taylor. 53. John Settell. 54. William Burrowes. 55. Percevall Stradling. 56. John Harrice. 57. Frauncis Pormoth. 58. Edward Baddiford. 59. Thomas Price. 60. Phillip Goulding. 61. Roger Morrice. 62. Stephen Burdall. 63. Nicholas Ragwood. 64. George Wattes. 65. Myles Berry. 66. William Mounke.

A note of the mens names deceased out of the Hector.

1. John Robinson. 2. Thomas Dassell. 3. Jeames Jefferes. 4. Morrice Webbe. 5. Mathew Starkey. 6. John Middleton. 7. Thomas Appollow. 8. John Fishaker. 9. George Parsons. 10. Walter Cobbe. 11. Edward Holte. 12. Richard Marshall. 13. John Ossever. 14. Morrice Hammont. 15. Thomas Wilkinson. 16. William Jones. 17. Edmund Faurcliffe. 18. Roger Moore. 19. Robert Ashplie. 20. Peter Johnson. 21 Adam Children. 22. Robert Burche. 23. Henry Great. 24. Nicholas Franke. 25. William Predam. 26. Emanuell Sims. 27. John Harris. 28. Maist[er] Henry Napper. 29. Christopher Cadde. 30. Thomas Pinchbanke. 31. Rowland Hils. 32. Oliver Adams. 33. John Endick, maister. 34. John Russell. 35. John Martin. 36. John Coman. 37. John Holliday.

A note of the mens names deceased out of the Ascention.

1. William Leake. 2. William Pizing. 3. William Whitting. 4. Gabriell Stone. 5. William Hambling. 6. Edward Carricke. 7. Arnold Malyn. 8. William Morgan. 9. Robert Savadge. 10. John Verker. 11. Richard Burrice. 12. John Griffeth. 13. Michaell Nicholson. 14. John Fare. 15. Thomas Daurell. 16. John Rowe. 17. Robert Double. 18. Robert Cooper. 19. John Hampton. 20. Thomas Cocklim. 21. William Betty. 22. Robert Batman. 23. John Badby. 24. Richard Horton. 25. John Syclemore. 26. William Williamson. 27. Richard Hamond. 28. Thomas Everet. 29. Augustin Jordan. 30. Thomas Way. 31. Methewsaleh Mountjoy. 32. William Brune, capt[ain]. 33. Thomas Ward. 34. Thomas Scriven. 35. William Maler. 36. Robert Pope, captain. 37. John Reddoe. 38. Thomas Salter.

A note of the mens names deceased out of the Susan.

1. Henry Page. 2. Christopher Scult. 3. John Church. 4. John Foster. 5. Edward Seely. 6. Martaine Joxes [Jones?]. 7. Gilbert Crippin. 8. Richard Pope. 9. John Smith. 10. Marchus Floud. 11. Nicholas Sims. 12. Edward Steele. 13. Richard Bowyer. 14. Michaell Allen. 15. Richard Smally. 16. Thomas Wilson. 17. Richard Spencer. 18. Thomas Joanes. 19. Jeames Sket. 20. Richard Whitehead. 21. Robert Michel. 22. John Earle. 23. Christopher Androws. 24. Jacob Johnson. 25. Anthony Younger. 26. Robert Powell. 27. John Bishop. 28. Morgan Priddis. 29. William Haward. 30. Richard Sprat. 31. Henry Johnson. 32. Richard Egleston. 33. Jeames Upgrave. 34. John Goulding. 35. John Browne. 36. John Haward, cap[tain]. 37. Phillip Winscombe. 38. John Samon. 39. John Fousticke.

FINIS.

III

A LETTER[1]

WRITTEN TO THE RIGHT WORSHIPFULL THE GOVERNOURS [sic] AND ASSISTANTS OF THE EAST INDIAN MARCHANTS IN LONDON, CONTAINING THE ESTATE OF THE EAST INDIAN FLEETE, WITH THE NAMES OF THE CHIEFE MEN OF NOTE DEAD IN THE VOYAGE.

At London.

Imprinted for Thomas Thorppe, and are to be sould by William Aspley.

1603.

Right Worshipfull,

My dutie remembred.

It may please you to understand that we wayed anchor the 20 of Aprill 1601, and set saile out of Torbaye, by Dartmouthe.

The 21 of June following, being in the heigth of three degrees to the northwards of the Line, wee tooke a ship of Vianna, bound for Brasill, of the burthen of 130 tunne. Her lading was wine, oyle, and meale, which hath stood us in great steede in this our voyage. Five or six dayes after, we turned her off, after we had pillaged her as we thought good.

---

[1] This pamphlet evidently reproduced one of the two letters which were read at a general court of the Company held on 6 June 1603 (*The Dawn*, p. 242). Both are described as having been 'received by a Frenchman which latelie departed at sea from one of our fleet, the ship *Assention*; which letters were written, the one from Roger Style, cape merchant of the *Assention*, and the other from Ed[ward] Highelord, purser of the same ship; bothe discoursing the state of the voyage, bothe concerning the partes which have bene visited for trade and howe many of our menn are dead in the voyage.'

It is impossible to say which of the two letters is the one printed, and we cannot therefore fix its authorship. Nor do we know the circumstances in which it came into the hands of the publisher. The pamphlet was not registered at Stationers' Hall, and no other copy is known to exist than the one here reproduced, which is in the Bodleian Library at Oxford (40, L. 81, Art. (15)). Included in the pamphlet is a folding sheet with a woodcut of a ship. From its lavish display of the royal flag it is evidently a vessel of the royal navy, and we may infer that the publisher used an old block which had really no reference to the subject. The illustration has therefore been omitted.

The 20 day of July we turned away the *Guifte*, beeing in the height of 19 degrees to the southward of the Line. The 24 day we came under the Tropicke of Capricorne.

The 19 day of September we came to anchor at Saldaiua[1], beeing in very great distresse, by reason of the scurvy disease then raging among us. The *Ascention* and *Susans* company were scarce able to let fall their anchors without the helpe of other ships. There we staied and refreshed our men with fresh victuals, as beefe and mutton in great aboundance, which cost us little or nothing. There we staied about seaven weekes; and had staied there longer, if the inhabitantes had continued to bring us fresh victuals. So we departed thence the 9[2] of October.

The 29[3] of December we came to anchor in the baye of Antoga [Antongil]. Here we trucked with the inhabitants for rice, lemmans, and plantaines and such like fruite. We sette up one of our pinnaces. Here also we lost diverse of our men, which dyed of the flix, by reason of the great heate and feeding of[f] the plantaines and lemmans, which they did devoure immoderately. This baye is the inland[4] of Saint Laurence, and standeth in the height of sixteene degrees.

The 4 day of March we departed thence in the evening, and the first day of June 1602 we discried the land Sumatra. The 3 day we anchored in the roade of Achin, in seaven faddome water. To make any large discourse of matters which passed whilst wee laye in the roade of Achin I omitte, because time will not permitte; but in few wordes you shall understand that heere wee found little pepper, not sufficient to loade the *Ascention*, having in her little above eight score tunnes.[5] We could not, I thinke, in all the East Indiaes have come to a worser place for loading.

The 30 of July the Generall sent away the *Susan* to Priaman to seeke her loading; being an iland[6] which lieth towardes the southwardes eight score leagues, a little distance from Sumatra.

---

[1] A printer's error for 'Saldania.' The date should also be 9, not 19, September.
[2] Should be '29.'   [3] Should be '25' or '26.'
[4] An error for 'in the iland.'
[5] Her cargo appears to have comprised 210,000 lb. of pepper, 1100 lb. of cloves, 6,030 lb. of cinnamon, and 3,420 lb. of gumlac (*The Dawn*, p. 247).
[6] An error.

And about 20 dayes before our comming to[1] Achin, the little pinnace came from her and certified our generall she was almost loden. [So] that we hope she will not be long after us.

The 11 of September we departed out of the roade of Achin for the Straights of Mallaca to seeke purchase: the *Red Dragon*, the *Assention*, the *Hector*, and a Flemming which came into the roade of Achin but 4 dayes before.

The 3 of October, beeing Sunday, about five of the clocke in the afternoone we saw a saile and gave her chase. About nine of the clocke wee fetched her up and hayled her, and found her to be a ship come from Goa and bound for Mallaca, laden with Portingals goodes, as pintados, calicottes and other stuffes great store. A great part of her loading was rice and victualls; and in her about seaven or eight hundred persons, men, women, and children, We had out of her 958 fardils[2], and divers chests, with other things, as canistees[3]. Wee were forced from her by force of weather; beeing put from our anchors.

The 25 day we anchored in the roade of Achin.

The 11 day of November, being Thursday, we waied our anchors and set saile from Achin, viz. the *Dragon*, the *Hector*, and a little pinnace, and the *Ascention*. They did keepe us company till the next day, being bound for Priaman unto the *Susan*, and so from thence they were purposed to goe for Bantam. God grant they may get thither in safety; for then it is not to be doubted they shall get their full lading of pepper, according to their desires, as shall appeare unto you hereafter. So wee, leaving them the day abovesaid, departed for England, to the great rejoycing of us all, that were to goe home into our country after so tedious a pilgrimage.

The 3 day of Februarie, about 10 of the clocke afore noone, wee had sight of the Cape Bona Esperanse; a Frenchman which we left in the roade of Achin being in our company, which came out a day after us; who together had determined to goe for Saldania, if two Flemmings who came then into our company had not altered our determination. For after wee had hailed them, wee understood they were unwilling to put in for that

---

[1] This should be 'from.'
[2] Fardels, i.e. bales.
[3] An error for 'canisters,' meaning baskets.

place, but to goe for Saint Hellena. So we stoode along with them, and altogether arived at Saint Hellena the 21 day of the same month: the *Ascention*, and the Frenchman (called the *Creset*, of Saint Mallowes), the two Dutchmen. The admirall was called the *Amsterdam* (about the burthen of 300 last[1]) and the other called the *Tergow* (of the bignesse of the *Ascention*); which shippe[s?] hath beene almost thirty three monethes from home, and (as they tould us) laden at Patania; most of her lading beeing pepper; and in their way homeward they touched at Banton. The people of Banton were glad when they came thither, because they thought they woulde have laden pepper; having great store lying upon their hands, and being cheaper then ours is. The generall of the Flemmings, whose name is Jacob Cornelius van Neskes [see p. 139], toulde us that there is pepper enough to lade foure or five ships. So that, if the *Dragon* came there in any time convenient, it is not to be doubted but they are uppon the waye homewardes, full laden with pepper &c.

The Frenchmen have determined suddainely to leave our companye to depart homewardes; which hath made mee to trouble you with this discourse, although not so large as willingly I would it were, for the time will not permitte mee to doe otherwise; hoping that it will not bee anything displeasing unto you, having (as I thinke) not before this heard any certainetye of us since our departure out of England; beeing verie willing it should come to your hands before you heare of us any more, the better to prepare your mindes for the setting foorth of a new voyage.

Wee shall bee readye to departe from hence the fifteenth day of this moneth of March. God send us home in safetye.

The names of the chiefe men of note which are dead in the voyage.

There was 182 men which were dead out of our fleete before we parted from our generall. Three of our men dead since.

Men of note which are dead are these: William Leake,

---

[1] One last equals two tons.

purser of this shippe: George Parsons, purser of the *Hector*; Maister Casell[1], Maister Horton, who married Alderman Wattes his daughter. Which foure dyed before we came to Saldania.

Bradbancke, maister of the *Dragon*; Maister Pullion, our preacher; Maister Winter, maisters mate; Maister Napper, maister of the *Hector*. These foure dyed at Antogill.

Maister Brand, captaine of the *Ascension*, going ashore in his boate to the buriall of Maister Winter, very unfortunately, by a shotte that was made by the gunner of the admirall, was slaine; with another called John Parker, who steered the boate.

The 27 of Februarie, being Satterday, Maister Haward, captaine of the *Susan*, dyed in the roade of Achin. Maister Stradling[2], Maister Winchcombe[3], John Hand, James Chamley, dyed in the roade of Achin. Maister Robert Pope, in the Straights of Mallaca. Maister Thomas Saltin[4], in the roade of Achin.

Thus being inforced to cut short, I cease for this present; praying for your prosperities in all your intended enterprises, according to your desires. Fare you well.

From aboard the *Ascension* at S. Hellena, the 9 of March 1602 [1603].

---

[1] An error for (Thomas) Dassell, a factor in the *Hector*.
[2] Percival Stradling, a factor in the *Dragon*.
[3] Philip Winchcombe, a factor assigned to the *Ascension* but afterwards transferred to the *Susan*.
[4] Also called Salter and Saltern; a *factor* in the *Ascension* (see p. 129).

APPENDICES

THE COMPANY'S COMMISSION AND INSTRUCTIONS FOR THE THIRD VOYAGE[1]

WHEAREAS we, the Governour and Companie of the Marchauntes of London Tradinge into the East Indies, have chosen you, Master [James] Lancaster, for the cheefe governour or generall, to governe or rule all such marchauntes, mariners, officers and other Her Majesties subjectes which are ymployed by us or are or shall be shipped in any of the fower shipps by us prepared and set forth for this present intended voiadge towardes the East Indies: and whereas the Queenes Most Excellent Majesty, approveing and allowinge of our choise of you to the said government, and favouring the said enterprize, hath by her gratious letters patentes under the greate seale of England, the better to inable you to keepe your wholle companie in good agreement one towardes another and in obedience and due respect towardes you, geaven you authoritie to chastice and correct such offences as shall aryse in the said voiadge, accordinge as in the said letters patentes att lardge appeareth. Which letters patentes extendinge onlie to the generall governmente of your wholle companie shipped in the said shipps, for their civill behaviour whilest the[y] are abroad in the said voiadge, and not unto the managinge and orderinge of the trade of marchandize, for which the voyadge is principallie appointed and sett forth: wee therfore, by theis our present letters or commission under our comon seale, for the orderinge and disposeinge of all such marchandize, gould, pearle, jewells and other comodities

---

[1] *Miscellaneous Court Book*, in the India Office Records, f. 2. Printed in *The First Letter Book*, p. 4. For another copy see *The Dawn*, p. 132. A few corrections have been made from this version. This commission, 'conceaved by the committies,' was read at a general court on 10 February 1601, and was 'well lykd of and agreed to be written in fowre severall partes, and unto everie part the comon seale of the Companie to be added, to thende that in everie ship one of the said comissions may be kepte in the handes of the principall merchauntes of everie ship' (*ibid*. p. 132).

which are to be bought, bartered, procured, exchandged, or otherwyse obtened in this present voyadge, doe for your direction and remembrance in that behalfe sett downe theis clawses, ordenances, and decrees heerafter followinge: declaringe heerby our purpose and intention how we appointe and ordeine that the traffique of this present voiadge shall be ordered and caried. Which ordenances and decrees wee will and requier you to observe and keepe, and doe give you power and aucthoritie to see the same executed and putt in use accordinglie, viz.

We doe ordeine and decree that all the preparations of moneys, marchandizes, and other provision for the said voyadge, and all comodities, moneys, jewells, and other marchandize retourned in the said voiadge shall be holden, reputed, and accompted, and be carried, managed, ordered, and handled as one entire accompt and comen stocke of adventure; wherein noe private traffique, barter, exchandge, or marchandizeing shall be used, practized, or admitted by any particuler governour, capten, marchaunte, agent, factour, master marriner, officer, or other person whatsoever imployed in the said voiadge or permitted to goe in the same, upon peine of the losse and forfecture, to the use of the generall Companie and adventurers in this voyadge, of all somes of moneys, jewells, wares, goodes or marchandizes which shall be found in the said shipps or ellswere carried forth or retourned home by any private or particuler man, and not conteyned and brought into the generall and comon accompte and joynt adventure of the said voyadge.

And to thend this prejudice of private traffique may the better be avoided, we doe ordeine and appointe that due inquisition be made in all and every the severall shipps of the said voyadge and elswheare, by search of all such chestes, boxes, packes, packettes, bookes, writinges, and other meanes whereby discovery may be made of the breach of this present ordenance.

And we doe in like manner ordeine and decree, for the avoideinge of all unfaithfullnes and deceipte to be used in the said voyadge in the defraudinge of the generall adventure, which is prepared and sett forthe att the great costes and chardges of such as repose their trust and confidence in the officers and mynestors imployed in the said voyadge, that what person soever shall be found unfaithfull and unjust in the said voyadge, by imbecillinge or withdrawinge of any the goodes, wares, marchandizes, jewells, or other commodities whatsoever, either belonging to the adventure sent out or being parcell of the retourne of the same, which was, is, or shall be either prepared, bought, or belonginge to the comon or generall stocke or adventure, that such person shall be barred and excluded to demaunde of the Governour and Companie of the said Merchauntes of London Tradeing into the East Indies any accompte, reckoninge, or payment of any wages, salarye, contract or interteinement for his ymployment in the voyadge, whereunto he was or otherwyse might have beene interessed, yf such offence had not been comitted. And further that every such person soe offendinge shall be prosecuted by the said Governour and Companie of Merchauntes of London Tradinge to theast Indies, accordinge to the qualitie of their offence in that behalfe, by the lawes and statutes of this realme.

And furthermore we doe ordeine that yf, uppon delivery of Her Majesties letters to the princes of those places where our shipps shall arrive, you shall be peaceablie received and enterteyned as marchauntes to comerce and traffique with the people of those countries or places, and be secured and warranted heareafter to frequent and visite those places, then we doe ordeine and decree that you shall select, out of the youngest sorte of our factours and others intertayned by us or voluntarilie suffered to goe in the voyadge, such and soe many of the aptest and towardest of them as you shall thinke meete, and as shall have best approved themselves fit for such an ymployment, to recide and abide in those places where you shalbe soe peaceablie received, yf you may be permitted thereunto; takeinge sufficient and carefull order for the defrayinge and supplyinge of their chardges untill those places shall be hereafter visited with another fleete sent from hence, and leaveing with them such advise and direction for their better information how to carrie themselves in those places as by your good discretion, with the advise of such as you shall conferr thereof, shall be thought meete, and as time and experience of those places shall direct you.

And forasmuch as the daies of mans lyfe are lymitted, and the certentie thereof for their continuance and end onelie knowne unto God, wee, the said Governour and Companie of Marchaunts of London Tradinge to theast Indies doe heereby ordeine and provide that, yf yt shall happen you, the said James Lancaster, to departe this mortall lyfe before the retourne of the said shipps, then, from and after the decease of you, the said James Lancaster, we doe, by this our present comission under our comon seale, constitute and appointe you, Master John Middleton, to be the cheefe governour or generall of the said marchauntes, marinours, officers, and other Her Majesties subjectes by us ymployed or otherwyse shipped in the said voyadge; willing and requiring you and geving you like power and aucthoritie to putt in execution the said ordenances and decrees concerninge the orderinge and disposeinge of the traffique and marchandizeinge of the said voyadge as we have donne to the said James Lancaster. And yf yt shall happen, by Godes appointment, that both you, the said James Lancaster and John Middleton, shall decease in the said voyadge, then we ordeine and appointe the principall and generall governmente of the wholle companie therein ymployed or shipped in this present voyadge unto you, Master William Brund, being alsoe one of our fower principall merchauntes whome we have chosen and interteined for the orderinge and disposeing of the marchandizes and traffique of the said voyadge; requieringe you, yf you shall fortune to survive the said James Lancaster and John Middleton, to observe and keepe the same our ordenances and decrees before mencioned, ordened, and appointed by us for the traffique and marchandizeing of the said viadge; geveing you the like authoritie to execute the same as is formerlie hearein geven to the said James Lancast[er] and John Middleton, or eyther of them. And yf you, the said William Brund, shall fortune to decease in the said voyadge, then we doe appointe the imediate succession and execution of the said chardge and governmente aforesaid unto you, Master John Havarde, one other of our said principall marchauntes; requiringe you to see our ordenances and decrees to be kept and performed; geving unto you the same power and aucthoritie as we have hereby geven to the said James Lancaster, John Middleton, and William Brund, or any of them.

And yf yt should fortune that all the said severall persons ymployed by us as our principall marchauntes in this present voyadge to decease, then we ordeine the wholle government and chardge beforemencioned to be undertaken by one of you foure which are of the second sorte of marchauntes or factours by us ymployed in the said voyadge; the same to be taken and executed successivelie one after another, as any of you shall happen to decease after the said chardge, by the true meaninge hereof, shall be cast upon you; which chardge we doe ordeine shall succeede in this manner, vizt.: first, to our second merchant shipped in the *Redd Dragon*; next, to our second marchaunte or factour shipped in the *Hectour*; thirdlie, to our second marchante or factour shipped in the *Assention*; and lastlie, to our second marchante or factour shipped in the *Suzan*.

And we doe further ordeine that, as we have appointed a succession [of] our principall merchaunte and governour of the wholle companie imployed or shipped in this voiadge, soe we doe order and decree that uppon whomsoever the said government in succession shall fall, by the decease of any the persons beforenamed, that he shall or may shipp or imbarke himselfe in the admirall of our fleete, and injoye and receave such place, cabbin, easment, and comaundment therein as our said generall and principall governour formerlie didd.

And lastlie, wheareas Her Majesty, by her comission under the greate seale, hath onelie appointed the generall government of all her subjectes ymployed in the said voiadge unto the said James Lancaster, without any appointeinge of succession by like warrant to any that is ymployed in the said voiadge,[1] and that yt lyeth not in us to give any warrant for the correction of offences by penall lawes to be executed upon the bodies of any Her Majesties subjectes, we doe in that behalfe, as to men haveinge reason and discretion and to men that feare God, offer unto your good considerations the beneficte of order and peaceable agreemente in matters and enterprises undertaken for a comon good; reposeing in you, our severall marchauntes, and

---

[1] This was doubtless an oversight. In the royal commission for the Second Voyage, the necessary authority was given not only to the general but to his second in command, should he succeed to the principal post.

all you, our severall officers appointed and interteyned in this voiadge, a spetiall hope, trust, and confidence that you will accorde and agree together, and joyne in freindshipp and amytie to doe and execute your uttermoste endevours for the benefitt of the voyadge, without contention, discorde, or emulation to be used amongst you; guideinge yourselves therein by that generall regiment and sea governmente which our English fleetes doe use when they sorte themselves together; haveing a spetiall and due respect to him that is your principall or cape marchaunte. And soe we comend you and your travels to Gods providence, who guide you with His feare and defend you from all daungers.

LETTER FROM LANCASTER *to* MR SKINNER, 1 APRIL 1601[1].

M[aste]r Skynner[2],

My very hartye commendatyons, etc.

I dyd, in my last letter I rote you, make accompt not to have trobled you this yere or too. But the contrarye winds haith so staied me uppon this cost of Englande that I cannot prosede uppon this Est Indea vyage which I have undertaken as y[e]t, but here abyde attendant at Gods plesure, to prosede when wynde and wether shall permyt; which vyage God graunt maye be to His glorye and the benefyt of our countre[y] and commonwelth.

Sir, according to your accostomed order, I praye you pase to the brynger hereof, M[aste]r John or M[aste]r Josefe Jacson, your warraunt for the twelfe pounds tenne shillings dwe to me out of Her Majestyes Excheker at Our Ladye Daye last past; for ether of thes ij men have poure by a letter of atorney from me, for the resete of soche rentes and dettes as are dwe to me in my absence.

[1] From British Museum *Add. MS.* 18738, f. 53. It was printed at p. 58 of the previous edition, but a few corrections have now been made.

[2] Vincent Skinner was one of the officials of the Exchequer, and is mentioned from time to time in the *State Papers, Domestic.*

Thus, hopinge, according to your accostomed kyndnese, you will accomplysh my request herein, I comyt you to the protectyone of the Allmyghtye, who sende you His blessinge and me His grace to serve Him in this my pretended [i.e. intended] vyage.

From the Downes, abord the Red Dragon, this fyrst Apryell, 1601.

Your Worshipes to use,
JAMES LANCASTER.

Addressed: To the Worshipfull M[aste]r Skynner, of Her Magestyes Excheker, deliver this.

THE GRANT OF PRIVILEGES BY THE KING OF ACHIN.

A[1]

I, moste mightie kinge of Dachem and Sumatra, to all persons that shall read this present writeinge [send] greeting.

In token of our espetiall freindshipp, and upon many good considerations us moveing, and cheeflie uppon the contemplasing of the gratious letters received from the most famous Queene of England, we, of our espetiall meere motion, doe signifie and declare to all people that we have intertayned into our freindshipp and holie league our well beloved, the Serinissima Regina de Englaterra: to hold and keepe true and faithfull league with her, according to the comendable course and law of all nations. Unto whose subjectes we wish much felicitie, and therefore doe give and graunte by theis presentes, for us, our heires and

---

[1] From a copy in the *Miscellaneous Court Book* (I.O. Records), f. 27. It has been printed in *The First Letter Book* (p. 69). There is another copy in the *Original Correspondence* (no. 1), printed in *Letters Received*, vol. 1; but this presents no important variation.

It is not the actual grant (for which see the next document) but the draft submitted by Lancaster, as related on p. 96. The demands it contained were agreed to in general, and a promise was given that they should be 'written againe' by a secretary. The result was Document B.

successours, as much as in us lieth, to the said subjectes of the most noble Queene of England, our confederate, and every of them theis articles, grauntes and priviledges expressed and declared.

Firste, we doe give and graunte free licence, aucthoritie, and power to all the people, factours, marchauntes or subjectes of the Queene of England, that they may att all tymes heereafter for ever suerlie and saffelie come into any portes or elswheare into theis our dominiones and kingdome of Sumatra with their shipps, goodes, and marchandize, without any deteinmente or hindraunce to them or to their goodes; and theare to abide, sojourne, buie and sell, barter and exchaunge, according to their owne manner and fashion, with all manner of nations whatsoever, as well as with our owne naturall subjectes, both in spices and all other marchandizes. And soe they may tarrie in our countrie soe long as they will, and goe away when the[y] list, without any ympediment, lett, or hindraunce, paying all such debtes as they shall owe to any of our subjectes within our said dominion.

Furthermore, our will and pleasure is that all such goodes and marchandize as any of the subjectes of the Queene of England shall bringe into this our kingdome, or any the partes thereof, shall be free of all custome or payment whatsoever; as well for that which shall be brought into theis our dominions as for all manner of marchandize they shall transporte out of the same for any forreine parte whatsoever.

Item, yf any of their shipps in tempest of weather shall be in daunger to be lost and perishe, and thereupon shall stande in neede of our helpe, wee will and comaund that our vessells with all speede doe helpe and succour them, to save the same shipps and goodes; and what may be saved to retourne to the said marchauntes or their assignes, they paying resonable consideration for their travell.

Item, yf any Englisheman shall make his will and testamente, to whomesoever by the same will he shall give his goodes, the partie shall have them accordinglie. And yf he die intestate, he to whome the cheefe factour or governour shall saie the goodes of the dead to belonge, he shall posses the same.

Item, that every bargaine made by the said marchauntes with any manner of person for any kinde of marchandize shall be firme and staple, and that noe man of either partie may shrinke or goe backe from the same. And yt shall be lawfull for them to goe before any of our justices and to register the same in a booke, according to the tenour thereof. Yf any controversie shall aryse, present justice to be done to both parties. And when they have sold any of their wares to our subjectes or any other, they shall not retourne the said wares upon the marchauntes handes, but paie for them, or ells they shall have present justice.

Item, yf any English marchaunte, factour, or servant shall offend the agent or cheefe governour of the factorie, yt shall be lawfull for the said governour to doe justice upon the said partie, or to send him home into England, att his pleasuer. And further we graunte unto the said governour power and aucthoritie to end any controversie that shall aryse betweene them, and to doe justice accordinge to their owne lawes and customes.

Item, we doe graunte the said marchauntes and to their successours that, yf any of them or of their servantes shall be wounded or be slaine in any parte or place of our dominion, then, information thereof being geven, we, our justices, and other officers will execute due correction and punishment without delaie, accordinge to the cause of the offence, soe that yt shall be an example to all others not to offend in the like. And yf it shall happen the factors, servauntes, or mynisters of the said marchauntes to trespasse or offend, whereby they or any of them shall incurr the daunger of death or of punishment, that then the goodes, wares, or marchandizes of their seniours[1] shall not therefore be forfected, confiscate, seazed upon, nor spoyled by us, our heires or successours, or by any of our officers, ministers, or subjectes, but shall remaine franke and free, as dischardged of all punishment and losse.

Item, we doe promyse the foresaid marchauntes, graunting yt for ever for us and our heires, that, yf any shall bringe any manner of goodes or marchandize meete for treasurie, that we will not cause anie staie or arrest to be made of their said goodes or marchaundize to us or for our uses, without present content

---

[1] 'Signiors' (*O.C.* 1).

to be made by our threasurer at such reasonable prises as the marchauntes could sell them for ready money; and that noe price or valuation shalbe set upon their goodes or marchandizes by us or any officers of ours.

Item, we of our goodnes have graunted to the said English marchauntes, their successours, servauntes, and deputies that doe or shall remayne in any parte of this our kingdome of Sumatra, whether yt be in Dachem or any other parte of our dominion, freelie to keepe their owne lawe, and in any wyse none of ours to force them to our lawe or faith against their wills.

Item, yf any man shall saie that theis, being Christians, have spoken anythinge to the derogation of our holie faith and religion, and have slaundered the same, in this matter, as well as in all others, there shall noe false witnes in any case be admitted.

Last of all, to thintent that this league with Her Majestie, and the aforesaid grauntes and priviledges with her subjectes, may the better be observed and inviolablie be performed, we, by the grace of God greate kinge of Dachem and Sumatra, for us, our heires and successors, doe promyse by our princelie word instead of an oath, inviolablie to maintaine and preserve, and will cause to be inviolablie kept, preserved, and mayntayned frome tyme to tyme and att all tymes heereafter. And for the more ratification we comaund all our captaines, judges, customers, governours, and servauntes, wheresoever theis letters or priviledges shall be seene, throughout all our dominions, that they be obeyed in all pointes accordinglie. As longe as the Queene of England of her parte shall duelie keepe and observe this league and holie peace expressed in this priviledge with us and our subjectes, we alsoe of our royall parte doe chardge and comaund the same soe longe to be strayghtlie kept and observed. And the contrarie to this divyne league and priviledge lett noe man presume to doe or saie anythinge.

B[1]

I am the reigning sovereign of these [countries] below the wind[2], holding the throne of the kingdom of Acheen and Sumatra and all the countries subject to Acheen. All ye who scan this letter shall [do so] with good will and peace, and listen to the words which it contains and understand them all.

It has been my pleasure to declare for your information as follows:—I have made friends with the king [sic] of England, and ye shall be friends with all the king of England's people, as ye are friends with all the rest of mankind in the world; and ye shall do them good, as ye do good to the rest of men. For I do good to them, and I receive them into my country and receive their gifts, and I look upon them favourably, for that I desire mutual affection with the king of England; and for that I desire to do good to all his people, I am treating well those who have now come, and [shall do so to] those who shall come hereafter. I have pledged my faith to those who come to Acheen and Sumatra, so that they shall no longer be afraid for their ships and their possessions and all the valuables which they bring, and they shall not be afraid or suspicious of me. And as for all of you my people, when they shall bring any valuables from their country to this country of mine, ye shall buy and sell with them, and shall exchange your valuables for any valuables of theirs; even as ye trade and exchange with other people by their charters [sic] from all the foreigners for trading and buying pepper and buying other valuables, so shall ye trade with the English people and shall buy and sell.

---

[1] This appears to be a copy of the grant actually made by the king. What became of the original is not known. According to the Court Minutes of 26 Feb. 1614, it was then supposed to be in the custody of Lancaster, who was to be asked for it; but there is no further reference to the matter. A copy, however, was discovered in the Bodleian (*Douce MSS*. Or. e. 5) by the Rev. W. G. Shellabear, who published, in the article referred to on p. 100, a facsimile, the Malay text, and an English translation, which is reproduced above, with the kind permission of the author. There is no date; but the document is on the same sheet as the fragment of a copy of the royal letter mentioned on p. 109, and this by itself would point to the conclusion that the grant is the one made to Lancaster, though his name does not occur in it.

[2] Dr Blagden has informed me that this expression means 'South-Eastern Asia, as contrasted with Arabia and Persia. The reference is to the strong S.W. monsoon which prevails in spring and summer; Burma, Malaya, and the Dutch East Indies are "below," Arabia and Persia are "above" the wind.'

And the English people, if they desire protection in my country, whatever their desire may be, I approve of it. And if they desire to sail away from my country, I approve; let no one forbid them thus to sail. But if anyone has any claim upon them, or if they are indebted to anyone, let them not sail until they have paid or until the judge has decided their cases; and when their cases are decided, they may sail. Now as for this order which I command, for trading and buying and selling with the valuables which they have brought to my country, let them no longer fear or suspect. And ye shall not take tithes[1] from any of the merchants who are in their ships, nor from any of the English people.

And as for all the English people who come to my country and anchor their ships in the sea of Acheen and in Sumatra and in the countries subject to Acheen, if a storm comes down upon their ships and they are afraid that their ships will be wrecked for the violence of the storm, should they desire to discharge all the ships' cargo, and request assistance from you, asking for small vessels and sampans[2] to discharge all the valuables in the ships which are about to be wrecked for the violence of the storm, ye shall assist them to discharge their valuables as far as possible. And when their valuables reach the shore, ye shall restore the valuables to those that own them. If they voluntarily give you anything due to you for discharging the above-mentioned valuables, ye shall receive it.

And if anyone of the English people shall die, and while he is sick unto death shall give an order to anyone to send his possessions and the possessions of the people whom [which?] he has brought, and shall order them to be delivered to his relatives and to the owners of the possessions, ye shall hold his will valid. And if anyone of the English people shall die[3], his property shall go to some English merchant, or to some other merchant; the property shall be determined as belonging to the person, his associate in trade and buying and selling; ye shall give judgment according to the law of the country.

And if any Englishman go to law, their charges being one against the other or against some other person, ye shall give judgment according to the laws of the people of the country.

---

[1] Customs dues.   [2] Boats.   [3] 'Die intestate' seems to be meant.

INSTRUCTIONS LEFT AT BANTAM BY LANCASTER[1].

A Remembrance for Master Keche, Master of the Pinnace.

Firste, as soone as I am gone, you shall procure from the marchauntes resident heare your ladeing of such and soe many goodes as they shall appointe you, and by all meanes, after you have taken them in, procure such provisions that they may be kept drie, for a little wett bringeth in theis goodes much damadge. I doubt not you will be carefull in this pointe.

Your ladeing being received, you are to take in Master Towerson, Thomas Tudd, William Chase, and Thomas Dobson; and then sale directlie for the iland of Banda, not touching in any place by the waie without greate cause. And wheresoever you be come, trust none of the Indians, for their bodies and soules be whollie treason, and yt will be very daungerous to touch in any unknowne place; therefore avoied yt.

When God shall send you to Banda and [you] have delivered your marchandizes, you maie laie upp your shipp, and you and your men lie att the marchauntes howse and assist them in their busines all you cann. But I thinke yt good to looke to your shipp, that she be not lost, but husband her, soe that, yf occasion should be proffered by any enymies aland, you maie have some helpe by her by the sea.

As my trust is in you, assist the marchauntes and give them all helpe, for I have placed you in the 4th place with them. In this pointe be verie carefull, as I hope you will be. And hereby I doe acknowledge to have consorted[2] with you from the 1 of Febr[uary] 1602 [1603], for as longe as you shall be in the marchauntes service, for 8*li*. the monneth.

Thus God send His blessinge upon you in all your affaires. In Bantam, this 12 of Febr[uary] 1602 [1603].

---

[1] *Miscellaneous Court Book* (I.O. Records), f. 12. Printed in *The First Letter Book*, p. 33.   [2] Agreed.

A Remembraunce for Master Starkie, Thomas Morgan, and Master Scott.

As sone as our shipps be dispatched from hence, with as much convenient speede as may be made I would have you to dispatch the pinnace for the Moloccos to the iland of Banda; and lade in her of all sortes of comodities as you can learne to be vented there. Onelie keepe your narrowe and Mallacoe fard[el]es to furnish you here, as your most staple comodities to trust unto. You may lade in her some 60 fardells; the most of blewes and checkered stuffes; some fine pinthadoes and some store of corse; some of your Sian[1] rowles, but not many; and some white cloth and some browne, and some of your stuffes that be checkered. In all theis thinges use your good judgmentes; onelie lett them be well furnished.

Alsoe lade in her 500 r[ials] of 8 att the least; for yt may chaunce they maie have neede to use some money.

The next busines that most importeth is your dispatch of your howse. Yf you could sett forward the one in dispatching the other, yt would doe very well. Onelie have this reguard in the building thies[2] yt be as free from fire as chardge will make yt.

For the sales of your comodities, you must use your owne discretions; alwaies holdinge this in mynde, the tyme of the comeing of our shipps; and procure 20,000 bagges of pepper (as neere as you cann) to be in readynes agay[n]st their comeing. And as much money as will dispatch them here of chardges for this next accompte I will not have willinglie to be mingled with any other. If yt please God to send me home, I will wryte to you att lardge about this pointe, for yt will importe us that are ymployed in this busines. Myne opinion is to putt yourselves out of comodities as soone as you cann and putt yourselves into peppers, for in soe doinge you may chaunce to benefitt the Company in the defraying your chardges, for they shall be at above 850*li.* the yeare chardge in theis partes.

When you have bought any store of pepper, yf the Holland shipps come and the prise ryse, you may take the benefitt and

---

[1] This is really more correct than the usual 'Siam,' as the name was originally a form of 'Shan.'   [2] 'That' appears to be intended.

sell to the Companies most proffitt; onelie, have a reguard not to be unfurnished at the expectation of our shippinge. You have the benefitt of 2 harvestes; I doubt not but you shall furnish the next shipps in good sorte.

Alsoe, I doe appointe you, Master William Starkey, to be head and cheefe commander over all in this place; but to take the councell and advise of Thomas Morgan and Master Scott in all matters, that the Companie may be the better assured of all thinges that passeth.

And yf yt please God [to lay His hand] upon you, Master Starkey, and to take you out of this world, I would have you to give over your chardge and accomptes to Thomas Morgan. And yf you, Thomas Morgan, die, then to Master Scott[1]. And yf you, Master Scott, then to whom you shall thinke moste meete; alwaies leaveing your things in the best manner you cann, and the playnest.

For such wages as shall be due to men that be here, you may allowe yt by the yeare or halfe yeare, as you see mens necessities. Allwaies have reguard that you be not necessited for want of money; lett not to have 1000 r[ials] of 8 at the least att all tymes by you.

And for the boyes, lett them not waunt apparrell and necessaries that apperteyne unto them, for soe they shall doe you better service. Lett the cookes boye be bound for 7 yeares; and to have the freedome of London in his tyme, accompte the 2 yeares that he hath served in our shippe.

Thus I end, desiering you to meete together in the morninges and eveninges in prayer. God, whom yee serve, shall the better blesse you in all your affaires. Thus I wish His blessing to be alwaies upon you, to preserve and keepe you, and to putt His feare in your hartes. Amen.

Forget not to husband your comodities, that there be nothinge spoyled nor come to decaye under your handes.

---

[1] Starkie died on 30 June 1603. Morgan had died on 26 April, and so Edmund Scott took charge of the factory. He returned to England with Middleton's fleet, and wrote an account of his experiences which was printed in 1606. Extracts from it were given by Purchas.

A Remembraunce for Thomas Tudd[1], Gabriell Towerson, William Chasse[2], and Thomas Dobson[3].

As soone as the pynnace is laden by the marchauntes resident here in Bantam, of such and soe many fardells of cloothes and pynthados as they shall appointe, you shall imbarke yourselves in her and, by the helpe of Master Ketch and his company, saile directlie with your said goodes for Banda, unlesse you touch in some place necessarie for your refreshing. And make no longe staye, and have espetiall care of your saffetie and how you putt any man aland in any place, for the people in those partes, their wholle bodyes and mindes be all treason; and therefore open your eyes in this behalfe.

And when God shall send you to Banda, take a howse or howses for your busines, as you shall thinke most fitt for the Companies best proffitt, and make sale of your comodities, alwaies advaunceing the price the best you may.

In your provision you shall make in nutmegges and maces, have you a greate care to receive such as be good, for the smallest and rotten nuttmegges be worth nothinge at home; soe that their fraight and principall will be lost. Of maces the fayrest and best will be soonest sould, and to best rekoninges.

Alsoe, be carefull to gett together all the cloves you can, and use all diligence to procure some 60 or 80 tonns att the least, and the rest of nutmegges and maces. All theis thinges must be carefullie husbanded; which you must have a spetiall reguard unto.

I make accompt the Companie will fraight some 2 shipps for that place of the burthen of 600 tonns, more or lesse; and therefore have a care to get their ladinge in tyme and aforehand, that it may be redie by such tyme as the shipps be with you (which I hope will be Michaellmas come twelvemonneth or before). Yt doth greatlie ymporte you to be carefull and procure ladinge, for this is your whole busines there, and therefore ar you sent.

---

[1] He came out in the *Hector* as a factor 'of the fourth sort.' He died at Bantam on 14 April 1604.
[2] He died in 1603, while on the voyage to Banda in the pinnace.
[3] Died, 17 July 1603.

Alsoe, I would have you to agree together loveinglie, like sober men; for your owne discordes, yf you suppress them not, will be to the marchauntes greate losse and hindrance and to your owne undoing. Therefore governe yourselves soe that there be noe brabbles amonge you for any cause.

I have appointed Master Ketch to be an assistant to you in your busines; and use him as one of yourselves, ymploying him in your busines as you shall have most neede. If you send him to any place, lett yt not be farr of[f], and without daunger of enymies; for I would not have him farr from you, whatsoever should befall; neither will I have that he putt himselfe in any daunger.

Alsoe, I doe appointe Thomas Tudd to be cheef factor and principall, and the rest to be at his comaund in this busines. Next him I appointe Gabriell Towerson, and next Gabriell Towerson William Chasse, and nex[t] William Chasse Thomas Dobson. And you, Thomas Tudd, I would have you to take councell of the rest in all this busines, that every mans advise may be geven, to the benefitt of the voyadge.

Alsoe, my will is that, yf yt please God to call you, Thomas Tudd, out of this world, then comitt the busines and your place to Master Towerson. And yf you, Gabriell Towerson, die, comitt your place to William Chasse. And yf yt fortune you, William Chasse, to die, comitt the factory to Master Ketch, master of the pinnace. And yf he doe chaunce to die, lett him comitt yt to Thomas Dobson.

Alsoe, I have geven order to the factours heare to supplie you with 500 royalls of 8, because we knowe not what neede you may have. And have a care to your money, and dispose yt not till greate occasion serve.

And for the paying of your companie their wages, doe yt sparinglie, and remitt soe much as you cann till their retourne. But when necessitie requireth, rather doe yt in comoditie then money, yf you in your discretions see such occasion.

I would have you to paie noe wages to Thomas the barber, and fitt him with clothes meete, not to exceede in any thinge, for he is another mans prentise, and seeketh onelie to wast his masters.

Alsoe, I would have you, Thomas Tudd, to keepe the accomptes of all such busines as shall passe.

Per me, Thomas Tudd.
Per [me], Gabriell Towerson.
Per [me], William Chasse[1].

LANCASTER'S HINTS FOR A VOYAGE TO THE EAST[2]

Firste, yf yt please God to send your shipps to the Cape Bona Speranza in time, that is, by the first of June, little more or lesse, and your people standing in health, myne opinion is that you stay not att Saldania to water or refresh, but rather hould on your course directlie for St. Lawrence, and touch att the ryver of St. Augustine[3]; for theare (as I have beene credibilie informed) is as good meanes of refreshing as is att Saldania. This course will advantage you much in your navigation to the coaste of the India; beside the avoydeinge of fowle whether, that in that monneth comonlie is in Saldania.

Haveing theare refreshed, have a greate care of the flattes of the ilandes of Judea[4], for many shipps have been lost theare; for the currant setteth from the coaste of St. Lawrence right upon them, soe that, yf you be not very carefull to looke out night and daye, you shall feele them before you see them. Therefore, have a diligent care of this pointe; for I myselfe (haveing twoe very

---

[1] These signatures were doubtless affixed to Lancaster's copy, as acknowledgments that those concerned had read and noted the contents.

[2] *Miscellaneous Court Book* (I.O. Records), f. 53. Printed in *The First Letter Book*, p. 136. These notes, prepared for the guidance of the Third Voyage in 1607 under William Keeling, are entered also upon the *Court Minutes* of 13 February of that year.

[3] St Augustine's Bay, on the south-west coast of Madagascar, in lat. 23° 28′. Keeling's ships called there accordingly, and it became a favourite stopping place for subsequent fleets.

[4] The *Bassas da India*, or Europa Shoals, in about lat. 21° 30′ S. The Portuguese called them the *Baixos da Judia* (rendered by the translator of Linschoten (vol. II, p. 199) 'Judas banks,' though in another place (vol. I, p. 22) he translates it as 'the flattes of the Jewes'); but the early English cartographers copied *Judia* as *India*, and this version has persisted in our maps.

sufficient masters in my shipp) was by the said currant much deceived; but that was in the monneth of September[1].

If by any misfortune you have further neede of refreshing, you shall fynde yt att the ilandes of Comora[2]. But looke to yourselves; for, after their tournes are served of such thinges as they need, they will imploye all their wittes to betray you in what they cann. Therefore trust noe men aland; for the Fleminges have lost men t[h]rice in theis ilaundes, and I myselfe once.

If the tyme soe serve you that you cann gett into Indea by the 5th of Julie, you may (as you see cause) first touche in the mouth of the Redd Sea; for although you make your staye there till the middest of October, yett you shall have wyndes to bring you to Indea; but not longe after. But yf yt soe fall out that you see yt will be the midst of August or thereaboutes ere you shall gett into the Redd Sea, then I would take my course directlie for Cambaia and follow my busines there; for by the 20th of December, or prime of Januarie att the furthest, yf you settle not your trade theare, the wyndes growe fayre to goe for the Redd Sea; whither at that tyme yf you take your course, you shall have 3 monnethes to staye, to see what you cann doe in setlinge your trades. And aboute Aprill the west and norwest wyndes begynning to blowe, soe that you may retourne agayne for the coast of Indea. But thinke not to touch upon the coast, for yt is exceeding daungerous at that tyme of the yeare, and from thence till August, and therefore come not neare yt, for till August yt is fowle weather and verie thicke and stormye upon the coaste of Indea, and the wyndes sett right upon the coaste, May, June, and Julie. But theis wyndes will carrie you to Bantam; but take not too high or sowtherlie a course, for then you will hem [out] of the way of the westerne monsond, that should helpe you in this navigation. But comeing to Bantam before September, you cannot goe for the Molloccos, for the westerne monsonde reacheth but to Bantam. Therefore, as you see cause, you may touch att Pryamon, where is good pepper reasonable good cheepe, and a good ayre.

Note that, yf you touch not upon the coaste of Indea before the 5th of November, you cannot doe yt till August or September come twelve monneth.

[1] During his first voyage (see p. 5).   [2] 'Comoza' in the MS.

INDEX

Achin, xvi, xxvi, 90, 129, 146; unimportant as a trading centre, xxix, xxxi, 100, 109, 133, 136, 145; Lancaster's proceedings at, xxx, 90–106, 108–9, 129–34, 135–7; various nationalities at, 90–1; 'Bishop' of, 96; a notable port, 98; cock-fighting at, 99; scarcity and dearness of pepper at, 100, 132, 134, 145; Portuguese envoy at, 100, 105, 131; intrigues of the Portuguese at, 101–5; French at, 133–4; Dutch at, 90, 91, 129, 130, 134; canoes at, 129; fires at, 133; English factory house at, 133; funeral customs at, 135; punishments at, 135; character of inhabitants of, 136; currency at, 136; price of provisions at, 136; unhealthiness of, 136

Achin, King of, letter from Queen Elizabeth to, xxvii, 91, 92, 93, 94–6, 129–30; presents to, xxvii, 92–3, 108–9, 130; foreigners seeking the protection of, xxvii, 90; Lancaster's friendly relations with, xxvii, xxx, 90–105, 108–12, 129–33; privileges granted to the English by, xxix, 96, 98–9, 132, 155–60; his dislike of the Portuguese, xxix, 101, 103–6, 132; his letter to Queen Elizabeth, xxx, 108, 109–12; his permit to Henry Middleton, 100 n.; his name, 92 n.; his appearance, 92 n.; his son, 132; his ordnance, 135

Adams, Oliver, 142
Addy, John, *see* Awdley, Capt. John
Agalega (Galega) Island, xxvii, 86 n.; description, 86
Agoada de S. Bras, *see* Mossel Bay
Albacores, 15, 138
Algoa Bay, 16
Ali-uddin Riāyat Shāh, Sultan of Achin, *see* Achin, King of
Allegranza Island, 77
Allen, Michael, 143
Allin, William, 141

Almeira, Francisco de, 3 n.
Ambergris, 14, 128
Amsterdam, the, 139 n., 147
Andavaka, Cape, 77 n.
Andrews, Christopher, 143
Andrews, Richard, 142
Angasija, *see* Great Comoro Island
Antongil Bay, xxvii, 82, 83, 84, 86 n., 145
Antonio, Don (Prior), xiv, 7
Appollow, Thomas, 142
Aqua vitae, 15
Arden, Ralph, 141
Arnold, —, surgeon, death of, 8
Arrack, 13 n., 93, 131
Ascension, the, xxv, xxxiii, 75, 76, 145; her captain killed, 85, 86, 126, 148; her lading, 105, 109, 145 n.; her master-gunner, 122; her surgeon, 125; her master, 126; her purser, 144 n.; returns to England, xxx, xxxii, 112, 137, 146, 153; at St Helena, 147; letter written on board of, 144–8; deaths in, 143; wrecked, 129 n.
Ascension Island, 120, 140
Ashplie, Robert, 142
Aspley, William, 121, 144
Awdley, Captain John, commands the *Virgin,* 32, 58; at Recife, 39, 48
Azores, the, 84 n., 120 n., 140 n.

Badby, John, 143
Baddiford, Edward, 142
Bahama Islands, 18
Bahar, content of a, 132
Bamboo, a liquid measure, 136
Banda, Lancaster's 'Instructions' for a trading voyage to, 161, 162, 164–6
Bandar, harbour, 111 n.
Bandolier, 46
'Banks', 36
Banning, Paul, 31, 32 n., 57
Bantam, 84 n., 108, 167; Dutch at, xxix; commercial importance of, xxx, xxxi, 109, 137; English factory settled at, xxxi, 115, 162; pestilential climate of, xxxi, 115;

INDEX

Bantam (*continued*)
the *Dragon* and *Hector* at, 113, 146; price of pepper at, 114, 147, 162; 'Instructions' left by Lancaster at, 161–6

Bantam, King of, xxx; letters and presents interchanged with, xxxi, 113–16; Lancaster's reception by, 113–14; his Regent, 114; trading agreement between the English and, xxxi, 114

Barbotiere, Monsieur de, relations between Lancaster and, 18, 26–8; his ship wrecked, 28; at Newfoundland, 30

Barker, Edmund, 11, 12, 16, 27, 39; narrative of, 1–21; Lancaster's lieutenant, 1; marooned at Mona, xvii, 19–20; rescued, 20; returns to England, xvii, 21; commands the *Solomon*, xix, 31, 34; killed, xxii, 48, 68, 74; verses in commemoration of, 70–1

Barker, John, 48; killed, 49
Barker, William, 142
Barley, W., 52
Barret, William, 142
Basingstoke, xiii; bequests, to, xxxv
Bassas da India, 5 n., 166 n.
Batman, Robert, 143
Bear, the, 4 n.
Beberibe, river, xx, 40 n.
Bedwell, the Rev. William, 111
Bengal, 90; goods brought from, 15
Bennet, Peter, 142
Bermudas, the, xvii, 18, 22, 28; Henry May wrecked off, xviii, 28–9; description, 29–30
Berry, Myles, 142
Betty, William, 143
Bezoar stones, 116
Bilbao, 35 n.
Biscay, province, 35 n.
Bishop, John, 143
'**Biskaine**', 35
'**Bitter**', 45
Blackwall, 32, 51, 58
Blanco, Cape, xix, 1, 33, 34, 35, 58, 59, 60
Boca de Dragone, *see* Serpent's Mouth
Bonitos, 9, 15, 138
Boreman, —, 57; owner of the *Solomon,* 58

Boreman, Simon, 58
Bowyer, Richard, 143
Brand, William, *see* Brund, Captain William
Brava Island, 36, 61
Brazil, *see* Pernambuco
Brazil-wood, 31, 32 n.
Brigges, Henry, 142
Broadebent, William (Brodbancke), master of the *Dragon,* 126, 142, 148
Browne, John, 143
Brund (Brand), Captain William, commands the *Ascension,* xxvi, 76; killed, xxvii, 85, 86, 126, 143, 148; linguistic attainments of, 76 n.; to succeed Lancaster and Middleton, 152
Buona Speransa, Cape of, *see* Cape of Good Hope
Burche, Robert, 142
Burdall, Stephen, 142
Burrice, Richard, 143
Burrowes, William (2), 142

Cadde, Christopher, 142
Caen, 26
Caicos Islands, 21
Calenture, 126
Calico, 14, 15, 23, 24, 162; seized in a Portuguese ship, 107, 135, 146
Calicut, 23, 90
Camlet, 13
Canary Islands, xix, 22, 33, 58, 77, 121
'**Can-hook**', 59
'**Canisters**', baskets, 146
'**Cannon-perer**', 52 n.
'**Canter**', 60
Cape Breton Island, 30 n.
Cape of Good Hope, the, *passim*; trade by barter with natives at, 3, 22, 80–1, 122–3, 145; inhabitants of, 3, 81, 123; fat-tailed sheep at, 3, 123; natural productions of, 3–4, 81, 123; Lancaster's measures of defence at, 80; *see also* Table Bay
Cape Verd Islands, xix, 1, 32 n., 34
Capibaribe, river, xx
Caravel, a Portuguese, captured, 2
Carricke, Edward, 143
Cash, value of a, 136
Casualties, in the first voyage, 2, 4, 5, 10, 23; in the second voyage, 49,

INDEX

51, 68, 70; in the third voyage, 79, 81, 85, 86, 115, 119, 121, 122, 124, 125, 126, 134, 136, 137, 138, 140-3, 147-8
Cavendish, Thomas, xi, 72
Caverly (? Chamley), James, 142
Cerne, Cirne, *see* Mauritius
Ceylon, xvi, 9, 14, 24, 133 n.
Chagos Archipelago, xxvii, 87 n., 128 n.
Chamley, James, 148
'**Champion**', 30
Chase, William, 161, 166; Lancaster's 'Instructions' to, 164-6; death of, 164 n.
Children, Adam, 142
Chudleigh, John, 17
Church, John, 143
Cinnamon water, 135
Clarkson, John, 142
Cloudie Islands, 19
'**Cloy**', 68
Cobbe, Walter, 142
Cock, Abraham, 41, 65; notice of, 41 n.
Cock-fighting, at Achin, 99, 137
Cocklim, Thomas, 143
Cole, Alexander, 119, 126; drowned, 119 n.
Coman, John, 142
Comorin, Cape, xv, 1, 8, 9, 10
Comoro Islands, xv, 1, 23, 167; inhabitants, 5, 23
'**Compeers**', 72
Consent, the, xviii, xix, 31, 57, 100 n.; fire on board of, 51, 70
Cony Island, *see* Dassen Island
Cooper, Robert, 143
Copang, *see* Kupang
Corbin, the, wrecked, xxviii, 133 n., 134
Cornelison, Martin, 142
Correntes, Cape, xv, 4
Corvo, 140
Cotton, Captain Randolph, xix, xxiii; commands troops at Pernambuco, xxi; killed, xxii, 49, 68; verses in memory of, 70-1; eulogy of, 72-4
Cotton cloth, *see* Calico
Counters, 128
Crippin, Gilbert, 143
Croissant, the, xxviii, 133 n., 138 n., 140 n., 147

Cuba, 18
Cumberland, Earl of, xxv, 41 n.; Twelfth Voyage of, xxiv
'**Cumray**', 68 n.

'**Dagges**', 92
Dame, Robert, 142
Dartmouth, xix, xxvi, 32, 58, 72, 76, 121, 144
Dassell, Thomas, 142, 148
Dassen Island, 124 n.
Daulat, 130
Daurell, Thomas, 143
Davies, Edmund, 141
Davis, John, of Limehouse, xxvi n., 80 n., 86 n., 87 n.
Davis, John, of Sandridge, xxvi, 73, 90 n., 92 n., 100
De la Bardelière, Michel Frotet, Sieur, 133 n., 134; death of, 134 n.
Deaths in the three voyages, *see* Casualties
Demi-culverin, 37
Dergoes, the, 139 n., 147
Dieppe, xvii, 20, 21, 41, 51
'**Disbocking**', 21
Dobson, Thomas, 161; Lancaster's 'Instructions' to, 164-6; death of, 164 n.
Dog, the, 6 n.
Dolphins, 9, 138
Double, Robert, 143
Downs, the, xxxii, 50, 69, 76, 120, 141, 155
Dragon, the, xxv, xxvi, xxx, 75, 76, 153, 155; sails to Priaman, xxx, 112, 146; at Bantam, 113, 146; her master, 148; damaged by a storm, xxxvi, xxxvii, 116-18; deaths in, 141-2; arrives in England, 120
Drake, Sir Francis, xi, 51 n.
Dudley, Sir Robert, xxiv, 4 n.
Duke, John, 142
Dutch, the, ships of, met with, xx, 36, 37, 139; co-operate with the English, 40, 44, 49, 63, 65, 105, 134; in the fight at Recife, 69; at Bantam, xxiv; at Achin, xxviii, 90, 91, 129, 130; information left by, at Madagascar, 84
Dysentery, 16, 69, 86, 126

INDEX

Earle, John, 143
East India Company, the, foundation of, xi; commission from, to Lancaster, 149–54; results of Lancaster's voyages for, xviii, xxii, xxxii
Edward Bonaventure, the, 4, 22, 23; struck by lightning, xv, 4–5; off Zanzibar, 6–8; off Malacca, 12; laden with prize goods, 12; parts company with the *Merchant Royal,* 27; return voyage of, xvi, 28; casualties in, 2, 4, 5, 10, 23; captured, xvii, 20
Egleston, Richard, 143
Elephants, in Achin, 136; fighting of, 137
Elizabeth, Queen, petitions to, xii, xxiv; charter granted by, xxv; her letters and presents to the Kings of Achin and Bantam, xxvii, xxxi, 76, 91, 92, 93–6, 113, 129, 151; the King of Achin's letter and presents to, xxx, 108, 109–12; her royal commission for the Second Voyage, 76, 153 n.; her letters patent for Lancaster's Third Voyage, 149; her death, xxxii
Endick, John, 142
'Ensign', 37
Europa Shoals, *see Bassas da India*
Everet, Thomas, 143
Exame, Richard, 142
Expedition, the, 100 n.

Faircliffe, Edmund, 142
'Falcon', 47
Falmouth, 30
Fardels, bales, 146, 162
Fare, John, 143
Faux Cap, 82 n.
Felix, Monsieur, 20
'Fetches', 43
Fishaker, John, 142
'Fisht', 8, 59
Flores Island, 140
Florida, Cape, 18
Floud, Marcus, 143
Flux, *see Dysentery*
Fogo Island, 120
Fortunate Islands, *see Canary Islands*
Foster, John, 143
'Fourteen score', 39

Fousticke, John, 143
Foxcroft, Captain Samuel, xii, 22
'Frame', 73
Franke, Nicholas, 142
French, the, ships of, met with, xvii, xxi, 20, 27, 146–7; their expeditions to the East, xxiv; in Achin, xxviii; relations between Lancaster and captains of merchant vessels, xvii, xxi, 21, 26, 27, 41, 64, 65, 69
Frotet, Michel, *see* De la Bardelière, Michel Frotet, Sieur
Fuerteventura Island, 77
Fullar, James, 142
'Furniture', 42

Galega Island, *see* Agalega
Gamryn (Gamram), Nathaniel, 129
Gaufe, Jeremy, 142
Gift, the, xxv, 75, 78; dismantled and abandoned, 78, 122, 145
Goa, xvi, 8, 12, 146
Gold, from Priaman, 113
Golding, Rainold, death of, 10
Gomes, Pulo, xvi, 1, 10
Gonave Island, 26, 28
Goulding, John, 143
Goulding, Philip, 142
Gracechurch Street, 52
Grampus, 124
Grand Canary Island, 77
Grave, Philip de, *see* Grove, Philip
Great, Henry, 142
Great Comoro Island, 5; ruler of, 6; English murdered at, 6
Griffith, John, 143
Grove, Philip, 129, 133 n.
Guest, the, *see Gift,* the
Guinea, coast, 8, 77, 120
Gujarat, 90

Hakluyt, Richard, his *Principall Navigations,* xxiii, 1 n., 22 n., 32 n.
Hall, John, 9 n.; death of, 10
Hall, William, 142
Hambling, William, 143
Hammont, Morrice, 142
Hamond, Richard, 143
Hampton, John, 143
Hand (? Hankin), John, 148
Hankin, John, 142
Hankin, Roger, 126

INDEX

Harket, John, 141
Harmensz, Wolphert, 84 n.
Harrice (? Harris), John, 142
Harris, John, 142
Haward, William, 143
Hawkins, Sir John, 51 n.
Hayward (Havard), Captain John, commands the *Susan*, xxvi, 76, 125, 129; to succeed to the command of the fleet, 152; death of, 133, 143, 148
Hector, the, *passim*; her master, 148; her purser, 148; attacks a Portuguese ship, 106–7, 134–5, 146; sails to Priaman, xxx, 112, 146; at Bantam, 113; stands by the *Dragon*, xxxi, xxxii, 117, 118, 119; deaths in, 142
Heemskerck, Jacob van, 84 n.
Highlord, Edward, 144 n.
Hill, Robert, 142
Hills, Rowland, 142
Holliday, John, 142
Holt, Edward, 142
Hope, John, 142
Hopgood, —, xxxv
Horton, Richard, 143; his wife, 148
Houtman, Cornelisz, xxiv, xxvi, xxviii, 80 n., 90 n.
'Hoyting', 120
Humber, John, 142

Ifrangi, 110 n.
Indeck, John, 126
Izard, Mrs., xxxv

Jackson, John, 154
Jackson, Joseph, 154
James I, Lancaster knighted by, xxxii; petition of the *Susan*'s crew to, 134 n.
Jamryn, Nathaniel, *see* Gamryn, Nathaniel
Javanese, the, reputed thieves, 115
Jeane, John, 142
Jefferies, James, 142
Jeffes, Abel, 52 n.
Jew, a, in Lancaster's employ, 97; account of, 97 n.; baptized, 124
Johnson, Henry, 143
Johnson, Jacob, 143
Johnson, John, 141
Johnson, Peter, 142
Jones, Richard, 142
Jones, Thomas, 143
Jones, William, 142
Jordan, Augustin, 143
Joxes (? Jones), Martin, 143
Judson, John, 142
Junk, significance of the term, 8 n.
Junkseylon, xvi, 13; ruler of, 14
Juraza, river, 32 n.

Kārkun, secretary, 130 n., 132
Keachinman, Robert, 142
Keall, Edward, 142
Keeling, William, 166
Kendal, Abraham, 4; account of, 4 n.; at St Helena, 16
Ketch (Keche), Master —, 164, 165; Lancaster's 'Instructions' to, 161
Kingsclere, bequests to, xxxv
Kintār, 13 n.
Kotaraja, *see* Achin
Kris, dagger, 93 n., 131, 132
Kupang, value of a, 136

La Noyer, Captain Jean, *see* Lenoir, Captain Jean
Laccadive Islands, xvi, 9
Lam, the, xxviii n., 133 n., 134 n.
Lancaster, James, birthplace, xiii; conjectural early career of, xiii; a member of the Skinners' Company, xiii, xiv; later career of, xiv; his character, xviii, xxxvi, xxxvii, 34, 35; First Voyage of, xv–xviii, 1–30; commands the *Edward Bonaventure*, xii, 22; ill health of, xvi, xxi, 15, 47, 134; his crew mutinous, xvi, xvii, 15, 17, 24, 25, 26, 27, 28, 33–4; marooned at Mona, 19–20; rescued, 20; returns to England, xvii, 21; Second Voyage of, xviii–xxii, 31–74; commands the *Consent*, xix, 31, 58; captures Recife, 39, 62–3; his protective measures, 63–4; his appreciation of French assistance, 41, 64; his dislike of the Portuguese, 43, 62–3, 66; his orders disregarded, 48, 67–8; Third Voyage of, xxv–xxxii, 75–141; commands the *Red Dragon*, xxvi, 76; his salary, xxvi; armed with letters of reprisal, xxix n.; commissions to, 76, 149–54; his friendly relations

Lancaster, James (*continued*)
with the King of Achin, 90–106, 108–112, 129; foils the Portuguese at Achin, 101–5; letters of, xxxi, 118, 154–5; his 'Instructions' left at Bantam, 161–6; his 'Hints', xxxiv, 166–7; pension drawn by, xxiv, 154; knighted, xxxii; last years of, xxxiv; his London residence, xxxiv; his death and burial, xxxiv; his will, xxxiv, xxxv; portrait of, xxxvi
Lancaster, James, of Basingstoke, xiii
Lancaster, John, xxxv
Lancaster, Peter, xxxv
Lancaster, William, xxxv
Lancaster Sound, xxxiv
Land's End, 120
Last, content of a, 147 n.
Le Havre, 21 n.
Leake, William, 143, 147 n.
Lenoir, Captain Jean, takes Lancaster to England, 21; at Pernambuco, xxi, 41, 65; his services appreciated, 41, 65; killed, xxii, 41, 49, 68
Leogane (Laguna), 27, 28
Levant Company, the, trade of, threatened, xxiv
Lisbon, 78
Lizard, the, 141
Lucland, Richard, 27
Luisa, the, 20

Mace, from Banda, 164
Mace, William, 6, 23
Madagascar, xxvii, 5, 15, 23, 82, 166; barter with natives of, 84–5, 124–5, 145; inhabitants, 127; language, 127; deaths in, 148
Madre de Dios, 41 n.
Maio, xix, 34, 60; a galley fitted up at, 35, 61
Maize, 5, 23
Major, Edward, 141
Malacca, 1, 9, 10, 12, 23, 24, 146; Portuguese envoy from, at Achin, 101–3; measures taken at, to oppose Lancaster, 103–4, 106; unhealthiness of, 136
Malacca, Straits of, 12; Portuguese ship seized in the, 106–7, 134–5
Malagasy language, specimens of the, 127

Malay language, specimens of the, 14, 137
Maldives, the, xxviii, 15, 97 n., 133 n., 134
Malé, 97 n.
Maler, William, 143
Malice Scourge, see *Dragon*
Malindi, 7, 9, 23
Malyn, Arnold, 143
Mammale Islands, *see* Laccadives
Manangkabo, 113 n.
Mansur Shāh, ruler of Achin, 92 n., 95 n.
Margarita Island, 59
Marshall, Richard, 142
Martaban, 11
Martin, John, 142
Mas, value of a, 136 n.
Masa, an alloy, 93 n.
Mauritius, the, 77 n., 82, 84 n.
May, Henry, purser of the *Edward Bonaventure,* xviii, narrative of, xviii, 5 n., 6 n., 18 n., 22–30; his knowledge of French, 27; wrecked, xviii, 22, 28–9; sails to England from Newfoundland, xviii, 30
May, Thomas, 141
Merchant Royal, the, her tonnage, xii n.; sent back to England, xv, 4, 22; at St Helena, 16
Mermaids, 138
Michel, Robert, 143
Middleton, David, notice of, 100 n.
Middleton, Captain Henry, commands the *Susan,* xxxiii, 100, 132; permit granted to, by the King of Achin, 100 n.; commands a fleet in 1604, xxxiii; notice of, 100 n.
Middleton, John, of Chester, 100 n.
Middleton, Captain John, 90; commands the *Hector,* xxvi, 76, 83 n., 100 n., 107, 113, 129, 132; to succeed Lancaster, 152; death of, xxxi, 100 n., 115, 142
Milho da India, maize, 5, 23
Minion, the, 41 n.
Moluccas, the, xxxi, 84 n., 139, 167; trade of Bantam with, xxx; a trading venture to, 115, 162
Mon (Talaing) language, specimens of the, 141
Mona Island, xvii, 18, 19, 21, 26, 41
Monk, William, 142
'Moor', Muhammadan, 5

INDEX

175

Moore, Roger, 142
Morgan, Thomas, Lancaster's 'Instructions' to, 162–3; death of, 163 n.
Morgan, William, 143
Morrice, Roger, 142
Mossel Bay, 2 n.
Mountjoy, Methuselah, 143
Mozambique, xv, 1, 5, 7, 23
Muhammadans, ships of the, seized, 7
'Murdering piece', 36

Nancowry Island, 88 n., 128
Napper, Henry, 85 n.; death of, 126, 142, 148
Neck, Jacob Cornelisz van, xxiv, 139 n., 147
Negapatam, xvi, 12
Newchurch, Christopher, poisons himself, 125
Newfoundland, xvii, 29; Henry May sails to England from, xviii, 30
Newhaven, *see* Le Havre
Nichols, Leonard, 142
Nicholson, Michael, 143
Nicobar Islands, xvi, xxvii, 1, 10, 82, 87; inhabitants, 14, 24, 88, 128, 129; trade by barter at, 14, 24, 88; curious animal at, 89, 129
'Nipar' wine, 15
North-West Passage, search for a, xxxiv
'Note', 39
Nottingham, Earl of, a tenth of prize goods paid to, 134 n.
Nueblas Islands, 19
Nutmegs, from Banda, 164

Olinda, xix, xx, 31, 32 n., 39
Orlop, 135
Ossever, John, 142
Owfield, Thomasine, xxxv
'Oxe-birds', 11

Page, Henry, 143
'Pangaia', sailing barge, 5, 6, 7, 23
Pangeran of Bantam, the, xxx
Paria, Gulf of, xvii, 17, 18
Parker, John, 85 n., 86, 148; *see also* Verker
Parsons, George, 142, 148
Patani, 90, 139, 147

'Pavilions', 15
Pedir, 104 n., 132
Pegoune, John, 141
Pegu, 9, 10, 24, 90; ships of, seized, 11, 12; goods brought from, 15
Penang Island, xvi, 1, 10, 23
Penelope, the, xii, 1, 4, 22; disappearance of, xv, 4, 23
Penguin Island, *see* Robben Island
Penguins, at the Cape, 123
'Penny fathers', 72
Pepper, whence obtained, 100, 113, 133, 139, 145, 162, 167; limited English market for, xxxiii; scarce and dear at Achin, 100, 109; price of, at Priaman, 113, 135, at Bantam, 114, at Achin, 132, 134, 145
Perak, 11
Peranjew, 50, 69
Perchet, Mathew, 142
Peregrine, the, 35, 60, 65, 69
Pereira, Duarte Coelho, 32 n.
Pernambuco, expedition against, xviii, xx–xxiii, 31–74; Portuguese occupation of, 32 n.; Lancaster's attack on, 36–8, 52, 61–2; measures taken for the security of, 64; new Portuguese fortifications attacked, 66; Lancaster's force defeated at, 66–8
Philip II of Spain, xi
Pinchbanke, Thomas, 142
'Pintados', 15, 24, 146, 162; seized in a Portuguese ship, 107, 135
Pizing, William, 143
Plague, the, in England, xxxiii
Plata, Rio de La, 41 n.
Plymouth, 1, 22, 51, 69
Point de Galle, xvi, 14, 15
'Policy', 43
Pome-citrone, 128
Pope, Richard, 143
Pope, Captain Robert, xxvii, 126, 129, 131, 132; death of, 134, 143, 148
Poppe, Robert, 142
Pormoth, Francis, 142
'Portcullis money', xxvi
Portugal, Lancaster's residence in, xiii
Portuguese, the, claim the monopoly of Cape route to India, xi; enemies of England, xi, 7, 57; at Zanzibar, 7; settlements of, xv,

INDEX

Portuguese (*continued*)
xvi, 6, 8, 9 n., 23, 32 n.; Lancaster's dislike of, xiv, 43; seizure of ships of, *passim*; unsuccessfully attack the English at Pernambuco, xxi, 40; attempt to fire Lancaster's fleet, 45, 46, 63; Lancaster's refusal to negotiate with, 42–3, 66; the English loss in action against, xxi–ii, 48–9, 66–7; unpopular at Achin, xxix, 101; intrigues of, at Achin, foiled, 101–5
Portuguese language, Lancaster's knowledge of, xiv
Potáju, 50
Powell, Robert, 143
Predam, William, 142
Priaman, 108; pepper obtained from, 100, 133, 135, 167; price of pepper at, xxxi, 113; the *Susan* sent to, 100, 112, 137, 145, 146; Lancaster's fleet at, 112–3, 137; description, 113
Price, Thomas, 142
Priddis, Morgan, 143
Prize goods, agreement regarding the distribution of, 134 n.
Puerto Rico, xvii, 18 n., 19, 26
Pullen (Pulleyn), the Rev. Thomas, 85 n.; death of, 126, 142, 148
Pyrard de Laval, quoted, 97 n.

Quitangonha Island, 1, 5, 23

Ragwood, Nicholas, 142
Raja Makuta, 95 n.
Ram, 133 n., 134 n.
Raymond, Captain George, commands the fleet in the First Voyage, xii, xv, 1, 4, 22; disappearance of, 4
Recife, xx, 32 n., 34; capture of, xx, xxxvii, 39; fortified, 39–40; described, 40; no fresh water at, 44
Red Dragon, the, *see* Dragon
Red Sea, 9, 167
Reddoe, John, 143
Rhinoceros, horn of, an antidote, 14
Rials of eight, xxv, 14, 24, 114, 163
Richardson, Daniel, 142
Ridge, William, 142
Robben Island, 3 n., 82
Roberts, Henry, his pamphlet, xxiii, 52–74; notice of, 52 n.
Robinson, John, 142
Rochelle, 41

Rogue-Pize Island, *see* Agalega
Romania, Cape, 77 n.
'Rough', 69
Rowe, John, 143
Royal Merchant, the, *see* Merchant Royal
Russell, John, 142
Rye, xvii, 21

St Antonio, the, *see Santo Antonio*, the
St Augustine, Cape, 36, 61, 78
St Augustine's Bay, 166 n.
St Elmo's light, 138 n.
St Helena, Portuguese at, 119; the *Edward Bonaventure* at, xvi, 25; an Englishman found at, 16, 25; provisions obtained at, 120, 139–40; natural productions of, 16, 17; the *Dragon* and *Hector* at, xxxii, 119; the *Ascension* at, 147, 148
St Lawrence, *see* Madagascar
St Malo, xxiv, 147
St Mary Island, xxvii, 83, 84; description, 83, 124; inhabitants, 83, 124
St Nicolas, Cape, 27
St Roman, Cape, *see* Romania, Cape
St Thomé, *see* San Thomé
'Saker', 36
Salang, *see* Junkseylon
Saldana, Antonio de, 3 n.
Saldania Bay, *see* Table Bay
Salisbury, Philip, 141
Salter, Ralph, 142
Salter, Sute, 57
Salter (Saltin), Thomas, 129, 143, 148
Samon, John, 143
Sampans, 160
San Bras, *see* Mossel Bay
San Domingo, xvii, 18, 19, 20, 21
San Francisco, river, 32 n.
San Juan, Puerto Rico, 19
San Thomé, 9; Portuguese ships from, taken, xvi, 12, 107
Santa Maria Island, 120
Santo Antonio, the, seized, xxx, 107, 135
Santo Antonio Island, xx
Saona Island, 18
Saragossa Sea, 140
Savadge, Robert, 143
Schaep, the, xxx, 133 n., 134 n.
'Sconce', 64

INDEX

Scot, Christopher, 141
Scott, Edmund, Lancaster's 'Instructions' to, 162-3; takes charge at Bantam, 163 n.
Scriven, Thomas, 143
Scult, Christopher, 143
Scurvy, the, ravages of, xxvii, 79, 82, 83, 122; antidote for, xxvii, 79, 83, 124, 145
Seals, at Table Bay, 123
Sebastian, Cape, see Faux Cap
Seely, Edward, 143
Sembilan Islands, 12
Serpent's Mouth, strait, 25 n.
Settell, John, 142
Shahbandar, 115
Sharīf, noble, 7
Ships, see Amsterdam, Ascension, Bear, Consent, Corbin, Croissant, Dergoes, Dog, Dragon, Edward Bonaventure, Expedition, Gift, Guest, Hector, Lam, Luisa, Madre de Dios, Malice Scourge, Merchant Royal, Minion, Penelope, Peregrine, Ram, Red Dragon, Santo Antonio, Schaep, Solomon, Susan, Tergozo, Virgin, Welcome
Siam, embassy from, to Achin, 103; cotton goods from, 162
Sims, Emanuel, 142
Sims, Nicholas, 143
Sket, James, 143
Skinner, Vincent, Lancaster's letter to, 154-5
Skinners' Company, the, xiii, xiv; Lancaster's bequest to, xxxv; Lancaster's portrait in the possession of, xxxvi
Smally, Richard, 143
Smith, John, 143
Smythe, Thomas, xiv, xxv
Sokotra, xvi, 9
Solomon, the, xviii, xix, 31, 32, 49, 57, 58; false report concerning, 33, 59; rejoins the Consent, 34, 59; returns to England, 69
Sombrero Channel, 88 n.
Sombrero Island, see Nancowry
Spaniards, the Edward Bonaventure surrendered to, xvii; perturbed by Lancaster's operations in Brazil, xxii; negotiations for peace with, xxiv; identified with the Portuguese, 57 n.

Spanish Armada, the, xi, xii, xiv
Speilbergen, Joris van, xv n., xxviii, xxx, 105 n., 133; Lancaster's agreement with, xxix
Spencer, Richard, 143
Sprat, Richard, 143
Starkey, Matthew, 142
Starkey, Randall, surgeon, death of, 69
Starkie, William, xxxi, 106, 132; left at Bantam, 115; Lancaster's 'Instructions' to, 162-3; death of, 163 n.
Steele, Edward, 143
'Stirke', 3
Stone, Gabriel, 143
Stradling, Percival, 142, 148
Styles, Roger, 106, 144 n.
'Suckets', 13, 135
Sumatra, xvi, 1, 10, 14, 82, 88, 145
Sunda, Straits of, 113, 116
Susan, the, 75, 76, 100 n., 125, 145, 153; laden at Priaman, xxix, xxx, 100, 112, 133, 145, 146; returns to England, 113; her captain, 125 n., 148; petition of the crew of, 134 n.
'Swads', 62
Syclemore, John, 143

Table Bay, xv, 3 n., 4, 22, 122; see also Cape of Good Hope
Table Mountain, xxvii, 82
Tael, worth of a, 134 n.
Taffeta, 13
Talaing words, examples of, 141
Tāmbaga, mixed metal, 93 n.
Taylor, Lancelot, 142
Tenasserim, 14, 15
Teneriffe, 33, 58, 59
Tergozo, the, 147
Thickpenny, Henry, 142
Thomson, William, 141
Thoroughgood,—, tried for mutiny, 132
Thorpe, Thomas, 121, 144
Tiburon, Cape, 18, 26
Tiku, xxix
Topsail, Martin, 142
Tor Bay, 77, 121, 144
Tornados, 2
Towerson, Gabriel, 133, 161, 166; Lancaster's 'Instructions' to, 164-6; death of, 133 n.
Treenails, 29

Trincall, John, 142
Trinidad Island, xvii, 17, 25
'Tuck', turban, 90 n.
Tudd, Thomas, 161, 166; Lancaster's 'Instructions' to, 164–6

Upgrave, James, 143

Venner, Captain John, 50; commands the *Peregrine,* 35, 60; cooperates with Lancaster, xix, 39, 44, 48, 49, 61; death of, 50 n., 69
Verker (? Parker), John, 143
Vianna do Castello, 78 n., 144
Vincent, Alfonso, 100 n.
Virgin, the, 32, 33, 58, 59; her tonnage, xviii, 31, 57; arrives in England, 69

Ward, Thomas, 143
Waterspout, a, 108
Watts, George, 142
Watts, Sir John, 31, 32 n., 57, 58 n.; his daughter, 148
Watts, John, son of Sir John Watts, 58
Watts (? John), master of the galley fitted up at Maio, 36, 61
Way, Thomas, 143

Webbe, John, 142
Webbe, Morrice, 142
Welcome, the, 35, 60, 63, 65, 69
West, John, 27
Whitehead, Richard, 143
Whitting, William, 143
Wilkinson, Thomas, 142
Williams, Nicholas, 142
Williams, Rice, 142
Williamson, William, 143
Wilson, Thomas, 143
Winchcombe (Winacombe), Philip, 143, 148
Windward Passage, 21 n.
Wine, seized in Portuguese ships, 13, 33, 59, 78, 122, 144
Winter, William, 85 n.; death of, 126, 142, 148
Wood, Captain Benjamin, his unfortunate voyage, xxiv
Woodall, John, 142
Woolwich, 76, 141

Younger, Anthony, 143

Zanzibar, the *Edward Bonaventure* at, xv, 6–8, 23; productions, 8; Portuguese settlement at, xv, 7, 8